CW00350404

The Building Blocks of Training

DEBBY LUSH

The Building Blocks of Training

A Step-by-Step Guide to the Gymnastic Development of the Equine Athlete

J. A. ALLEN • LONDON

This book is dedicated in loving memory of

Jennifer Sewell

Indomitable, forthright and passionately caring, Jennifer's vision and enthusiasm in founding and nurturing the *Teachers of Tomorrow Trust* (TTT) enabled me (and hundreds of others) to access top international trainers on a regular and ongoing basis.

Her generosity in allowing her farm and her home to be taken over by hordes of like-minded strangers was without limits, and I shall endeavour to uphold and further the aims of this registered charity, which owes everything to such a unique and special lady.

First published in Great Britain 2008

ISBN 978 0 85131 932 2

J.A. Allen
Clerkenwell House
Clerkenwell Green
London EC1R 0HT

J.A. Allen is an imprint of Robert Hale Limited

A catalogue record for this book is available from the British Library

Edited by Martin Diggle
Designed and Typeset by Paul Saunders
Photographs by Mick Green
Line illustrations by Maggie Raynor

Printed in China
and arranged by New Era Printing Co. Limited, Hong Kong

Contents

Acknowledgements x
Foreword xi
Preface xii
Introduction xiii

Part One – **The Foundations**

1 **Goals and Principles** 2
The Goals of Training 2
Basic Principles 3
A Systematic Approach – Effective Communication – Your Body as the Template – Horses Learn Continually – Training Should not be Limiting – Help Your Horse by Doing What He Finds Hard – When to Revert to Simpler Exercises – The Value of Accuracy – Train *with* Figures, not *for* Figures – It's not Just About Test Movements – Schooling is not Boring – Check with the Scales of Training

2 **Basic Requirements** 7
You, the Rider 7
Position – Suppleness and Balance – Body Awareness – Muscle Control, Coordination and Fitness – Feel – Understanding Your Horse's Natural Responses – Patience – Empathy – Honesty
He, the Horse 12
All Horses Deserve Some Training – The Effects of Conformation

3 **Definitions and Techniques** – Your Plans and Toolkit 17
Definitions 17
Arena Dimensions and Markers – Quality of the Gaits – Rhythm and Tempo – Activity – Impulsion v Speed – Forward – Engagement – Cadence – 'Throughness' – Connection – Submission – Self-carriage – Collection – Lateral Flexion and Bend – Straightness – Natural Crookedness and the Soft/Hard Sides – Inside and Outside – Tracking – Balance – Contact – Evasions – On the Aids – Correct Posture (Outline) – Independent Seat – Reward – Schooling v Competing
Techniques 29
How to use Your Body – Direct and Indirect Reins – Combination Aiding – Passive Resistance – Half-halt – Inside and Outside Leg Positions – Position Left and Right – The Corridor of the Aids – Inside Leg to Outside Rein – Correct Use of a Schooling Whip – Correct Use of Spurs

4 **Think Like a Horse** 44

Basic Nature 44

Herd Instinct – Herd Hierarchy – Need for Security – The Instinct to Follow – Laziness – Excitability – Nervousness – Sensitivity – Memory – Ear Positions – Love of Routine

Learning and Teaching Strategies 47

Habituation– Conditioned Response – Trial and Error – Latent Learning – Insight – Imprinting

Factors Involved in Learning 49

5 **Early Training** 51

Foals 51

First Days – Introducing Leading – Leading for the Show Ring – Picking up Feet – Tying up – Moving Over

Weanlings 54

Manners – Proper Leading, Starting and Stopping – Backing up – Loading and Travelling

Youngsters up to Backing 56

6 **Lunge Work** 57

Equipment 57

Key Points of Control 59

Voice – Lunge Line – Lunge Whip – Side Reins

Basic Lungeing Techniques 60

Sending Forward/Upward Transitions – Moving Outward – Asking for a Downward Transition

Lungeing Exercises 61

Alternative Lungeing Equipment 63

The Chambon – The Harbridge – Elastic Bungee

Troubleshooting 66

7 **Transitions** 70

Introducing Transitions under Saddle on the Lunge 70

Start – Stop – Next Steps

Transitions between Gaits 73

Upward Transitions – Downward Transitions

Training Value 76

Exercises

Troubleshooting 77

8 **Steering** 87

Body Position and Weight Aids 87

Rein Aids 89

The 'Wheelbarrow Push'

Leg Aids 90

Displacing the Ribcage – Controlling the Haunches

Troubleshooting 91

9 **Balance and Outline** – Why 95

Biomechanics in a Nutshell 95

The Postural Ring – Using the Postural System

Signs of a Correct Outline 102

Balance 105

10 **Balance and Outline** – How 107

Acceptance of the Bit 107

Chewing Down onto the Inside Bit – Alternating Rein Contact – Vibrating the Inside Rein – Passive Resistance: the Side Rein Effect

Contracting the Horse's Stomach Muscles 113

Waking Up the Stomach Muscles – The Pelvic Tuck – The Three Bascules

Putting the Horse on the Aids 114

Troubleshooting 115

11 **Riding the Gaits** 129

Walk 129

Variations of the Walk

Trot 130

Rising Trot – Sitting Trot – Variations of the Trot

Canter 133

Troubleshooting 136

Part Two – **The Building Blocks**

12 **Bend and Straightness – Circles** 148

Do Horses Really Bend? 148

The Illusion of Bend – Why is Bend Important?

Circles 150

Requirements – Aids – Patterns – Training Value

Troubleshooting 155

13 **Bend and Straightness – Straight Lines and Changes of Direction** 163
Straight Lines 163
Requirements – Riding a Centre Line – Training Value
Turns and Corners 165
Requirements – Riding Turns and Corners – Training Value
Changing Direction 167
Requirements – Aids – Patterns – Training Value
Troubleshooting 174

14 **Going Sideways** 177
Turn on the Forehand 177
Requirements– Aids – Training Value
Troubleshooting 180

15 **More Sideways** 184
Leg-yielding 184
Requirements – Aids – Patterns – Training Value
Troubleshooting 191

16 **Improving Straightness and Strength – Shoulder-fore, Shoulder-in and Sitting Trot** 202
Shoulder-fore 202
Requirements – Aids – Training Value
Shoulder-in 204
Training Value – Caution
Sitting Trot 206
Patterns
Troubleshooting 207

17 **Direct Transitions and Simple Changes** 211
Direct Upward Transitions 211
Halt to Trot – Walk to Canter – Training Value of Direct Upward Transitions
Direct Downward Transitions 214
Trot to Halt – Canter to Walk – Training Value of Direct Downward Transitions
Progression 217
Simple Changes 217
Requirements – Aids – Patterns
Troubleshooting 219

18 **Square Halts and Rein-back** 224
Square Halts 224
Requirements – Aids – Training Value

Rein-back 226
Requirements– Aids – Patterns and Outside Assistance – Training Value
Troubleshooting 230

19 **Lengthening and Collecting** 236
Lengthening 236
Requirements – Aids – Priorities – Patterns – Training Value – Progression
Collection 242
Requirements – Preparatory Exercises – Aids – Training Value
Troubleshooting 244

20 **Counter-canter** 251
Requirements 251
Aids 252
Patterns 252
Training Value 254
Troubleshooting 254

21 **Building Blocks of the Higher Movements** 257
Travers and Renvers 258
Travers – Renvers
Walk Pirouette 260
Half-pass in Trot and Canter 261
Flying Changes 262
Tempi Changes
Half-pass Zigzags in Trot and Canter 263
Canter Pirouettes 264
Piaffe 265
Passage 266

22 **Timescale for the Building Blocks** 267
Prior to Backing 268
First Six Months under Saddle 268
Second Six Months under Saddle 268
Year Two 268
Year Three 269
Year Four 269
Year Five 269
Summary of Goals of Training 269

Index 270

Acknowledgements

I would like to thank all at the TTT including my long-term trainers, Charles de Kunffy, Arthur Kottas and Stephen Clarke. Their differing coaching styles have complemented each other and enhanced my journey towards becoming both a rider and teacher, demonstrating clearly how many different valid approaches there can be to achieve the same goals.

Thanks are also due to Annie Pye, who told me firmly to 'stop talking about it and get on with writing it', and to Kimberley Battleday for keeping me in touch with the real world.

Nikki Green's generosity, both in her assistance with the photographs and her continuing support in allowing me to train and ride Merlin, is beyond measure. My thanks also to her husband, Mick Green, for his photographic skills.

Author's contact details

www.debbylush.co.uk

Teachers of Tomorrow Trust contact details

www.ttttrust.com

email: secretary@ttttrust.com

Foreword

This book will provide a valuable insight into the training of all riding horses, whether for competition or for pleasure.

As well as being a simple, practical, easy-to-follow guide for the less experienced rider it will give plenty of food for thought to even the most experienced trainer!

The depth of knowledge that is clearly demonstrated in this book comes from the author's wealth of experience in training all types of horses throughout every level of dressage whilst maintaining the genuine feel of empathy with her equine partners.

STEPHEN CLARKE

Preface

To develop a harmonious partnership with your horse, whether you have ambitions in the competition arena or not, you need to develop a two-way communication system that is clear to both of you.

Without external guidance you may develop your own 'system', which might work brilliantly with one horse, but if you put a strange rider on him who doesn't 'push the same buttons', or if you ride another horse who is trained to a different system, then you are going to have problems.

To give both you and your horse a fair chance, adherence to a simple, logical system based upon classical principles should be your goal. 'Classical' in this context refers to means tried and tested over hundreds of years, not 'old-fashioned', as many a result-driven competitor or trainer proclaims it to be.

Many different systems exist and this can be confusing to less experienced riders as they struggle with conflicting suggestions. For the good of the horse you should pick one well-established system and stick with it – mixing differing systems will only result in a confused horse and a frustrated rider.

In every good system each response and movement that we teach our horse is placed in a logical, progressive order that is easy for both horse and rider to understand. Our ultimate goal must be to enhance our horse's mental and physical capabilities and so allow him to move easily and happily forward from the earliest simple steps to the more complicated efforts required further up the competition ladder.

This book is designed to provide an easy-to-use reference guide to that order, and also offers solutions to a wide range of problems you may encounter along the way.

NOTE

Throughout this book I refer to the horse as 'he', and the rider as 'her', or 'she'. I make no implications by this, merely use these references as a simple and consistent means of identification.

To all male riders and female horses, I apologize.

Introduction

As a result of the ever-decreasing interaction of human beings with Nature, and the social changes that have resulted in many adults with no childhood equestrian background taking up riding, training (and handling) problems now occur that would have been unlikely in years gone past.

One of the biggest culprits is the modern desire to *anthropomorphize.* Defined in the dictionary as 'the attribution of human behaviour to an animal', and encouraged in our minds by books and films featuring animals expressing human thoughts and emotions, anthropomorphism is one of the greatest causes of misunderstanding in a human/equine relationship.

To train a horse successfully we must first appreciate that he thinks *like a horse!* Next, we must acquire some level of understanding of *how* a horse thinks before finally learning to translate our requests into terms that are logical to *him.*

Some of the things we will ask him to do will fit comfortably within his view of life: others will not. This does not mean that it is 'wrong' to ask such questions (one, for example, is that he allows you to sit on his back), merely that we should not try to impose our will upon him without taking into account his natural instincts. Modern labels for this approach include 'natural horsemanship' and 'equine ethology'. Scientific studies into behaviour, genetics, perception and biomechanics have greatly enhanced our understanding of how the horse's mind and body function, yet this new knowledge only serves to support and clarify the basic principles of classical training – principles that are being lost in the drive towards competition success and the desire for quick results.

This 'instant results' culture is the other big problem in modern equestrianism. Raised with the expectation that one can either buy success, or find short cuts to any goal, riders today often lack the patience needed for a long-term project; and their horses bear the brunt of unreasonable and damaging demands. Like children, horses need time to mature both mentally and physically – even if they look big and strong. Many of today's riders neglect the gymnastic work needed for strengthening and suppling because it takes (in their minds) too long and is too boring. These people miss out on the joy of riding a willingly cooperative partner who is comfortable to sit on and will stay sound into advanced age regardless of the use to which he is put.

The aim of this book is to provide a guide to this gymnastic development which is relevant to all riding horses, and especially to those who will compete at some time in their lives. It outlines the order in which exercises should be introduced, along with some idea of a likely time frame, detailing the basics that *all* competition horses should cover, irrespective of discipline. It is not designed to take the place of a trainer, or even a good set of 'eyes on the ground', but should be used in conjunction with such essential assistance. It can be read as a whole, or used as a reference book to look up individual topics with links to related information, and while it would be impossible to cover all eventualities, you will find in the *Troubleshooting* sections the most common problems outlined, with detailed suggestions for tackling them.

Part One

The Foundations

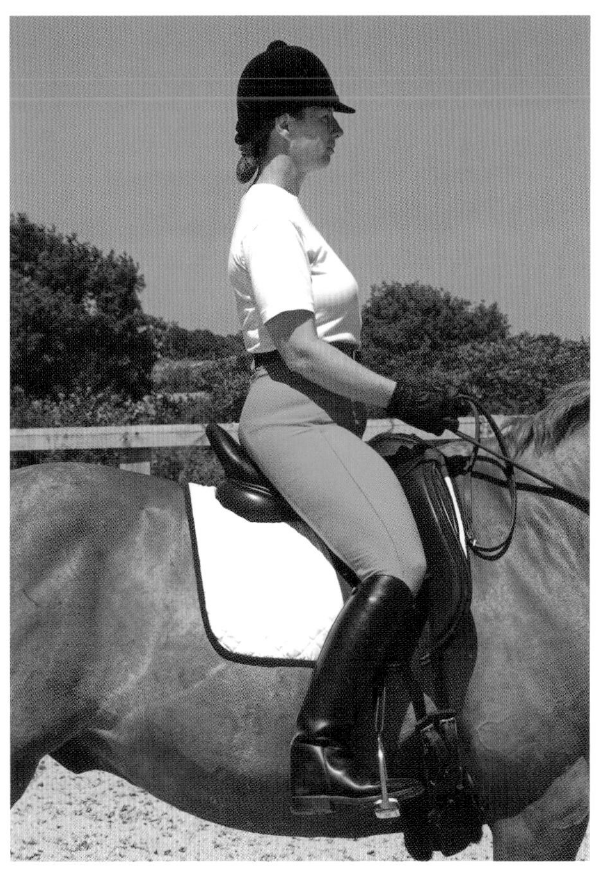

1 Goals and Principles

The Goals of Training

These can be identified as follows.

1. To interact safely with your horse by developing clear lines of communication. These must be based on an understanding of his natural responses and, as a result, the clear behavioural boundaries that you set.
2. To redevelop his balance with your added weight on his back.
3. To straighten his body. Just as humans are born right or left-handed, so horses are born with unequal sides. To some extent this evens out as they grow and play, but some vestige of this inequality will still exist when their ridden career begins. For this reason all early training must be therapeutic until he uses both sides of his body equally.
4. To supple and strengthen his joints and muscles to prolong his health and soundness.
5. To identify weak areas in his body or in his basic training and address them, not disguise them.
6. To develop an equine athlete and gymnast – supple, ambidextrous and strong in his body, confident, attentive and keen in his mind – within the limits that his conformation, character and talent permit.
7. For both partners to enjoy their ridden work. Only those who seek to train with knowledge and sensitivity as opposed to crude strength, and who allow their horse to develop at a pace which his mind and body can tolerate, will achieve the art form of perfect harmony that produces true beauty in motion.

Basic Principles

A Systematic Approach

A systematic approach is the only logical and humane way to train a horse.

Successful progression from backing to fully developed athlete depends entirely upon you tackling the **building blocks** in the correct order: from easy up to hard. This is essential not only for the horse's understanding, but also to his physical development – strength, suppleness and motor skills.

Effective Communication

Effective communication, known as aiding, has three essential components.

1. *Pressure,* appropriately applied by seat, leg and rein.
2. *Response:* the pressure is maintained until the horse gives you the response you want.
3. *Release:* you confirm to him that he has given you what you want by releasing the pressure and finding harmony with him.

Only if you follow this sequence will he learn in a relaxed and enthusiastic manner.

Your Body as the Template

Your body is the template to which the horse will conform.

Put simply, this means that whatever you do with your body, your horse will mirror with his own: if you turn to the right, so will he; if you hold a well-toned posture as you ride, so will he.

This is the best possible reason for developing your position and body control, because it makes communication so much simpler.

Horses Learn Continually

To a horse, everything is a learning experience.

This means that there is no 'neutral', so be consistent and take care what you teach him!

Training Should not be Limiting

Never train in a way that limits the horse's possibilities.

Clearly, not every horse has the capacity to become a Grand Prix dressage star. At the same time, you cannot predict with any accuracy how far up the training ladder he might go. Horses have an amazing ability to confound predictions based on conformation and breed, but if you start his training with a preconceived limit in mind, that will certainly become his achievement ceiling.

Should you change your goals later, you could find that the way you've trained him prevents him from going further. Aim to give every horse, for every purpose, the same thorough grounding in developmental work.

Help Your Horse by Doing What He Finds Hard

Your horse doesn't need to do what he finds easy – he needs to do what he finds hard.

Horses will, by nature, try to find the easiest option. Their instincts guide them to conserve energy so they have reserves when they need to flee from danger. Enthusiastic and energetic horses are being produced nowadays by selective breeding but even this does not wholly negate instinct. The crooked horse will try to avoid the effort needed to straighten. Suppling and developing his muscles takes effort, as does holding a good balance with the added inconvenience of your weight. For the sake of maintaining and enhancing his physical well-being he must be guided to make the efforts he does not wish to. As his body strengthens, the effort required to make these changes will become less, and what was once hard will become easy.

When to Revert to Simpler Exercises

When something is confusing or stressful for you or your horse, go back to a simpler exercise.

In such cases, return to a simpler but related exercise in which the horse is already confident. Repeat the stages leading up to where he became uncomfortable to re-establish his confidence and reinforce his understanding of the earlier **building blocks** that form the foundation for the exercise you are introducing. Only when he is calm and responding correctly to the simpler exercises (the lower level of **building blocks**) should you try again with the new demands.

The Value of Accuracy

Accurate riding of figures is not just about gaining marks in a dressage competition.

While insisting on accuracy at the expense of quality (looseness and freedom of his gaits) is stupid, being lazy about figure riding is also detrimental. Only if he is proceeding along a correctly shaped figure will his body and limbs be aligned as they need to be for that figure to have value in developing both sides of his body.

Train *with* Figures, not *for* Figures

Figure riding (including all lateral work) should be used to train your horse's body – not vice versa.

Many people believe that they are training their horses to enable them to perform the more complicated movements required by the higher levels of competition. This assumption is only correct insofar as these movements will become easier for the horse to perform as he becomes stronger, more supple and better balanced. School patterns and movements are the *key* to these physical developments: each one specifically targets individual joints and muscle groups and, if they are first used diagnostically to reveal weak/stiff areas, and then as remedial and therapeutic techniques, the eventual result will be an athletic, happy horse.

It's not Just About Test Movements

You cannot train just by practising test movements.

Training involves riding movements and variations of gait that differ from those you will eventually show in competition. For example, introducing a new movement is best done at a slow gait – this gives both of you more time to think about what you are doing and to correct things when they go wrong. Sometimes, however, you will want to ride an exercise at the same gait but at a faster speed to push the horse into making greater effort than is his natural inclination.

Also, versatility and variability should be developed within his gaits – both speed of footfall and length of stride, so that in the future you can produce exactly the gait variant you want, when and where you want it, with ease.

Schooling is not Boring

It is a fallacy that schooling is inherently boring for horses.

Schooling should never be boring, but you may become bored if you lack understanding, 'feel' or goals, and you may bore *the horse* by repeating exercises endlessly without responding to how he performs them. Vary your schooling sessions by, for example, changing the order in which you ride the gaits and using lots of different patterns to change rein. Training must be a mixture of aids and patterns.

Hacking, jumping and lungeing all have their places, especially when the horse is young and weak, but you will find that, the more feel you develop, the more absorbing the interaction between you and your partner will become.

Check with the Scales of Training

Constantly check your work against the Scales of Training: rhythm, suppleness, contact, impulsion, straightness, collection.

Especially when things go wrong, take a mental step back and begin your corrections in the following order.

1. Is he relaxed? If not, deal with that first.
2. Is he supple? You may be asking him to do something he is not yet supple enough (either laterally and/or over his back) to do.
3. Is he accepting the contact properly? See Chapter 10 for how to teach acceptance of the contact.
4. Does he have impulsion? Don't even bother to ask for more impulsion if 1, 2 and 3 are still not right – only once they are.
5. Is he straight? Straightness needs attention from the start, but will only be achieved fully at a late stage in training.
6. Collection is the ultimate goal, and develops gradually as a result of the correctness of the other Scales. Whilst the full collection of the Grand Prix horse will not be achieved by all, collection begins in a miniscule way as soon as you begin riding correct transitions, and continues to develop throughout training.

The Scales are interdependent upon each other, but if you use this order whenever you need to sort out a problem, you won't go wrong.

2 Basic Requirements

You, the Rider

As a rider you take on responsibility for your horse's well-being – both physical and mental. To accomplish even the most basic level of training – essential for him to carry you without damaging his own body – you will need to train him with patience and consistency. If your work is either too intensive or too infrequent you will fail to lay the firm foundation for his future that he deserves.

There are certain prerequisites in terms of both understanding and skill levels required before you can train a horse effectively. You should be clear in your mind about what you are aiming to accomplish during each moment of a schooling session and how exactly you are going to impart this information to him.

To deliver aids with clarity and subtlety you will need to develop:

- A secure position.
- Suppleness.
- Balance.
- Body awareness.
- A refined degree of muscle control.
- Coordination.
- Fitness (muscle tone).
- Feel.
- In-depth understanding of the horse's natural responses.
- Patience.
- Empathy.
- Honesty.

Only when you can control yourself (both physically and mentally), can you control and influence your horse in any meaningful, subtle way. The greatest riders are those who look as if they are doing nothing.

Position

To develop and maintain this position takes time and effort and is best worked upon on the lunge when you can focus just on yourself – see photo opposite.

Ridden work without stirrups is also invaluable, but *only* if you already have a correct feel for how to move your seat in harmony with the horse. Clamping your legs on for grim death and bouncing round for hours on end might give you plenty of pain, but no gain!

Suppleness and Balance

These qualities go hand in hand, as one is not possible without the other.

Each of your horse's gaits – walk, trot and canter – has movement components in three different planes:

1. Horizontal.
2. Vertical.
3. Lateral.

Your body must be able to absorb and influence each of these vectors. This requires a supple lower back and hips, and an ability to produce a degree of tone in individual muscles without becoming tense.

A good contact requires a stable upper arm with softly flexed elbow and a relaxed forearm and wrist, yet with a closure of index finger and thumb to maintain a constant length of rein – see photo on p. 10.

When you can stay in balance with your horse without tension and without relying on the reins for support, you will be able to *harmonize* with his movements.

Body Awareness

This is essential in order for your position to become self-maintaining and self-correcting, as even the most experienced riders can develop bad habits if not frequently monitored. You can only correct such faults if you are (a) aware of where each part of your body is, and (b) you know where each part *should* be!

Again, riding on the lunge is ideal for developing a muscle-memory template for the correct position. Other disciplines, such as the Alexander Technique, Pilates and T'ai Chi can all help develop your body awareness and fine control.

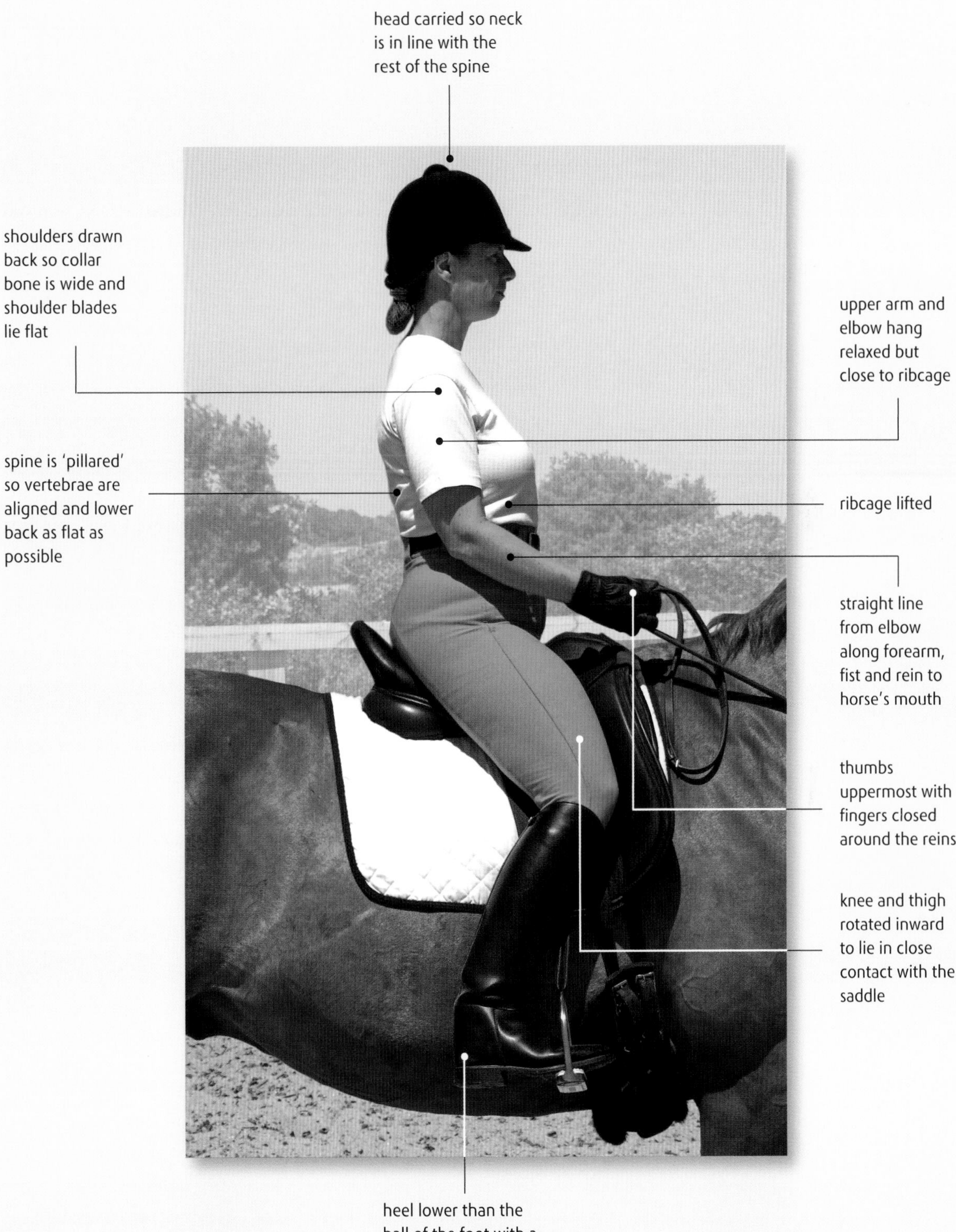
head carried so neck is in line with the rest of the spine
shoulders drawn back so collar bone is wide and shoulder blades lie flat
upper arm and elbow hang relaxed but close to ribcage
spine is 'pillared' so vertebrae are aligned and lower back as flat as possible
ribcage lifted
straight line from elbow along forearm, fist and rein to horse's mouth
thumbs uppermost with fingers closed around the reins
knee and thigh rotated inward to lie in close contact with the saddle
heel lower than the ball of the foot with a supple, flexed ankle

Elements of correct posture.

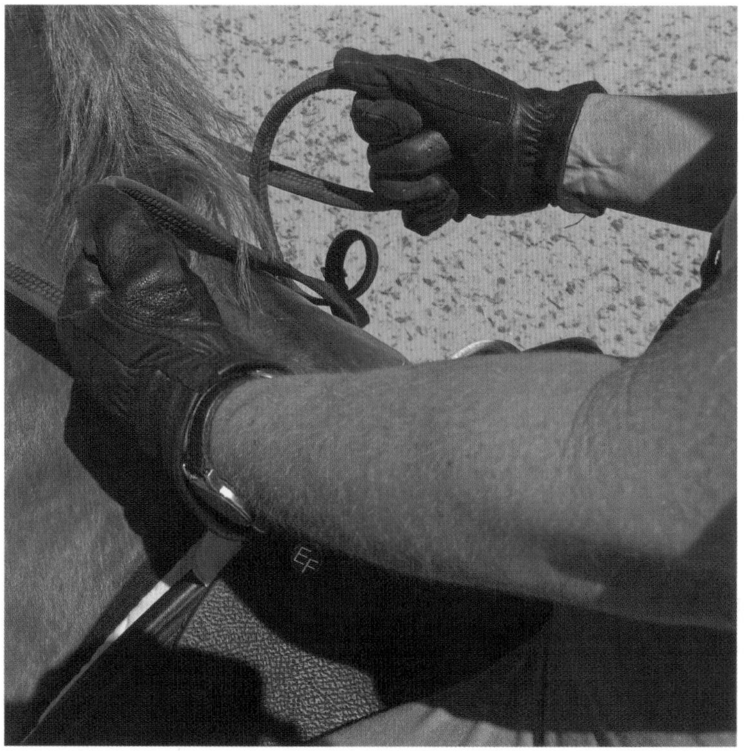

Correct hand position: thumbs uppermost, with rein held between thumb and fore-finger. Knuckles lined up, fingers closed but not clenched. Forearm, hand and rein in a continuous straight line, both along the back of the wrist, and along the underside. Little fingers slightly closer together than thumbs.

Muscle Control, Coordination and Fitness

These are the necessary tools by which you adjust your body when you feel your position go wrong, and also the means by which you give clear aids.

To maintain a correct position yet at the same time harmonize with your horse's movement *and* influence it takes skill. Those riders deemed 'talented' possess these physical requirements in natural abundance, but they can also be learned.

You will need to develop the ability to maintain an overall degree of tone within your body for posture and adhesion to the saddle, whilst at the same time flexing and relaxing individual muscles and muscle groups to give aids without corrupting your position.

You will require *fitness* to sustain your position and enable your aiding.

Feel

This is acquired by comparison. This is most easily achieved by riding a good schoolmaster who can give you the correct sensations for how a horse/movement *should* feel and giving you muscle-memory templates against which to measure all further rides. Failing this, you should be guided by a good trainer who can tell you instantly when you have things right so that you can build up a repertoire of 'correct' feelings.

Understanding Your Horse's Natural Responses

Every horse's strengths and weaknesses are different. Never forget that your horse is *an individual.* As you get to know a horse you should endeavour, without anthropomorphizing (p.xiii), to become clear about what motivates his responses to enable you to develop his character as a willing partner, not a miserable slave.

In general terms his reactions will be predictable, but to train him successfully you will need a greater depth of insight into his personal slant on life. Is he:

- Sharp or genuinely nervous?
- Lazy, or in discomfort, or lacking nutrients?
- Bold or bolshy?
- Laid-back or withdrawn?

Your ability to discern the different causes of what may be apparently identical behavioural patterns will improve with experience, so in the early days you should be prepared to take professional advice.

Once you are clear on *why* he reacts as he does, you can decide how you need to either utilize or modify his reactions. In the long term, his desire to work *with* you will depend on the fairness of your demands and your consistency in terms of *how* you ask and *how quickly* you reward.

Patience

This is essential because the horse's development must not be forced – he will mature mentally and physically at his own speed. You are trying to develop his body into something that would not occur entirely naturally and cutting corners will only result in physical and/or mental damage that may not become evident until later in his life.

Often the biggest challenge will be to keep his brain occupied whilst his body develops.

Empathy

While it is crucial not to anthropomorphize, it is equally as important to treat your horse fairly and with encouragement, as you would wish to be treated yourself. Empathy will also allow you to detect those tiny signs in either behaviour or movement that can be the first indicators of something going wrong. With horses there is vast scope for injuries large or small, for saddle-fitting problems as his shape changes and develops, and for behavioural problems as a result of pain, routine change, hormonal swings, etc. – the list is endless. Being sensitive to minute changes can enable you to prevent such issues developing into major problems.

The end goal of your training is to produce a partnership that finds movement together easy and enjoyable – whether hacking through the countryside or competing at the highest levels. To achieve this, your horse must *want* to please you, and he should be able to enjoy his work as a 'happy athlete'.

Honesty

This is a demand you must place upon yourself for the good of your horse. If you are beyond your skill level, out of your depth or just plain stuck, find help. There is no stigma attached to taking lessons, or getting an experienced rider to sit on your horse and perhaps explain something to him that you cannot. Even Olympic riders work with coaches. Learning to ride takes time, and learning to ride well takes a very long time.

Choose an instructor or coach with great care: success in competition is not a good guideline to a professional's coaching abilities. Rather, experience of training a wide range of horses (ages and breeds) plus willingness and ability to *correct your equitation* in terms that are clear and easily put into action are better guides.

At the same time, there are responsibilities you must take upon yourself – your instructor cannot be there to tell you every move you must make all of the time, and because of the vocal nature of instructions, they will most often come too late for your horse's ideal moment.

Only *you* can make the changes to yourself that are needed.

Bear in mind that, in today's commercial era, riding instructors earn their living from teaching and while those who possess integrity will not compromise their observations or instructions, they are still subject to subtle pressures from you, the client. Do not be tempted to try to dictate what you want to learn; remember that you are not the expert – that is what you are paying for!

You will find that truly excellent instructors are rarely short of clients and if you find yourself at odds with such a one, you should ask yourself who is at fault.

He, (the Horse)

All Horses Deserve Some Training

Whatever your goals, be they competition at the highest level, doing a bit of everything or hacking pleasantly and safely through the countryside, a certain level of training is not only beneficial, but truly essential if you want your horse to enjoy things along with you.

The first thing you do when you mount him is to destroy his natural balance. You also sit on a relatively weak part of his anatomy. Without basic re-balancing, straightening and strengthening work you condemn him to discomfort, anxiety and possible physical breakdown. Consider how many vets earn a living from the riding fraternity!

Training a horse is a fine example of the classic 'chicken and egg' syndrome: to accomplish schooling patterns successfully you need him relaxed, attentive, supple, balanced and physically strong. To achieve this way of going you need to ride the patterns that will supple and strengthen his body. To start with, when he is less than balanced with your unaccustomed weight on his back you will need to take things slowly, often introducing new work in the walk where you will both have time to make adjustments and become familiar with new feelings. This will also enable him to find his balance and, as a consequence, feel relaxed.

A correctly rounded outline should be your goal from the outset, with his back raised and him seeking forward and down for the contact. This posture can and should be established right from the start – if his lunge work (Chapter 6) has been carried out correctly this shape will be familiar and comfortable for him, and his muscles will already have started to strengthen.

It is never too early to address his outline. In fact, leaving him in an incorrect outline is damaging to his body (see text on basic biomechanics in Chapter 9).

Of necessity, his earliest outline will be long and low. This does not mean slopping along on the forehand with inactive hind legs, nor does it mean going with his nose poked out and his neck stiff and straight. He must at all times be in a *round* outline with his nose just in front of the vertical, and his hind legs stepping forward underneath his body.

It is also fallacious to think: 'Let's get him going forward first and then worry about his outline.' While it is true that he must react by going forwards from your legs when you apply them, *it is impossible for a horse to be genuinely forward unless he is in correct posture.* This will be explained in greater detail in Chapter 9, but put briefly: only when his muscles are being used correctly can he both support the weight of his rider *and* move his limbs efficiently.

If you want to compete in a specific discipline you should try to begin with a horse who is as ideally suited for that sport as possible, within your budgetary limitations. If you begin with one who has non-ideal conformation (some examples of which are discussed in the next section) you must accept that it will be unfair to expect him to perform on a par with animals who find the work physically easier. Having said that, horses are a constant source of surprise despite physical characteristics that would seem to disadvantage them. Probably the most important factor is his mind – a willing and easily focused horse can be a pleasure to work with even if he has physically limiting factors.

The Effects of Conformation

Not all horses have the physical capabilities to become equine athletes. Like us, their physiques vary, as does their mental makeup and so their 'talent' for one job or another. Training can help minimize the effects of some conformational difficulties, but only to a certain degree.

Nowadays, selective breeding is producing horses who are 'bred for the job', with conformation and trainable attitudes that are a joy to work with. However, these paragons do not come cheap and most of us have to train horses we can afford, or those we already have.

A basic understanding of how conformation can affect your horse's ability to achieve your goals will help you to target his weaker areas, yet at the same time sympathize with his limitations, and so be fair in what you ask of him.

A large head will not only look less attractive than a small, neat head, it will also be hard for the horse to carry easily in any but the lowest of neck positions. For its size, the horse's head is the heaviest part of his body and if a horse has a big, heavy head, his neck muscles will struggle to lift it above the more basic outline.

A thick jowl (the space between the lower jaw and the neck) can make it severely uncomfortable for him to come 'on the bit'. At its worst the jawbone will press against the wings of the atlas (first) vertebra, and the salivary glands will be compressed.

A short neck will cause problems with producing an arched neck and is often associated with thickness through the jowl. Horses with short necks often have long backs, making for an unbalanced appearance, no matter how well you train them.

A long neck can produce difficulties as it is easy for the horse to overbend, or to have a high point several vertebrae back from the poll (sometimes called a 'broken neck'). If, however, the long neck is well set on (arching upward from the withers) and the horse is correctly trained, it can present a most elegant picture.

A low-set neck makes it impossible for the horse to raise his head and neck into a more advanced frame. If such a neck is also long it is likely he will try to carry it in a 'swan-necked' shape, which will develop a large under-neck muscle.

Upright shoulders will restrict stride length. Not only will the horse be unable to produce medium or extended gaits – his working gaits will be choppy and uncomfortable.

A long back can make it more difficult for the horse to lift his shoulders correctly, as he must use his back like a lever to lift his forehand (see picture, p.126). As mentioned above, long backs and short necks often go together, and such an appearance will never be pleasing. On the other hand, long-backed horses often find lateral work easy. If the neck is also long (and well set on) they can make an impressive picture.

Short-backed horses can find it hard to bend, especially within lateral work. They do find engaging and collection easier, but can be uncomfortable to sit on as the short spine has less shock-absorbency and more movement must be absorbed by your own back.

Dipped backs are never ideal as one of the main goals of training is to raise and round the back, with the accompanying tucking of the pelvis to bring the hind legs forward under the body. Some low backs may be simply the result of a lack of muscle that will resolve as the horse strengthens, but a downwardly arched spine cannot be corrected and the ability of such a horse to engage will be limited.

Pelvis set on too open means that the horse with this conformation has his hind legs naturally built out behind him, which is considered desirable in certain breeds, but makes flatwork training difficult, as he will be asked to do something his body is not built to allow. Such a horse will find *pushing* easy but *carrying* difficult and engagement or collection nigh on impossible.

Croup-high conformation is another limiting shape as such a horse will never be able to raise his shoulders enough to appear truly engaged. He will always appear to be travelling downhill.

A low-set tail can give the appearance of tightness over the top-line as it may look to be clamped down as opposed to the raised and gently swaying tail that accompanies a loose and swinging back.

A big front may appear impressive at first glance, but if the hindquarters are too small to lift the weight of those large shoulders the horse will find engagement hard.

Long hind legs are another difficult shape from a training viewpoint. Even if the horse is not actually croup-high he will find it harder to lower his rear end than a horse whose relative leg lengths are more equal. This horse will be likely to have plenty of power, (and should jump well) but will not collect easily.

Straight hind legs do not bend well at the joints so, no matter how hard such a horse tries (not to mention the rider!) he will never look quite as active as one whose joints flex easily, nor will he have any great ability to engage.

Crooked limbs are predisposed to soundness problems. This category includes 'back at the knee', 'cow hocks' and any deviations of upper or lower limbs from plumb line straightness.

Weak hocks may not stand up to a great deal of intensive ridden work, so such a horse should not be asked to move on to more advanced levels as you may put his soundness at risk.

Long pasterns make for a comfortable ride as they act very effectively as shock absorbers. They are, however, prone to injury as they stretch the ligaments and tendons of the leg excessively with their over-flexible action.

Short pasterns are not so good at shock absorbency as the longer versions, tending to make the ride jolty. The horse's gaits may also appear less than elastic.

Foot shape is one of the most crucial factors in how a horse moves. Feet that are not symmetrical can affect the evenness of the strides, and feet that are not big enough for the horse's weight are unlikely to remain sound in the long term.

3 Definitions and Techniques – Your Plans and Toolkit

The issues discussed in this chapter might be described as the basic plans and toolkit that facilitate your training.

Definitions

Arena Dimensions and Markers

The markers K, H, M and F are known as *quarter markers.*

E and B are *half markers.*

Those on the *centre line* – D, X and G, plus L and I in the long arena – are unmarked and must be found by visualizing the intersection of lines joining other markers e.g. the intersection of the centre line from A to C with the *half-school line* from E to B will give you the position of X – see diagram overleaf.

Quality of the Gaits

At all times the quality of your horse's gaits should be maintained and, ultimately, enhanced. To achieve this goal, the correct sequence of footfall of each gait must never be compromised.

Walk

Walk is the easiest gait to damage and, once lost, the true four-beat sequence is almost impossible to regain.

The correct sequence is: left hind, left fore, right hind, right fore. The gap between each hoof striking the ground should be exactly equal. Listen to your horse walking on tarmac – you should hear 'clip-clop-clip-clop', *not* 'clip-clop --- clip-clop', with a gap between the two pairs of footfalls. Whatever movement you are

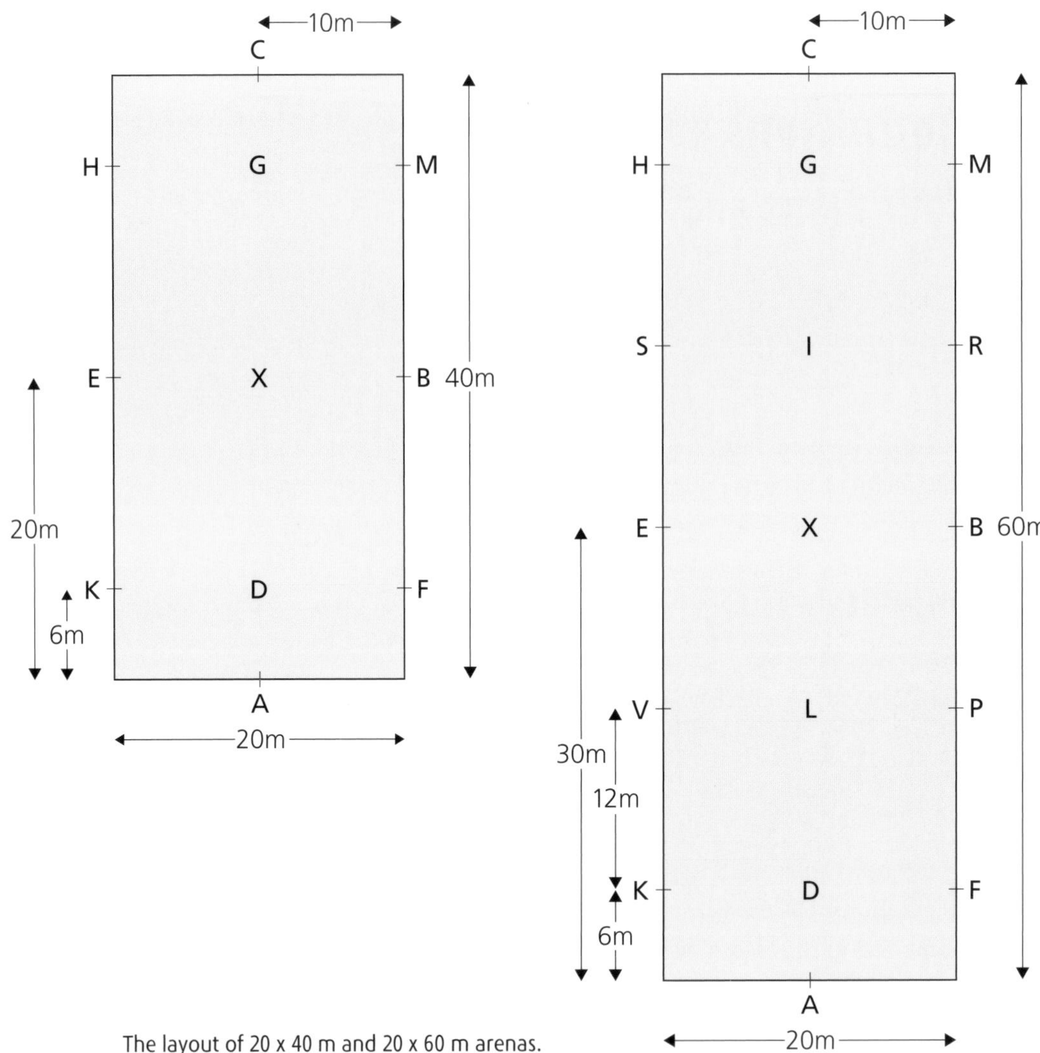

The layout of 20 x 40 m and 20 x 60 m arenas.

performing, and whichever variation of the gait you are in (collected, medium or extended) this sequence must be maintained.

Watching from the side, focus on the front hoof on the ground – does is appear to wait for the hind hoof to start descending (correct) or does it start to lift whilst the hind hoof is still travelling forward (incorrect, known as a 'lateral walk')? You should be able to see a 'V' between the two legs nearest you if the walk is correct.

The quality of the walk is measured by the security of this correct sequence, and by how much *overtrack* there is. Overtrack is a measure of how far the hind foot comes to the ground *in front* of the print left by the forefoot on the same side – a good overtrack in medium walk would be two shoe lengths. It is also important that both hind feet take equal length steps. The amount of overtrack achievable will be, to some extent, dependent on your horse's conformation, but the biggest factor is relaxation: a tense horse will always have a short (poor-quality) walk.

Trot

Trot is a gait with a moment of suspension between diagonal pairs of footfalls. Right hind and left fore touch the ground together, then the horse springs into the air before coming down with left hind and right fore together. He should look as if he is using the ground as a trampoline, whilst still maintaining a positive forward tempo.

If this airborne moment is diminished, or lost altogether, the quality of the trot has been compromised.

In the long term, with correct gymnastic development of his joints and muscles, your horse will gain greater suspension than he had when you began to ride him.

Canter

Canter is a bounding gait with three distinct footfalls: left hind, followed by right hind and left fore together, then right fore, followed by a moment of suspension when all four feet are off the ground (in right-lead canter). The exact opposite sequence constitutes left-lead canter.

The moment of suspension is again your measure of quality. If the canter becomes ground-bound, or the hind legs lose their separation (the distance apart that they land on the ground) or, at worst, the diagonal pair lose their coordination and do not touch the ground at the same time, you have a problem. Certain exercises can be used to recover the quality of canter to a degree, but not losing it in the first instance is preferable.

Rhythm and Tempo

Rhythm

Rhythm is defined as 'any sequence of regularly recurring functions or events'. In this case, the regularly repeated footfalls in correct sequence for each of the three gaits.

Like people, certain horses are born with a more innate sense of rhythm than others – such horses are easier to ride and train. As training progresses, rhythm will gradually become more consistent, displaying its clearest definition in the fully trained Grand Prix dressage horse.

Tempo

Tempo is the speed of the rhythm. For example a trot may have a true rhythm with evenly placed footfalls, but be too fast. This is particularly seen when a rider tries to achieve more impulsion, but instead pushes the horse to a faster speed.

Activity

Activity describes *the amount of energy put into the bending of the horse's hind leg joints* – *not* the speed with which he propels himself along the ground!

Impulsion v Speed

Impulsion is likewise not a measure of how fast the horse can go, but a combination of *activity* (see above) and a general looseness of his frame that permits his whole body to move effectively.

Impulsion cannot be achieved by running the horse faster, as this makes his body stiffen (through loss of balance), which shortens his strides.

Forward

Forwardness is as much an attitude of mind as it is about how the horse uses his body and, as such, it cannot be manufactured by driving him fast around the arena.

While he must respond to your driving aids, he must also *want* to go forward, and to do so he must feel capable in his own body – relaxed, supple, balanced and confident. This means he must be 'through' (see below) in his outline, and physically strong enough to carry your weight. If he is not naturally confident, you need to build him up by attending to his balance, not destroy it by running him off his feet.

Engagement

To be engaged the horse must move with *activity* (see above), but also with his hind legs travelling *forward* beneath his body (for carriage), not out behind his buttocks, which produces only propulsion. As his hind legs move further under his body, with actively bending joints, they begin to support a greater proportion of his bodyweight.

Engagement describes the ability to increase his degree of self-carriage and so the quality (cadence) of his gaits.

Cadence

Cadence is the result of a clearly defined rhythm with impulsion, good balance and great elasticity of body and limbs, resulting in an increasingly marked period of suspension. As the walk sequence has no moment of suspension, cadence is a term that can only apply to trot and canter.

'Throughness'

A lack of stiffness, tension or resistance anywhere in the horse's body or mind characterizes 'throughness'. This lack of any blockage allows a clear flow of energy from his active hind legs, over a swinging back, through his body to his rider's soft hands to form an elastic contact.

Connection

Connection is the result of *throughness* (see previous page) with no slack in the circuit that joins horse and rider into a single harmonious unit. Your seat and leg actions produce energy that flows in an unrestricted manner through your horse's body and arrives as a consistent small weight that is equal in both your hands.

A secure connection from your seat and legs to your hands produces a total mutual focus that eliminates the effects of any outside influences and so enables unimpeded two-way communication.

Submission

This is characterized by the horse's willing acceptance, both mental and physical, of your aids, and by his *attention* to you. Attention can be gauged by:

1. The attitude of his ears – see Chapter 4, p.47.
2. The soft (inward) focus of his eyes.
3. His willingness to work with a lowered head carriage – the order of hierarchy in a group of horses is denoted by the relative heights of their head carriage: high – dominant, low – submissive. The more dominant horse keeps his head high to scan his surroundings for trouble – if he lowers his head for you he is trusting *you* to see any danger for him.

Other aspects of submission include:

- Relaxation.
- Acceptance of the bit, shown by a relaxed jaw, quietly chewing the bit to produce a wet mouth.
- Confidence.
- Harmony.
- Ease of execution of school movements.
- Balance appropriate to his level of training and to the task at hand.

Self-carriage

A horse can be said to be in self-carriage when he can maintain his outline and balance without support from your hands. If you were suddenly to cut the reins with a pair of scissors, what would happen: would his head snap up, would he fall flat on his face, or would he carry on as if nothing had happened? This last is a horse in self-carriage.

Your ridden test for self-carriage is the crest release – the longer you can sustain this without him altering balance, stride or outline, the better his self-carriage – see photo below.

Collection

Simply put, this is when the horse is gathered together, much as when a well-ridden horse is approaching a large jump. It has far more to do with the relative height of his withers and steps than with shortening of his strides and is a product of a strong back and lowered hindquarters that raise his forehand. In the earlier levels of competition he need only be 'collected' to the degree necessary to perform the required movements easily.

Lateral Flexion and Bend

Lateral flexion describes the turning of the horse's head to one side or the other *at the poll*. It does not involve any other portion of the horse's spine. *Bend* requires (as far as the horse's anatomy allows) a continuous curve throughout the body from head to tail (see Chapter 12).

Thus you can have *flexion without bend*, but you *cannot have bend without flexion*.

Crest release in canter. *Holme Grove Merlin*, 12-year-old, 15.3 hh Trakehner, also known as the '*Grand Prix Midget*'! Owned by Nikki Green and ridden by the author.

Straightness

A horse can only become truly straight when he is equally supple on both sides and his hind legs take strides of equal length and height. They must also always travel directly towards the prints left by his forefeet, so he can be described as 'straight' when he is correctly aligned on a circle, not only on a straight line.

Only a straight horse can be balanced, relaxed and engaged, so promoting soundness by equalizing the loading of his hind legs.

There is another factor to consider here, and that is the relative width of the horse's shoulders to his haunches. A horse's shoulders are narrower than his haunches, and this means that his forefeet touch the ground slightly closer together than his hind feet.

As a consequence we have two different but equally valid definitions of straightness:

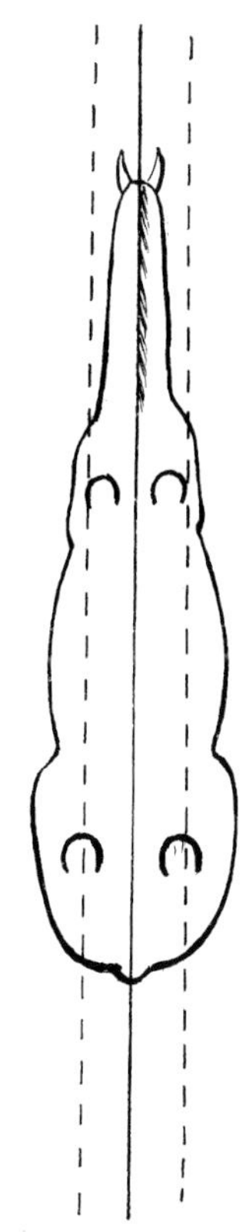

The relative width of the horse's shoulders and haunches. Note that his forefeet are placed closer together than his hind feet.

True straightness is when the horse's spine is perfectly aligned with the line along which he is travelling – straight or curved (corners, circles etc.), or is correctly aligned for the task at hand e.g. shoulder-in, travers, etc.

Functional straightness is when you have the two hooves on the inside of his body aligned, particularly relevant to curved lines, but also to the gait of canter when performed even on a straight line.

Curved lines (circles, serpentines, etc.) are used to supple the horse, and also to engage his inside hind leg by demanding that the joints bend (to carry the leg forward under the body), and that it bears weight (for increased strength and improved carriage). These effects will be maximized by positioning his shoulders very slightly to the inside, resulting in his inside hind leg being placed slightly more beneath his body mass.

In canter, as a consequence of the canter sequence, horses are prone to 'curling up' laterally according to which lead they are performing. In, for example, right-lead canter they will tend to lean out onto the left shoulder, with the neck and haunches curling to the right. To correct this you must ride the canter in a *slight* shoulder-fore, i.e. functionally straight – see diagrams overleaf.

Natural Crookedness and the Soft/Hard Sides

Horses are often described as having a soft and a hard (stiff) side, depending on the ease with which you can bend them each way. This is brought about by the fact that *horses are born crooked.* Possible reasons for this include:

- The horse's brain determines left- or right-handedness, as does ours.
- Foals in the womb lie predominantly curled to one side so the muscles on one side develop longer than on the other.

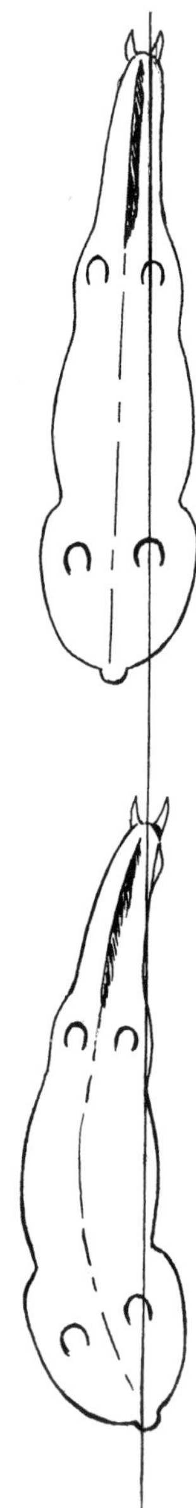

The functionally straight horse – note both inside hooves are on the same line (parallel to the wall)

The curled up horse – whilst inside hind is on the line, both his front feet are to the side and his whole body is shorter on the right side than the left

Functionally straight and crooked horses.

- Traditionally, we handle horses from the left side, which encourages them to bend their necks to the left and move with their shoulders to the right.

Whatever the cause, it is the rider's job to straighten the horse so that wear and tear over the years will be distributed equally on the two sides.

Each side has a positive and a negative aspect: his *soft* (easier to bend) side is *weaker* while his *stiff* side is *stronger* which means that, when schooling, you should perform the same exercise on each rein, but with a different goal on each rein: to strengthen the soft side and to supple the stiff one.

Inside and Outside

In training horses the terms *inside* and *outside* are always relative to the horse's bend, *not* the direction of travel. For example, if you are in left-lead canter, but travelling around the school to the right (counter-canter), the inside is the left side of your horse's body, despite his left side being closer to the fence than his right.

Tracking

This refers to the placement of the horse's feet on a line. For example, if he is tracking straight, each hind foot will be travelling along the same path as the forefoot on the same side (allowing for the hind feet being slightly wider apart than the forefeet). This may be on a straight line, or a curved figure.

If he is *not* tracking correctly, his hind feet will travel on different lines from the corresponding forefeet.

Incorrect tracking indicates crookedness, which may be natural or as a direct result of evasion. In either case, it will prevent him from developing the two sides of his body equally and must be addressed as a matter or urgency.

Balance

The simple act of mounting a young horse for the first time disturbs his natural balance. However, with patient

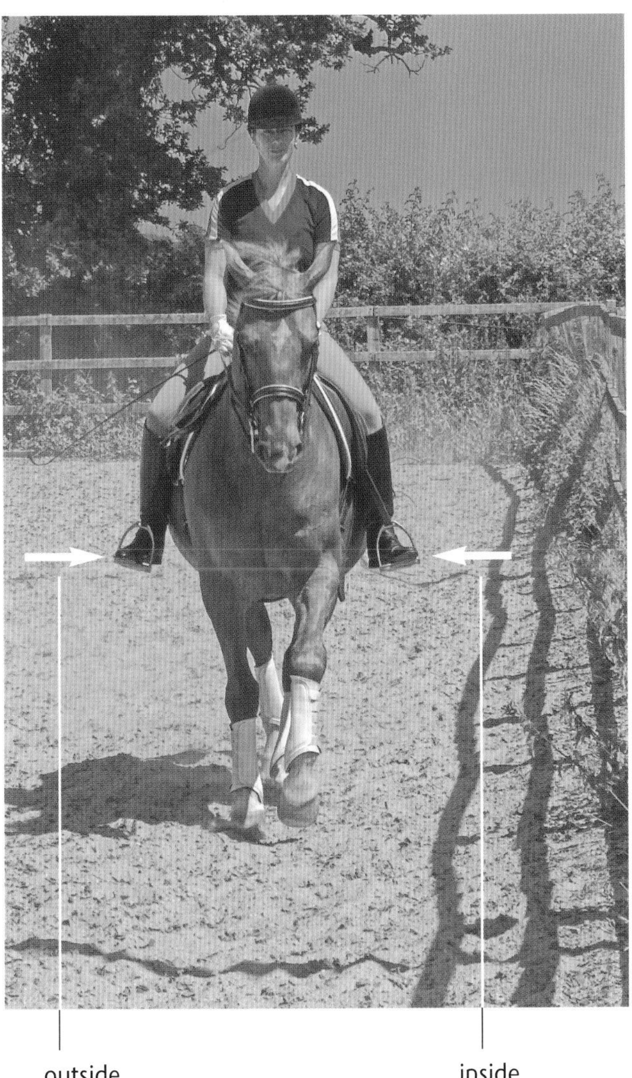

Left lead counter-canter: a small flexion left whilst travelling clockwise round the school.

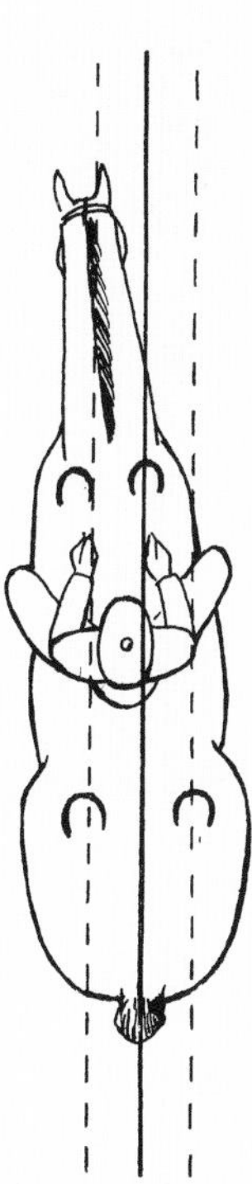

Incorrect tracking – the front feet travel on different lines from the hinds

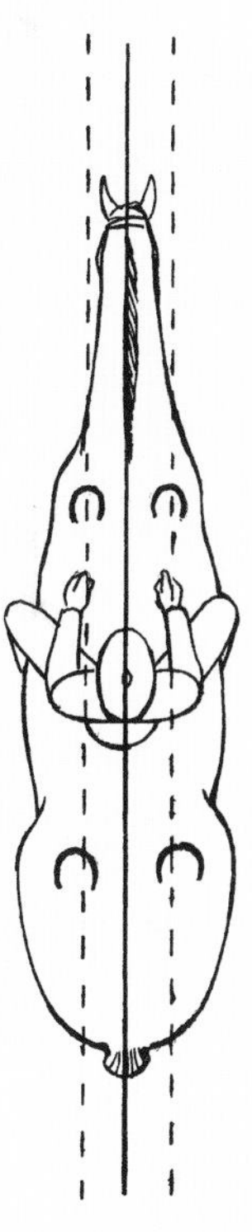

Tracking correctly – the front and hind feet are on the same lines

Incorrect and correct tracking.

long-term training any horse can be taught to carry this weight with increased ease, within the limits of his conformation.

His ability to balance will vary throughout his training under saddle, but his fundamental response to lack of balance will always be one of *panic*. This is because, to a horse, balance is one of his greatest assets. Put in a wild herd context, the horse who loses his balance is the one who falls over and gets eaten! In practice, this instinctive response will be displayed in differing forms depending on the precise circumstances and the horse's temperament, and may vary from mild anxiety to apparently disobedient and outrageous behaviour. If you understand why a horse values his balance so much and why he is upset when he feels it compromised, you should find some behaviours easier to understand and sympathize with, and you can tailor your approach to be more logical to him.

Contact

Of all the rider's skills, contact takes the longest to develop because of its inconsistent nature. The contact taken by a young horse will be quite different from that of a fully trained horse, and it can vary from movement to movement (even stride to stride) depending on changes in balance. Your goal will be a light, elastic contact that should be between his mouth and your still *elbows*, with your hands as modifiers. (Rein aids should be given only by small finger/wrist movements, never with your whole arm or by drawing back your elbows.) To achieve ideal contact with any horse will take several years and it is advantageous to have experienced help to guide you through the various stages.

Evasions

Horses have three basic types of evasion:

1. Inversion – above the bit, hollow, 'upside down', etc.
2. Speed – running too fast or dropping behind the leg and not going forward (too slow).
3. Crookedness – the horse has three parts of his body – head/neck unit, shoulders and haunches – which can be used to produce a multitude of deviations from straightness – and he may use all of them at various times!

All other evasions are variations on these three themes.

On the Aids

'On the aids' is a more holistic way of viewing how correctly your horse is going than 'on the bit', which focuses on the position of his head and neck. 'On the aids' is about the whole horse, both his mental and his physical states.

To produce an athletic and harmonious partnership we need him to be *alert yet calm* and *attentive yet relaxed*. In these mental states we have a willing and submissive partner.

The physical side of being 'on the aids' depends on him having reached a certain stage of balance. Balance will, of course, continue to change throughout his training, but he will need some development of his coordination, strength and suppleness before he can be said to be 'in balance', and therefore ready to be put 'on your aids'.

To determine if he is 'on your aids' you need to be able to tick all items on this checklist. He must:

1. Accept (a) your seat (weight) in the saddle, (b) the contact of your legs against his ribcage, and (c) the rein, allowing you to find an elastic contact.
2. Respond to your leg by moving willingly forward without running.
3. Allow you to slow him without pulling on the reins.
4. Allow you to turn him without falling in or out.
5. Understand that he should stay within the appropriate limit provided by your contact (i.e. rein length).

When you can complete this checklist and genuinely say he is 'on your aids' he will move with rhythm, freedom, straightness (equal bend on both sides) and impulsion and is ready for serious training in a chosen discipline.

Correct Posture (Outline)

'Correct' does not necessarily refer to the FEI definition of a horse working in an ideal outline. For your individual horse, 'correct' will depend on a number of factors including conformation, age, stage of training (not necessarily related to age) and his job in life. The important thing is that he is *muscularly functional.*

For example, a horse who is mostly hacking or doing endurance rides will work with a more forward-craning neck in a longer outline than a dressage horse or a showjumper. This long frame is a functional posture for his job and means that he is less likely to break down. For the dressage horse the shorter, taller frame with the poll at the highest point will be your end goal, but it must be reached by training him as a whole, not by artificially shaping his neck.

To identify correct carriage you need to look at the three bascules his body should display:

The neck should show an arched crest that is matched by the line of his underneck. This means a concave shape to the underside of his neck with no bulging underneck muscles. There should be a clear delineation between the top-line neck muscles and those underneath, with the windpipe hanging loosely.

The middle bascule is demonstrated by a clearly seen 'heave line' as a result of his abdominal muscles contracting to raise his back. Blowing and snorting during the warm-up are not just signs of mental relaxation, but also result from these contractions expelling excess air from his lungs.

The hind bascule is more difficult to see: his pelvis will change angle (tuck) with the bottom drawing forward (carrying the hind legs forward) and the top tipping slightly back, showing a slight lowering of his tail. This is most easily seen in rein-back when he appears to 'sit down'.

These three bascules are interdependent, highlighting the need to address training the whole horse, not just bits of him, as is done by the use of certain gadgets.

For more detail of the above, including photographs, see Chapter 9, p.103–4.

Independent Seat

To many, this means the ability to stay on board a horse without using the reins to assist balance.

For training purposes it must mean more than this: in order to influence your horse's gaits in both length and height, to encourage him to lift and swing his back correctly, and to make effective half-halts, you need to be able not only to follow his movement with your seat – you must be able to move your pelvis independently whilst staying totally adhesive to your saddle. In other words your seat must move pro-actively, demanding that he follows your motion, not the other way around.

Reward

We want our horses to want to work for us, in a willing and happy manner. To achieve this we contrive (without force or coercion) to place the horse in a position where he performs a step or a movement that we are attempting to teach, and then reward him so that he wants to do it again.

Reward is not about wildly enthusiastic patting sessions, nor quantities of carrots, polo mints or sugar: reward is given by cessation of the aid.

You will have asked him by positioning and aiding to perform a certain task. The most effective reward you can give him is that in the instant he obeys, you relax the demand, i.e. the aid. This requires quick reactions on your part: horses live 'in the moment' – a stride or two too late and he will not associate the reward with his response. Practice will improve your reaction time.

While he is still learning, many repetitions of demand and reward will be needed to achieve a clear connection in his mind, and you must be consistent to keep from causing confusion.

In addition, you can praise him with your voice, and also with a small touch of your knuckles (still closed around the rein) to his withers – this small gesture involves both touching him and a brief release of the rein contact for one stride only – but it must still be performed at precisely the right moment, instantly he has given you the answer to your question.

In contrast, patting and praising before he has answered you, in the hope that you might encourage him to do so, might make you feel better but will only serve to confuse him!

Schooling v Competing

The aim of schooling is to expose weak areas in your horse's abilities and training, then address and correct them. In competition, your goal is to *disguise* any problems so that the judge does not see them!

These are two totally different techniques, and need to be learned and used as such. If you have no desire to compete, then you have no need of one of these skills, but if you are to compete on a horse you train yourself you will need to know both, and to realize the effects of each on your horse.

Unless you are willing to train your horse at least two levels above the one in which you aim to compete prior to taking him out, you will quickly discover that competing is detrimental to your schooling. While, in both cases, you should take great care in the preparation of transitions and movements, in training you will wait until precisely the right moment before you make a demand. In competition you do not have the luxury of waiting, being required to perform at a given place whether your horse is ready or not. This not only has the potential to cause anxiety (loss of confidence), but may also make him realize he can do things in a different (wrong) manner.

Having said this, competition can be a good way of measuring the success of your training. It just needs to be approached with the pitfalls in mind, and in a manner appropriate to your horse's age and experience.

Techniques

These are your 'toolkit' – how you make things happen.

Always remember that any aiding can only be effective if you have sufficient control of your own body and riding position, otherwise your horse will receive lots of meaningless tweaks and random sensations. It is not his job to try to sort out the intended aid from the unintentional movements on his back. This is why cultivating a correct, well-controlled position is essential – it isn't just about looking pretty!

How to use Your Body

You have three body parts that you can use in various different ways to influence you horse: seat, legs and hands.

Seat

Your seat is responsible for the length and height of his strides. We have seen in 'requirements of the rider' (p.8) that your seat must be able to follow all three aspects of movement: horizontal, vertical and lateral. By varying the combination of these components you can influence how he moves.

More *horizontal* and less vertical movement will increase his stride length. Do this by pressing your seat from the back to the front of the saddle in a longer sweep, but without increasing the speed of the movement. Rising trot also makes this use of your seat easy: as you rise, swing your hips forward in a larger motion. You should feel almost as if you are going into slow motion because your air time out of the saddle will be greater.

More *vertical* and less horizontal movement will lift his steps higher and make them cover less ground. Do this with a feeling of pressing more down into the saddle then 'sucking' it upward with your seat. Make sure you don't leave the saddle but stay 'stuck' to it like glue, and that you keep your buttock muscles relaxed – you should be using your deep abdominal muscles (see p.132).

More *lateral* movement is mostly appropriate to the canter. In the canter sequence both legs on one side of the horse (the side of the 'leading' leg) are in advance of those on the other side (the outside). Increasing the lateral movement of your seat can help make a tense back softer and improve the lateral positioning towards his leading leg that is essential in canter to keep him functionally straight (see Definitions, p.23). This is done with a slight movement of the torso from side to side, in rhythm with his movement, and a deepening of your inside heel at each stride.

Legs

Your legs have four functions:

1. **To activate** – by using the lower leg with a slight inward/forward pressure against the horse's sides, making this movement rhythmically with his steps. Leg aids should never be given by contracting your calf muscles as this will pull your heels up – keep the muscle up the front of your shin contracted to lift your toes/foot (so lowering your heel). The adductor muscles on the inside of your thighs must make rhythmic contraction/relaxation pulses to swing your lower legs in and out, tighter and less tight against his belly – your stretched calf should never actually leave his skin.

   Try standing with one foot off the floor. Bend your knee and ankle as if your leg was in riding position. Now swing it in towards the other leg and feel which

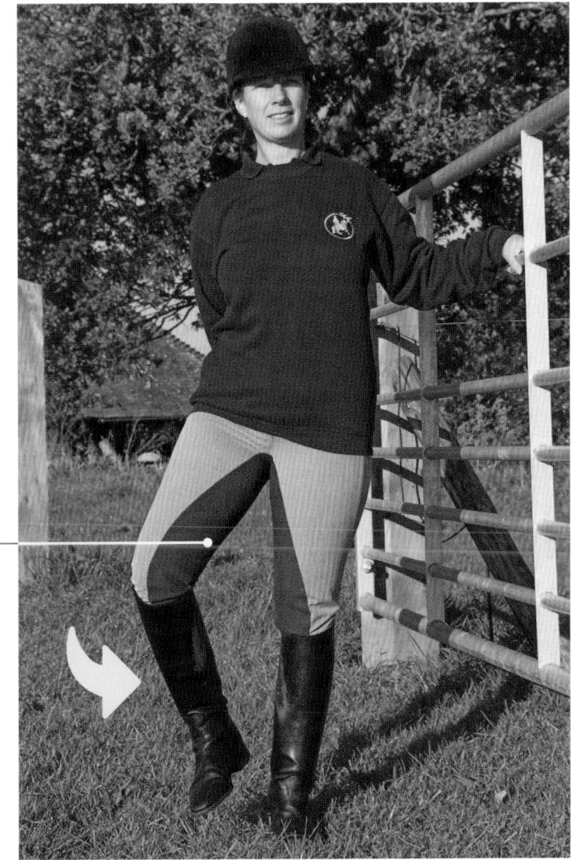

Dismounted exercise to feel the thigh adductor muscles.

muscle you used. Make absolutely certain you are not using your buttock muscles – these must always stay relaxed.

If the horse ignores your leg aid, use a larger version of the action just described, this time swinging your leg out to the side away from his belly and returning it with as much strength as you can, still *without* pulling your heel up. If it is truly necessary (and it certainly can be), this is the correct way to kick! Always do this at the correct moment in his stride – in other words, in rhythm with his footfalls – remember *he takes the speed of his steps from the speed of your aiding.*

2. **To support his posture.** This is about persuading him to contract his abdominal muscles, which in turn raises and rounds his back and enables his hind legs to travel forward underneath his belly.

   Try for yourself: get onto your hands and knees on the floor and tighten your abdominal muscles. What happened? Your back lifted and rounded. Now try moving one leg forward – that happens easily.

   Now arch your back and drop your tummy towards the floor. In this position try moving a leg forwards: it won't move far, will it? This is how your horse feels if his back is dropped.

These photographs show how a rounded back (top) facilitates hind leg movement, whereas a hollow back (below) restricts it.

Asking him to contract his abdominal muscles is done by closing both lower legs at the same time in a steady squeeze, and not letting go until you feel his back lift you up. You may need to repeat the process several times until he keeps the contraction for more than a few steps at a time, but this is essential to his ability to carry you effectively.

3. **To restrain** as a means of controlling excess speed: done by closing your *upper* legs in a consistent tighter hold on the saddle *without* clenching your buttock muscles (gripping up). Imagine that you are trying to hold the saddle at a slower speed than the one he wants (you may also need to hold your pelvis stiller to gain maximum effect – again using no buttock clenching, just core muscles). Tightening your thighs will slightly inhibit the action of his shoulder muscles, helping to slow him without having to resort to the reins.

4. **To displace him to the side,** as in lateral movements. This occurs as a result of combining leg pressure with your other aids to partially inhibit his forward travel, and redirect his impulsion instead into the sideways direction of lateral

movement. (All of the lateral work we teach has both a forward and sideways component – if his energy level remains constant, as it should, the less forward he goes, the more sideways he will travel.)

NOTE: *all your leg aids must be given without contracting your buttock muscles.* At all times your seat must remain relaxed and fully connected with your saddle. You may find this hard to do initially; practise off your horse – move your legs from side to side without clenching your seat muscles – this is essential for clear communication and to maintain relaxation in both of you.

Precise timing of your leg aid, coordinated to the lifting of the horse's hind legs, will make your aids far more effective (i.e. less effort) but this can be developed as you go along and I will discuss it whenever appropriate to an individual movement.

Hands

Your hands, through the reins and bit, have three possible actions:

1. **To follow the contact** – also known as a 'floating' contact and involves your hands being able to follow the horse's head wherever it goes – nose poking, dropping behind the vertical, up, down – so that you maintain a constant weight in your hands. This is not easy!

   This technique is most appropriate to a horse who lacks balance and is still using a varied head position to help rebalance himself. In no way should this horse be restricted by your hands. As his balance improves his head carriage will gradually stabilize. This contact then becomes the elastic soft contact you want.

   In some cases of evasion this can also work; the horse will eventually come to terms with the idea that no matter where he puts his head, he cannot evade your hands. As it gains him nothing he will gradually stop moving his head around and settle to a steady position and contact.

2. **To provide appropriate limitation to the posture of his neck.** Such a limit can be needed when a horse tries to poke his nose out, or put his head up above the bit, but should not be used to 'shorten' his neck artificially in an effort to collect him.

   To achieve this limiting you must develop a *contact point,* also known as the *base of hand,* so that whatever he tries to do with his head, your hand will stay in exactly the same spot. This is not easy when he is trying to pull you around, but with practice it can be achieved. It involves *isometric tone* in the muscles of your torso and in your upper arms. ('Tone' = partially contracting a muscle without reaching clenching or tension point; 'isometric' = toning two sets of opposing muscles.)

   Put your arms into riding position. Now try to push your elbows backward and your fists forward at the same time. The result is your hands will stay still, but your upper arm muscles will have tone. Your elbows should be lying close to your sides, not sticking out, and your forearms should be relaxed, with your wrists soft.

Body tone is created in the same way, using the muscles on the front of your torso in opposition to those on the back, but with no tension in your waist or seat.

These two muscular efforts together will enable you to prevent the horse from moving your hands from the place where you want them to stay.

A good way to think about contact is that your upper arms belong to you; your forearms belong to the horse. Contact is really made between his mouth and your elbows – your hands simply hold the reins.

3. **To yield forward.** This can be used to (a) reward, (b) test for self-carriage (see Definitions, p.21) or (c) alter the horse's frame, such as when stretching his neck down.

   To yield one rein, push your hand forward towards his mouth until your elbow is straight (see photograph, p.111). This can also be done with both reins at the same time (see photograph p.22).

   To retake the rein use a slight D-shaped action that will encourage softness.

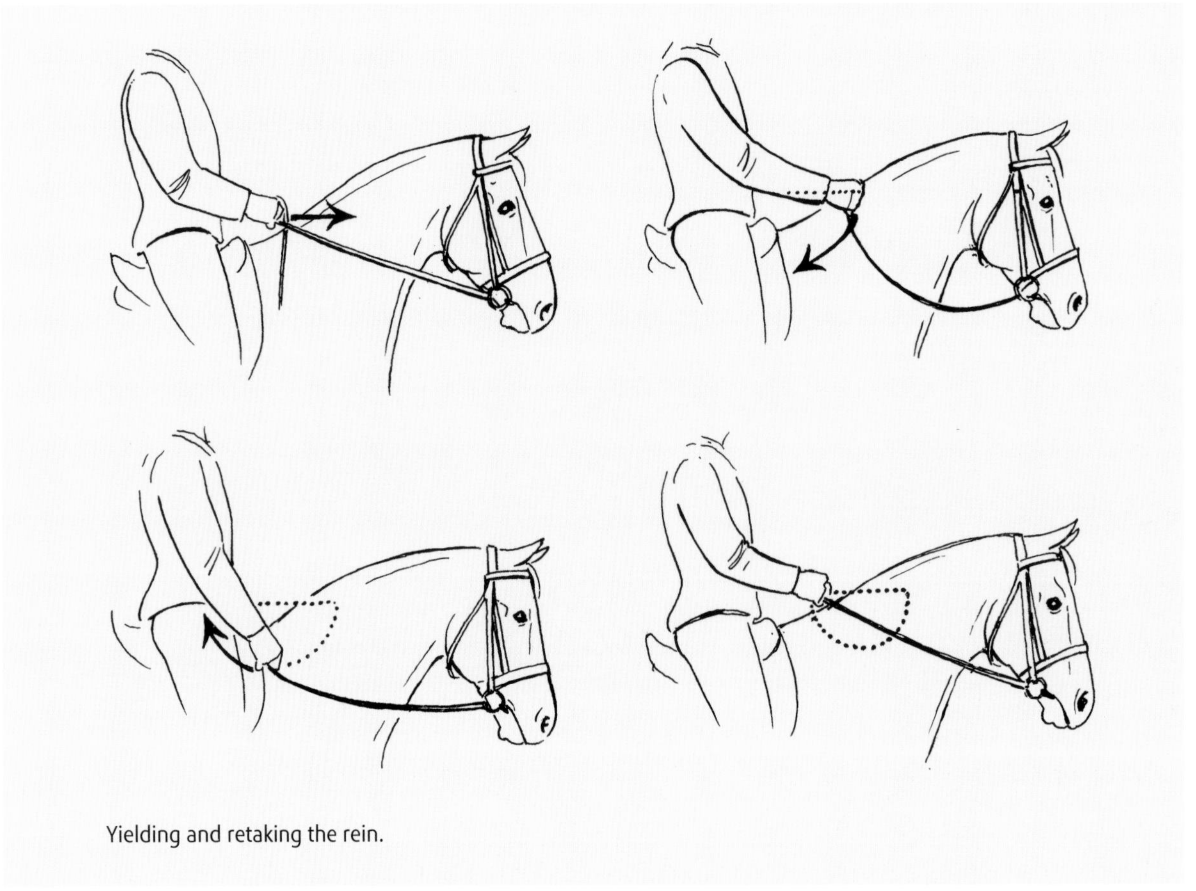

Yielding and retaking the rein.

Direct and Indirect Reins

These are your steering and bending rein aids.

Direct Rein

The direct rein, also known as the open or leading rein, is used for exaggerating your turning aid, especially with a young or uneducated horse. Keep your inside elbow close to your side and move your forearm towards the inside of your circle/turn. Support this with your outside rein, still in contact but slightly allowing forward, to permit the outside of the horse's body to stretch so he can bend round to the inside – see photograph overleaf.

Indirect Rein

The indirect rein is used to position/re-position the horse's shoulder towards the outside of a bend. By taking your inside hand inward and even slightly across his neck at the withers (without altering its height), you can cause him to move his shoulder out and at the same time bend his neck to the inside.

Use this only as a brief corrective aid (you must return your hand to its normal position as soon as you have his shoulders where you want them) or he will begin to use your hand as a prop and quite happily lean on it – see photograph overleaf.

Combination Aiding

Clearly, most aids are a combination of seat, leg(s) and rein(s). With experience you will learn to balance the ratios of all three in a wide variety of circumstances.

Your aids will also sometimes multi-task, e.g. in lateral movements where your legs activate and displace at the same time.

Passive Resistance

This concept follows on from 'rein action no. 2' above, and is the basis of the aids for the *half-halt*, but it may also be used in other circumstances, such as a means to correct hollowing, to deal with resistance to your contact, or to slow and thus rebalance a running horse.

1. Find a base position for your hand as described above. This is to limit how far he can dispute your contact.

2. Tone your lumbar (lower) back muscles and your deep abdominal muscles to find a feeling of pushing your seat slightly forward and down into the saddle, so increasing your vertical pressure. He should feel that he cannot dislodge you.

3. At the same time, support his ribcage with a closure of your legs – the upper legs (inside thigh muscles toned but without tightening your buttocks) to help

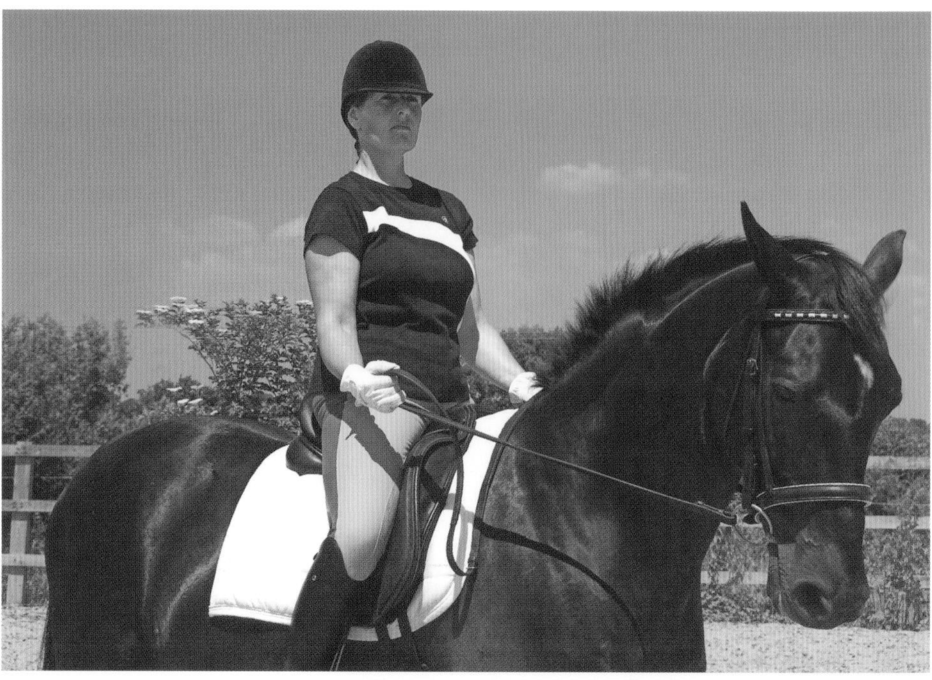

Direct rein – elbow close to ribcage; forearm moves to the side but stays at the same height.

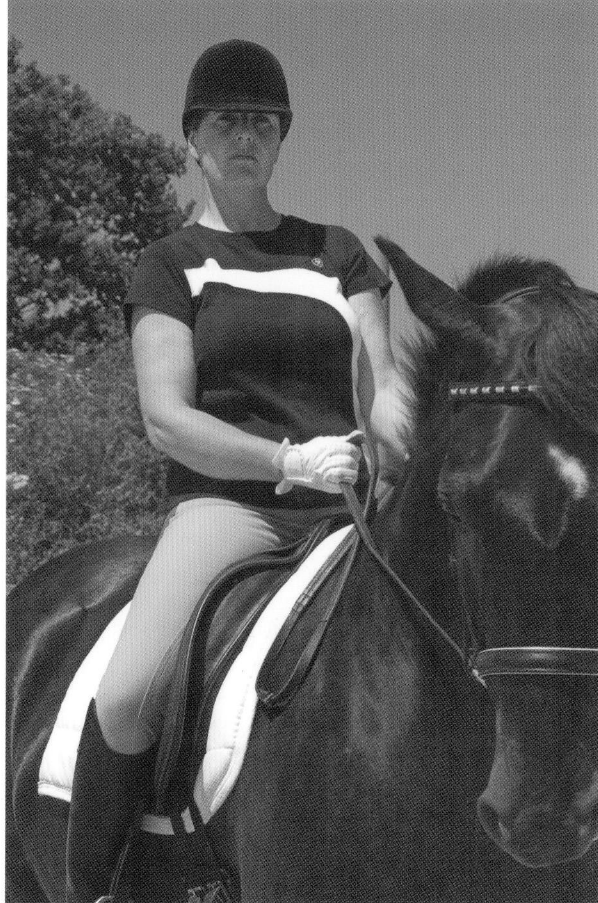

Indirect rein – hand moves in towards the withers (with no pulling backwards); forearm stays at the same height.

restrain, lower legs squeezing rhythmically with the gait to encourage his hind legs to step forward under his body.

The contraction of his abdominal muscles, which causes his back to lift, also pulls the pubic arch (bottom front of his pelvis) forward. His hind legs are moved forward by this action, so your seat and legs are working here to produce the same effect (see Biomechanics in Chapter 9).

When you have your desired response: a rounding of his outline; a polite seeking forward for the contact; a slowing from a run; a rebalancing – you relax all three aiding components to harmonize:

1. Change to a floating contact.

2. Swing along with a more horizontal seat action.

3. Relax your legs.

Remember, harmonizing (release of pressure) is both reward and confirmation that he has given you the answer you wanted.

Half-halt

The half-halt can be defined as 'a momentary rebalancing and activation of the horse whilst in motion'.

In simple terms – persuading his front end to wait whilst his back end catches up and his hind legs step further forward under his body.

The aids are a momentary application of those described earlier in 'passive resistance', although the ratios of your seat, leg and rein aids may well vary according to level of training and thus his ability to respond. 'Momentary' may be as brief as half a stride with an educated horse, or as much as half a circle (and sometimes more!) with a green horse. The secret to a successful half-halt is to feel for your desired response (a change in balance towards his hindquarters, and a stepping under of his hind legs) and to:

1. Keep your aids in place until you feel him give this response.

2. Respond *immediately* yourself by relaxing and harmonizing.

Half-halts cannot be used until the horse is submissive to the rein contact, and the demands should be progressive – you should not expect great results before his second year of training.

Inside and Outside Leg Positions

Every book on riding will tell you that you need your inside leg at the girth and your outside leg slightly behind the girth. Many leave it at that.

Inside and outside leg positions do not apply only when riding circles or asking for canter on a particular lead. They should be in position *all* the time with the exception of centre lines and other straight lines away from the track, when they should both be in girth position.

This is not a case of being picky, but of function. If your horse swings his hindquarters to the outside, he should meet your outside leg before he has deviated more than a few centimetres (an inch or so). Unless you are using it for a specific purpose, your outside leg may hang quite passively, just touching his side, *but it should always be in place.*

Looking further ahead, as he becomes more advanced in canter work this difference between inside and outside leg positions is crucial to keep him in your chosen canter lead, especially when riding counter-canter, or if he has started to learn flying changes. (Many horses learn changes when they showjump – this is not the sole domain of the dressage horse.)

Position Left and Right

The basis of all steering and bending, whether on a simple curved line such as a circle, or in a complex movement such as a half-pass, is the ability of the rider to sit in either position left or position right.

By way of example, the following are the steps to attain position left:

1. Turn your upper body (including your head) to the left, *from the waist* upward.
2. Keep your elbows in position near the points of your hips. This naturally moves your inside (left) hand slightly towards the inside of the curve whilst moving your outside (right) hand towards the neck and slightly forward. This closes the outside rein snug against the horse's neck, controlling his shoulder yet at the same time allowing the right side of his body to lengthen, whilst the left shortens: in other words *left bend.*
3. Your head (face) should remain at 90 degrees to your shoulders.
4. Move your outside (right) leg slightly back *from the hip*, (not the knee). You will feel this raise your right seat bone upward inside the buttock muscle, away from the saddle. This puts greater weight into your inside (left) seat bone – one of the components of the turning aids (Chapter 8).
5. Ensure that your inside leg remains stretched down with your *inside hip forward.* You should now feel that you have more weight in your inside stirrup iron than in your outside.

Position right entails the opposite of the above.

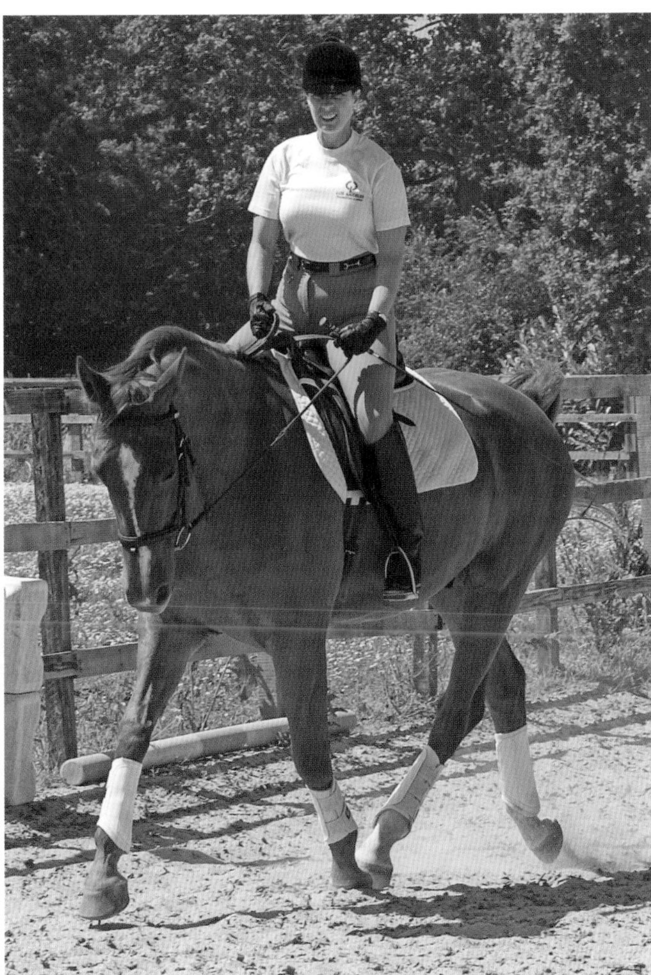

Position left, seen from the inside. 5-year-old Hanoverian/Belgian, *Lover Boy*, also known as *Stanley*.

Position left, from the outside. *Stanley's* full brother, 10-year-old *Leo's Orlando*, also known as *Ollie*, ridden by his owner, Nikki Green.

The Corridor of the Aids

This is a training concept designed to assist in the development of straightness.

- Imagine your horse moving along a corridor.
- The walls of the corridor are defined by the reins, your hands, your forearms and your elbows.
- Your horse cannot move his shoulders beyond the walls of the corridor.
- If the corridor is wide, he can move his shoulders quite a way from side to side. This is necessary to some extent on a young horse as he lacks the ability to maintain his balance with ease (self-carriage). With a more educated horse any extra width in the corridor, such as elbows sticking out, can be exploited by him to evade your controls.
- As his training progresses you will gradually narrow the corridor by moving your hands closer together, gaining more precise control over the placement of his shoulders.
- Ultimately, your guidance of his shoulders will be so refined that you will carry your hands no more than a hand's width apart and you will feel as if you have his shoulders threaded 'through the eye of a needle'.

The corridor of the aids.

The wider 'corridor' for the younger horse

The narrower 'corridor' – hands closer together – of the more advanced horse

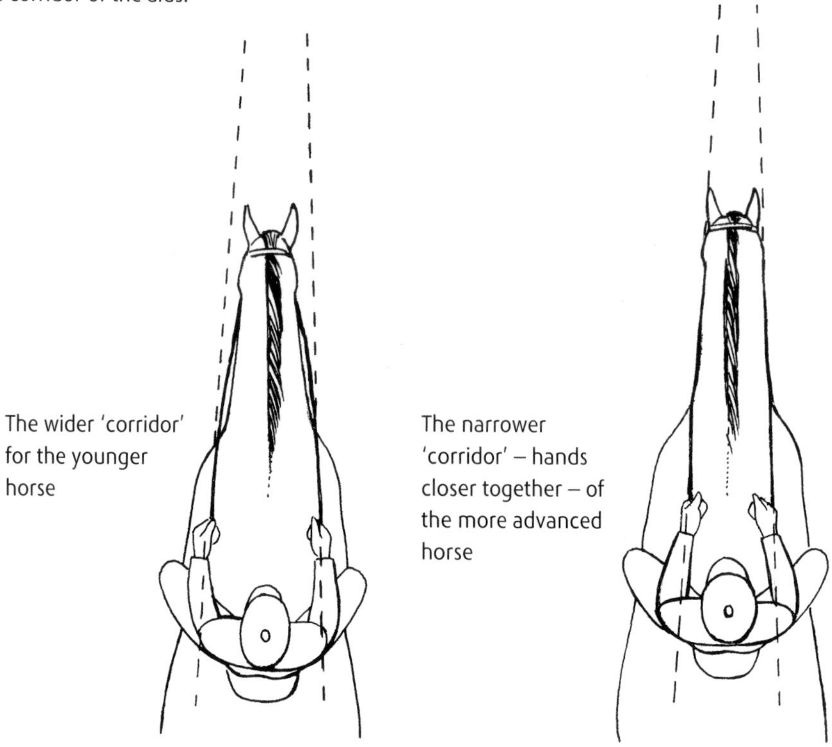

Inside Leg to Outside Rein

Achieving a correct connection from inside leg to outside rein is one of the most important skills you will develop. It allows you to position your horse's forehand wherever you want to without compromising the engagement of his hind legs by pulling, or restricting with the inside rein. Even slightly too strong a contact in the inside hand will have a blocking effect on his inside hind leg, preventing it from stepping fully forward.

The best place to gain a feeling for this connection is on a circle.

- Ride an accurately shaped 20 m circle.
- Ensure that you have clear inside bend. Feel that you are pressing his ribcage outward away from your inside lower leg, and add knee and thigh pressure if he does not yield easily. Check that you can see his inside eye (without leaning over!) and that his haunches are correctly aligned.
- Now give your inside rein away – see photograph, p.111. Initially do this for three or four strides only, and maintain a steady outside rein contact.
- If his bend does not change, you have achieved your goal.
- If he loses bend, or changes it altogether, check first that your outside rein has a 'forward' enough feel to allow his body to bend.
- If he still loses bend you will need to use exercises such as leg-yielding (Chapter 15) on straight lines and on spirals, to confirm more clearly in his mind that he must move away from your inside leg.
- You may also need to work for longer at equalizing the muscle lengths on the two sides of his body – you will probably find you can get the connection in one direction (with his shorter side on the inside) but not in the other.

Correct Use of a Schooling Whip

With young horses a short jumping whip is best – the flap on the end makes a noise that may be effective at startling him forward without much force behind it. A long, sharp whip will often have the opposite effect – he will back into it in protest.

Once he is forward-thinking, you can change to a long schooling whip that you can use without taking your hand off the reins.

The next point to consider is where to apply the whip: different horses are sensitive in different places on their bodies. In general, the correct place to use the whip is *just* behind your leg, so the horse thinks that your leg has suddenly become sharper and thus gains more respect for your leg aids. In some cases, however, you will find more response by touching him further back and/or higher or lower. Experiment to find out what works best with your individual horse.

Swish your whip from side to side, but keep it straight upward – you don't want unintentionally to clip him around the ears!

To help him understand to *sit* more, as opposed to go more forward, you can touch him on top of his croup. If he responds by pushing his croup up, or by threatening to buck, you need to repeat the tap but keep your weight firmly down in the back of your seat (even leaning back if you have to) and maintain a light contact with slightly raised hands to help him understand that he is to lower his croup and raise his forehand. If he goes above the bit in the short term, this does not matter and can be corrected when you have the desired response from his haunches.

In canter it is often more helpful to use the whip on the *outside*, as this encourages the quicker movement of the first leg in the sequence (outside hind) which improves impulsion.

Generally, the whip should be applied as a single tap with more or less sharpness depending on the response you want. If the horse does not respond you must apply it again *immediately* and if necessary keep doing so until you get a response – he *must not* be allowed to ignore it, or it becomes useless as an aid. Even if his response is not what you wanted (e.g. he bucks), you must at first accept it – at least he did respond. In the long term, however, bucking as a response is not acceptable and you must smack him again, sending him more forward regardless of how he goes (head up, wrong gait, out of control, etc.). In time he will accept that it is not worth the hassle of ignoring you.

Nappy horses will often back up against the whip – try using it upright in front of your face, swishing it from side to side to make a whistling noise. Just be careful the first time: he may over-react.

You can also use it by waving it outward beside him, as if you were going to smack him, but without connecting. Watch jockeys 'scrubbing' with their whips towards the end of a race – this encourages without actually hitting him.

Initially you don't need to be too fussy about timing the whip aid. However, as you progress you may want to influence an individual lazy hind leg, or ask his inside hind to step further forward on a circle or in say, shoulder-in. The only time you can influence an individual leg is during its flight phase – when it is in the air – so this is the moment to tap.

In walk this is the same moment as when you apply your inside leg (see Chapter 11, p.129). In sitting trot you must feel for the same thing as in walk (his belly swinging away from your inside leg), or in rising trot it is as you *rise*, not as you sit. In canter it is the same time as when you use your leg – during his moment of suspension.

Correct Use of Spurs

Spurs should only be used to emphasize a leg aid if the horse has been slow to respond or ignored you, *never* to prod him at every stride just to keep him moving.

With your legs correctly positioned your spurs will not touch his sides. They should be used only when required by a brief outward turn of your foot to press them once, as sharply as required, against his side before returning your foot to its usual position. Your goal is to remind him to respect and listen to your legs, not to bruise his sides.

4 Think like a Horse

Basic Nature

To develop clear lines of communication you first need to understand *how* your horse thinks and what is *important to him*, and then you will be better able to anticipate his reactions and form requests that make sense to him.

First and foremost: *your horse thinks like a horse, not a human.* Imagining that he processes thought like a human is at least stupid, and at worst, dangerous. To communicate safely and sensibly with him *you* must learn to think like a horse.

Horses are grazing herd animals. No matter how we keep them now, that is their origin and they are supremely adapted to that lifestyle. Their time in the wild was split between searching for food and avoiding predators. Along with the seasonal urge to breed, these two factors were paramount to the horse, and they still colour his life and responses today. Whilst domestication and selective breeding have gone some way towards modifying these natural traits, they are never far below the surface.

The horse's natural instincts and reactions may affect his training in the following ways.

Herd Instinct

This tells him that he is safer in a crowd – the greater the numbers the better his odds of surviving an attack by predators. Examples can be seen at every dressage or jumping show – the horse who warms up happily with the crowd then refuses either to leave the warm-up area or to enter the competition arena where he will be alone. Overcoming this natural instinct requires training in both obedience and trust. In the early days it can be exploited by using an educated horse as a lead, or by asking the green horse to do something (like a small jump) when heading towards others. It is quite likely that he will have more impulsion in an arena when heading towards the exit (i.e. towards his stable and companions) – the ideal place to teach lengthened strides!

Herd Hierarchy

Studies have shown that our previous belief in dominance within herd structure by means of 'pecking order' is erroneous and largely based on domestic horses thrown together in groups in enclosed fields – a highly unnatural situation. In the wild there is no competition for small piles of food or space in gateways and although some individuals are undoubtedly more aggressive than others, this has nothing to do with the organization of social hierarchy in the natural state. The more dominant animals appear to be those who are the *focus of attention*. In training terms, aggression produces fear that will cause some horses to submit, and others to attempt to escape, or even to fight back. Whichever reaction occurs (depending on that individual's own natural degree of aggression), fear will *always* serve to confuse and so limit learning. Successful training is better based on the 'focus of attention' approach, initially using familiar and thus relatively calming surroundings to minimize the horse's loss of attention from you. An indoor school is ideal, as there will be a minimum of distractions. Failing that, use an all-weather school or an enclosed field where you can control the surrounding environment as far as possible. Ideally, this should not be situated too close to your horse's stable or grazing field (see below). Once you are established as the focus of his attention he will keep it firmly on you wherever you take him, making him a reliable partner so long as *you* do not become distracted! A horse who has been trained in this way would become very upset if a new rider were to use heavy-handed dominance, just as a horse who has been dominated may at first take advantage of a less aggressive approach.

Need for Security

This, both in terms of companionship (herd instinct) and knowledge of where food can be found may be displayed in ways ranging from nappiness at one end of the scale to a calm and receptive individual at the other. Schooling in his grazing field, or even having your school near his stable can often be the cause of problems as his mind is more likely to be on the food he associates with those locations than on his training. On the other hand, if he has done an exercise particularly well, then finishing a schooling session early and returning him to his box/companions is a great way to reward him. Taking time to develop his sense of security is hugely important in training a young horse as, without it, he will never be able to truly focus on anything beyond his basic instincts.

The Instinct to Follow

Most horses are by nature followers, not leaders. In the domestic situation these individuals are quite content to follow a human instead of another horse. Those few who are, by nature, leaders (often stallions) are more safely left to very experienced riders.

Laziness

Laziness (energy conservation) is natural to a horse. In his wild state the mature horse may cover long distances in a day seeking water and fresh pasture, but he will do so with a minimum of effort, only truly exerting himself when fleeing from a predator. Youngsters, on the other hand, will use energy to play, and selective breeding is going some way towards producing horses who, even at maturity, are more willing to expend energy on activities unnecessary to survival. Many horses, however, are still governed by the natural urge to conserve energy, and these are your 'lazy' individuals.

Excitability

Excitability is a natural result of conditions that are reminiscent of the horse's wild state, or occurs when he is asked to do something that he would not do in natural conditions. Galloping (or a speedy, unbalanced canter) simulates flight from a predator. Jumping is unnatural to horses, as herds tend to live on open grassland, so this may also be a cause of excitement. Fear is another cause of agitation, as may be the approach of a strange horse. You cannot prevent a horse from becoming excited, but by training him to be obedient to your aids, and by accustoming him to the causes, you will be able to control and contain it.

Nervousness

This is an integral part of the horse's survival mechanism – to shy, spin round and run off are all part of his natural instinct to flee from danger. You must never punish him for spooking, either deliberately or by accident (losing balance and jerking on his mouth) as this only makes him more nervous. He needs you to be confident and, as far as you are able, to ignore the object of fear – this will suggest to him that it is not worthy of his attention.

Sensitivity

Sensitivity is apparent in the way a horse will feel a fly touch his skin anywhere on his body. If you believe that your horse is insensitive to your aids you are mistaken – he has simply learned to ignore them or react against the discomfort you are causing. Pulling on the reins causes him to run faster – away from pain in his mouth. Kicking hard can often cause him to go even slower as he tenses his muscles rigidly against your hammering heels or spurs. What you create with force you must hold with force and, if it comes down to a straight contest, the size of his muscles compared to yours should tell you who will win! Try using light, small aids and praise him for even the tiniest correct reaction so that in the long term he will *want* to give you the responses you desire. Horses are by nature cooperative, and many show a delight in learning if they are confident and trusting.

Memory

The horse has an excellent memory – for both good and bad experiences. As he has no powers of *reasoning* his reactions are always based on memories. Instant reward and instant punishment (for example, a swift smack if he bites) will determine his future actions. What he *does not* understand is *delayed* reward or punishment – he has no ability to link things across a time delay and any response you want him to take note of must be given within *one second* for the two events to be associated in his mind.

Ear Positions

The attitude of a horse's ears is a dead give-away for his emotional state: laid back warns of temper, pricked up tells you that he is attentive to his surroundings, not to you. Flicking backward and forward means he is dividing his attention between you and what he sees in front of him. When riding, you ideally want to see his ears turned back towards you – partly as a sign of attention, but also because this shows submission – he cannot hear what is going on ahead but listens only to you.

Love of Routine

This is not derived from Nature, but is a result of the domestic state. Routine helps make for a relaxed horse although, if followed too strictly, it may cause problems when, for example, an outing to a show calls for changes. Try to keep such things as grooming and feeding as regular as possible, but vary the time of day at which your horse works. Also, once he is attentive to you, take him to other places to work and ask him to stay in strange stables – all things he may have to do if he is to handle change/competition later in life. Initially these variations may cause him anxiety, but with repetition he will learn to cope and will hopefully enjoy his outings.

Learning and Teaching Strategies

An important rule to remember is: with horses, *every experience is a learning experience – either for good or for bad. There is no neutral.*

The consequence of this is that any undesirable behaviour you might permit from the horse because you are tired, in a hurry or simply don't think it will matter 'just this once', will have ramifications further on in his training. You must be absolutely conscientious at all times when handling or riding him, and if you are short of time, don't start something you cannot be sure to finish.

Learning is *a change in response as a result of experience.* There are several different types of learning.

Habituation

This is a temporary learning *not* to respond to a stimulus and can be both useful and a problem. On the positive side, you can teach your horse not to be afraid of say, a noise, by frequently exposing him to it. After a few times his startle response will lessen, although the exposure may need repeating several times over a number of days to become truly successful. On the downside, he may learn to ignore say, a leg aid if it is repeated too often. Consider the rider who kicks constantly just to keep moving. Her horse has learned to 'switch off' to the leg aid because of repeated exposure to it.

Habituation does not always carry over to a different *place*; the same stimulus at a show may have completely different results!

Conditioned Response

Horses will learn to connect a signal with a behaviour pattern. For instance, when you lunge him, if you say 'Trot' just *before* he is about to trot (either because you can see him about to jog on, or because you have flicked the whip at him), after a few repetitions the word produces the action. *Timing* and *repetition* (to increase strength of habit) are the important factors, not reward or punishment.

Trial and Error

This involves the horse learning a new response in order to get a reward. This is particularly appropriate to more advanced training: first you reward him for any slight effort in the right direction whether you asked for it of not (e.g. if he volunteers a flying change you have not requested he should be rewarded, not punished, because you will want that reaction later on). As he progresses you gradually begin to reward only the perfect response.

Latent Learning

This describes learning without reward or stimulus, e.g. knowing where he will regularly be allowed to canter whilst out on a hack, or finding his own way home after you have parted company!

Insight

This is largely absent from horses, who are not by nature problem-solvers; *so don't expect your horse to work something out as you would.* This is why he needs building block training – and not just the physical build-up to make his body capable of performing what you want. He also needs you to teach him each individual stage until he clearly *understands* it before you can link responses together to bring about more complicated exercises. Once he does understand, his excellent memory will retain that knowledge.

Imprinting

This is how a horse knows he is a horse! He is born with an innate desire to follow anything that moves, especially anything large. After a few days he becomes choosy and follows only the one who has given him what he wants – his mother. This can be a problem with orphan foals who tend to imprint on a human, making later interactions complicated and not always safe!

Factors Involved in Learning

The most important factors in learning are:

Timing – reward (relaxation of aid) must occur immediately the horse gives the right response, or *within one second*, otherwise the connection between the two will not be made.

Repetition – essential to form strong habits.

Reinforcement by reward also strengthens the habit you are cultivating, and is even more successful if it is not used every time, becoming less frequent as training progresses. Punishment only works if it stops the response before it is complete – *there is no point punishing the horse after he has completed the response* as this won't mean anything to him and will cause anxiety that inhibits learning.

Negative reinforcement is a tool for discouraging unwanted responses merely by ignoring them. If a response earns neither reward nor punishment the horse will gradually cease to offer it. With a spooky horse, for instance, ignoring the spooks will gradually reduce them, whereas attempting to correct him by punishment or by patting and offering titbits as a bribe will only focus his attention on his incorrect response and may actually reinforce it.

Consistency in training is essential and something many riders are poor at. Most understand the principle but lack the self-discipline to give commands in a consistent fashion and to insist on obedience every time. Lack of consistency causes the horse to become confused and upset and to lose confidence in his handler/rider. Also, every time he is allowed to get away with behaviour you don't want ('It won't matter, just this once', you might think), he remembers. To repeat: *to a horse, every experience is a learning experience* – he has an excellent memory but no ability to differentiate between the human concepts of good or bad – he simply learns from us what we will accept. In the ideal situation, if you never give him cause for anxiety by being inconsistent, he will accept whatever you ask of him with ease and confidence. Try to use your brain and think situations through in advance – in theory your mind is your biggest advantage over him.

5 Early Training

There are many good texts covering the starting of a young horse from foal to early ridden work. The aim of this chapter is not to cover what is a large topic in brief, but to point out those behaviours and responses that are so essential further down the line, but which may easily be glossed over if their importance is not recognized.

It may seem obvious, but obedience to basic handling procedures is the basis for all other work. It is essential both from a *safety* aspect, and as a young horse's first real introduction to *submission*. These will be the first demands we place upon him for *attention*, and thus the first steps to gaining his *respect*. It should also be where you confirm his *trust* in you – that you will, in fairness, ask only things he can answer, and put such questions in terms that are logical and understandable to him, not just to you.

Foals

First Days

The first few days after birth are a good time to accustom the horse to a human presence and to being touched. Start by caressing him along the top of the neck, as the mare does. Do not approach him directly from the front – with their eyes on the sides of their skull, horses have a blind spot directly in front of their face and anything moving in that general area will be distorted. If you make him anxious he will move away to avoid contact – not what you want.

Within a week he should be haltered. His natural reaction to restraint will be to dispute it, so this is the time to teach him that he cannot break away from you. Once he is accustomed to wearing his foal-slip, attach a long rope and restrain him when he tries to move away. If you are fortunate, he will do little more than pull against the rope for a while before yielding to you. If not, you will discover that even a small foal can put up a strong battle and may lose balance and fall over, so ensure he is on soft ground. If, when he regains his feet, or simply stops struggling, you are still attached to the other end, he will have made his first mental steps towards accepting that the rope means restraint.

Losing his first dispute this early on directs his mind along the right lines – with a belief that people cannot be resisted. If this is not firmly established at the start and he learns that he can successfully resist over any matter, convincing him otherwise will be extremely hard.

Introducing Leading

To start with, lead the foal alongside his mother. This does not actually teach him to lead, but he will make attempts to rush forward and the rope will restrain him, confirming the lesson above.

To teach him to walk independently, use a soft rope around his rump (to push him forward) combined with the foal-slip, and begin to introduce the verbal commands you will use later in his training.

Verbal commands should be single words where possible, and certainly no more than two, with crisp sounds: 'Walk on', 'Stop', 'Stand', and 'No' for disobedience. Always use the same inflection.

Do not hide the command in the middle of a sentence.

When he does as you ask, praise him with a softer sound: 'Good' or 'Brave', stretching the sound and expressing pleasure with your tone.

Leading for the Show Ring

Showing a mare with a foal at foot is excellent education for the foal. Not only will he have to travel, giving him experience of loading with (hopefully) the calm influence of his mother to reassure him, but he will also be exposed to the sights and atmosphere of a show with that same reassuring presence.

In addition, he will get extra training beyond that of a normal foal, in terms of learning to trot up in hand beside his mother, and also to stand in line whilst she is taken away and trotted up on her own.

This sort of education makes for far less 'culture shock' when he is older and taken to his first shows under saddle.

Picking up Feet

Again, this is a job for the earliest days, when he is still too small to argue effectively. Hoof care and eventual shoeing are your primary goals, but should you choose later on to use in-hand work, he will need to lift each leg in turn to the light touch of a whip on his leg. A relaxed but sensitive response will be facilitated by his earliest lessons in lifting each leg obediently to command.

Tying up

Horses who will not stand when tied up are difficult in many ways. All the usual handling tasks – grooming, clipping, shoeing, tacking up, travelling – are made infinitely easier if your horse will stand patiently tied up.

This is yet another lesson best tackled while he is small. Start by simply slipping the end of his lead rope through a ring and holding on to it. Do this when you give him his hard feed, allowing the rope to be long enough so that he can reach his bucket with ease. Keep him there for a while after he finishes until this becomes a regular routine.

If he pulls back you can reprimand him with a sharp 'No!' and if necessary a tap on the rump to send him forward until the strain is off the rope.

Once he becomes used to the routine and the restraint, tie the rope to a piece of string, which in turn is tied to the tie ring. This will be strong enough should he argue, yet will still break should he fall. Ensure he can still reach his bucket with ease and do not leave him alone.

If this lesson is left too late, he will have both stronger opinions and greater bodyweight with which to argue.

Moving Over

Moving over on command is your very earliest step towards lateral work – even if you only wish to train your horse as far as opening and closing gates!

Accompanying the verbal command, 'Over', you should place a hand on his flank and push until he moves his entire body or his rear end away from you. Praise him when he does so, as this is not a natural response for him.

In a natural situation horses *answer pressure with pressure*. The best example is bucking – a natural response designed to dislodge a predator landing on his back. So, when you first ask him to move over, he will push back at you and it is your task to teach him to *yield to pressure* – an essential concept for a riding horse.

Ideally, you will do this while he is still small enough for you to use your own bodyweight to push him over despite his protests. If you do not have enough weight on your own, get someone else to help.

Slapping him on the flank is another option that may startle him into moving away from you, but is also likely to cause him to kick at you and is better left until later when it can be used as a reminder for a lesson already learned.

Weanlings

This next phase of the youngster's education should follow on directly from his lessons as a foal. He will be gaining body mass and developing an individual character, and will be continually testing his boundaries. Handled sensibly, you can use this time to direct his development along the lines you want.

Keep the lessons short, as his attention span is limited at this age.

Manners

The young horse should be civil at all times. He will have plenty of playtime in the paddock, so when he is being handled he should give you *attention* and *obedience*, and understand that he cannot intrude on your personal space (barging). *This is not too much to ask.*

Horses who have never learned manners or respect are not only difficult to train, but can be dangerous. If he steps out of line you should use a sharp verbal reprimand: 'No!' If this proves insufficient you may need to back it up with an open-handed smack, or a sharp tap with a whip. It is not wrong to smack him, no matter what his age; young horses are very quick to sense an advantage and if he is allowed to get away with anything he will develop a wilful and stubborn streak – it is better that he is never allowed to get his own way in the first place.

Having said this, it is crucial that you do not destroy his confidence in you by being overly aggressive. You must reprimand only when necessary, and be absolutely quiet and consistent in all your other handling of him.

Proper Leading, Starting and Stopping

Until now, leading will have involved the youngster following his mother. After weaning he has to begin obeying you without the lead of another horse. In his terms he is ready to start interacting with the herd as an individual, and he must now acknowledge you as herd leader – the one to whom he pays attention.

Be sensible – think. Begin your training in a controlled environment. A well-fenced small area: a small school or a round pen would be ideal. A large open field is inviting trouble.

Starting

This involves him walking forward in response to the verbal command 'Walk on'.

If his lessons as a foal were well learned you should find this stage relatively easy. However, if he needs a little encouragement, try the following:

1. Leading him towards other horses.
2. Carry a short jumping whip and tap him on the belly behind you.

3. Have an assistant walk behind you with a longer whip and have them tap him on the rump, ensuring they are out of reach of his hind legs in case he should kick out.

Always remember – horses can kick forward as well as backward. Be aware and position yourself sensibly.

Hopefully none of these extras will be needed, but ease of leading and obedience to the command to 'Walk on' are essential as they impact on all handling and, later on, lungeing.

Stopping

Stopping should be achieved by the combined use of a verbal command of your choosing ('Whoa', 'Stop', 'Stand', 'Halt') and restraint on the lead rope. Once you have made your choice of command word, stick to it and always use it with the same inflection – the same word given in a different tone will have no meaning to him.

Backing up

Asking him to step backwards should be an easy progression from teaching him to move over. As you have already instilled in his mind that he should yield to a pressure applied by you, you can now use the same concept for backing up.

Stand in front but slightly to one side (not directly in front of his foreleg, in case he strikes out), put your hand against the middle of his chest and, accompanied by the word 'Back', apply pressure to his chest.

If he does not step backwards, apply more pressure to his chest, repeat 'Back' and if he still does not comply, try a small slap to his chest – this may startle him into moving back.

Whenever he does what you have asked, no matter how hard you have had to work to get the response from him, or how small a response he gives, you *must* praise him – he will associate the praise directly with his response. If you withhold praise simply because he took time to respond, he will not understand.

Teaching him to back up now not only makes general handling easier, it also has implications later on for the ease with which he will learn rein-back, and is also a requirement of the vetting process (for sale or insurance purposes).

Loading and Travelling

Travelling can be one of the most stressful aspects of a competition horse's life but, even if he is not going to compete, it is rare for a horse not to have to travel at some time in his life.

Early introduction of loading and travelling, so that they are simply a normal part of his life, can make a great deal of difference to his stress levels and hence (for the competition horse) his performance.

Youngsters up to Backing

For the most part, youngsters should be left to grow up as young horses, with others of similar age for social interaction, and in as natural conditions as possible.

Handling generally need be only as frequent as required for health reasons – hoof trimming, vaccinations, etc. However, occasional revision periods are a good idea, if possible involving trips to in-hand shows with all the attendant grooming, bathing, trimming, travelling and leading, reinforcing the early lessons.

If attention is paid to these early lessons, backing will come as no great shock to the youngster and you will then be ready to progress with his training as a riding horse with all his basic responses in place.

A final word on handling: always remember that, no matter how much you love and trust your horse, *do not treat him as a pet.* He is a horse: a large, heavy animal, often with steel-shod hooves and a natural heritage that makes him prone to unpredictable sudden movements – no matter how quiet you think he is.

He does not process thought in the same fashion as a human being – *he thinks like a horse and should be treated as one.*

6 Lunge Work

Again, there are many texts covering this topic in detail and this chapter will merely point out those responses that are essential to have in place before you progress to ridden work, and the most common exercises you can use to continue the horse's schooling from the ground.

Equipment

Introduce each piece of gear you want the horse to wear gradually. For effective lunge work, i.e. for training as opposed to exercising, you will need:

- **A bridle.** If the horse is not to be ridden immediately after lungeing, strip it down (remove the reins and noseband) to avoid too many straps around his face. If you intend to ride afterwards, you will need the bridle complete, with the reins twisted up into the throatlatch.
- **A lunge cavesson.** Many people lunge with the line attached to the bit – this can damage the horse's mouth and makes it impossible to give correct half-halts on the line.
- **A lunge roller** with rings at varied heights or, if you intend to ride afterwards, a saddle.
- **Side reins,** long enough to have plenty of adjustment.
- **A lunge line.**
- **A lunge whip,** long enough to be able to reach the horse with the tip of the lash if necessary.
- **Boots** for the horse's legs/feet, as necessary.
- **Sturdy gloves.**

Lungeing equipment for groundwork – roller and stripped bridle.

For riding afterwards – saddle with stirrups secured up and reins twisted into throatlatch.

Key Points of Control

Voice

This will be an extension of the horse's leading lessons when he learned to walk, trot and stop to your voice commands. When lungeing, use *exactly* the same words and inflections to make your wishes utterly clear and logical to him.

Lunge Line

At all times you should try to keep the horse out on his circle to the full extent of the length of lunge line you have allowed him. With a young, green horse you will need a larger circle (about 20 m diameter) than with an older, more supple and balanced horse.

Hold the lunge line in your hand in the same way that you would hold a rein – never wrap it around your hand or wrist. Treat the contact you have along the lunge line just as you would the contact you want in the reins when you are mounted: elastic but connected, not loose (non-existent!) or too heavy (leaning).

When you give a vocal command to slow down or make a downward transition it should be accompanied by 'half-halts' given along the lunge line: make several small quick 'tugs' on the line using just your fingers and wrist, *not* your whole arm. Initially, try one half-halt to each stride. If he ignores this or is slow to respond, increase to two per stride or a continuous vibration along the line, again using just your fist, not your arm.

This is his introduction to the ridden *half-halt*, and will also be the basis of your control if you choose to pursue in-hand work.

Lunge Whip

There are several uses and positions for the lunge whip, all of which you should use precisely, according to the result you want (see below). Waving a lunge whip with no clear aim will only serve to frighten or confuse the horse.

To begin with, he should be accustomed to the whip and not frightened of it: it is as much an aid as your legs will be when mounted. Start at the halt and hold it up beside his head so he can see it clearly. Talk to him in calming tones and use praise words ('Good boy', 'Brave', 'Yes').

Next, run the whip carefully along the top of his crest several times. When he accepts this, continue on with the whip along the top of his back and over his croup, finally running it down the back of his hind legs, always remembering to stand in a safe position. If he fidgets or lifts his hind legs when the whip touches them, praise him – you want him to react, so long as he is neither frightened nor kicking out aggressively. Later on, if you wish to do in-hand work, this reaction is exactly what you want – so don't stop it now.

Side Reins

Initially, these should be fitted very loosely, just to get him used to the idea of something attached to his bit.

For the young horse, side reins should be attached to the girth just below the saddle flaps, or, if fitted to a roller, at around the same height – see photographs p.58. They should be gradually shortened during a lungeing session until they begin to encourage the horse to arch his neck, but not so tight that he is forced into an outline. In subsequent sessions you should be able to shorten them a little more until he is working in a comfortable rounded outline. This will help him develop strength in his top-line muscles to enable him to carry you in a correct outline from the beginning.

As he develops over the next few years, you will gradually attach the side reins higher on the roller to encourage a taller but still rounded posture. If you also choose to pursue in-hand work, he will need to be used to a fairly short side rein, although, as in everything else with horses, this is achieved by gradual changes over a period of time – months or even years.

Basic Lungeing Techniques

Sending Forward/Upward Transitions

Use your voice to make your requirement clear:

For more energy, use the word for the gait he is already in, but with more enthusiasm and an upward lifting tone at the end of the word.

For an upward change of gait, precede the transition command (word for the required gait) with 'And…' as a warning of change. For example: 'And…trot', with the word 'trot' in a higher tone of voice. Hold the whip level with the ground and pointing towards his tail. Flick the lash back then forward, towards the point of his buttock.

Moving Outward

To move the horse outward onto a bigger circle, hold the whip level with the ground, but pointed towards his shoulder. Use 'Out' or 'Away' as a command word. He may respond simply to your positioning of the whip, or you may need to flick the lash out towards his shoulder. This can be done underhand (from the ground

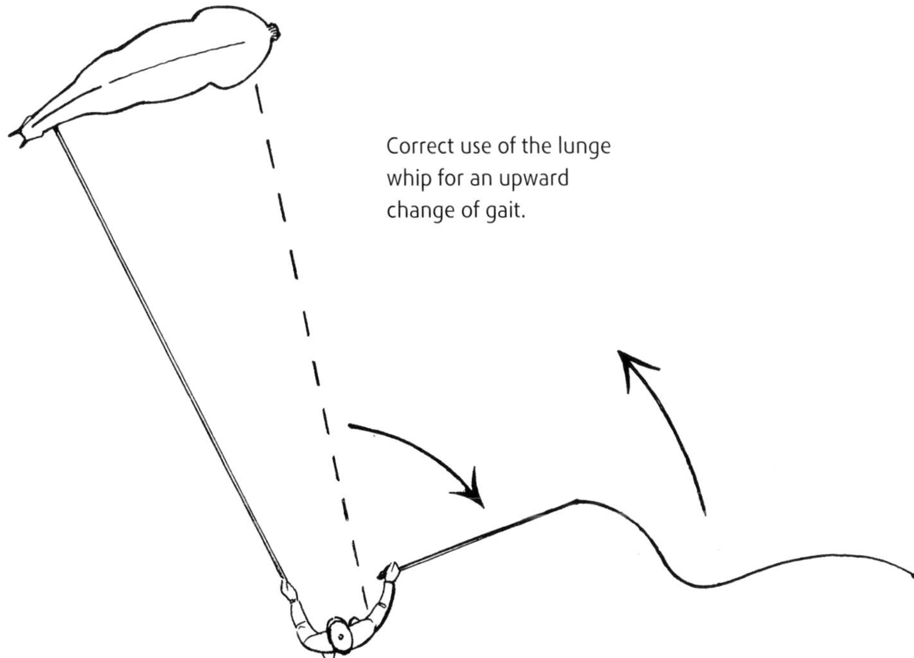

Correct use of the lunge whip for an upward change of gait.

in an upward direction) or overhand (lift up and back, then flick out and down), depending on his reaction. You want him to move steadily away from you to a larger circle, not spook and run sideways, or spin round.

If he ignores you, try to just catch him with the tip of the lash on his shoulder or on his girth area, around where your leg will lie. Practice will perfect your aim.

Asking for a Downward Transition

This is done with the voice and small half-halts on the lunge line, but you must also remember to drop the tip of the whip to the ground so that it no longer asks him to go forward. Use trial and error to find how far you need to drop it with your own horse – they are all different. Try just lowering it a little for trot to walk (when you need him to keep moving), and to the ground only for halt.

Lungeing Exercises

There is plenty of work that can be done on the lunge to strengthen and supple the horse, rather than just exercise him. Not only will this keep him from being bored whilst lungeing, it will help continue his physical development. The following exercises are laid out in the order in which they should be used during an individual lungeing session.

Using the lunge whip underhand.

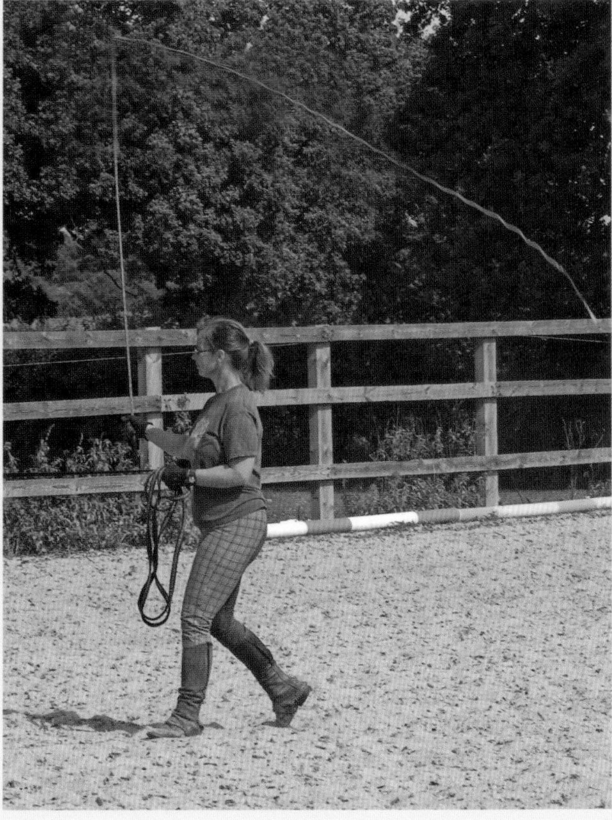

Using the lunge whip overhand.

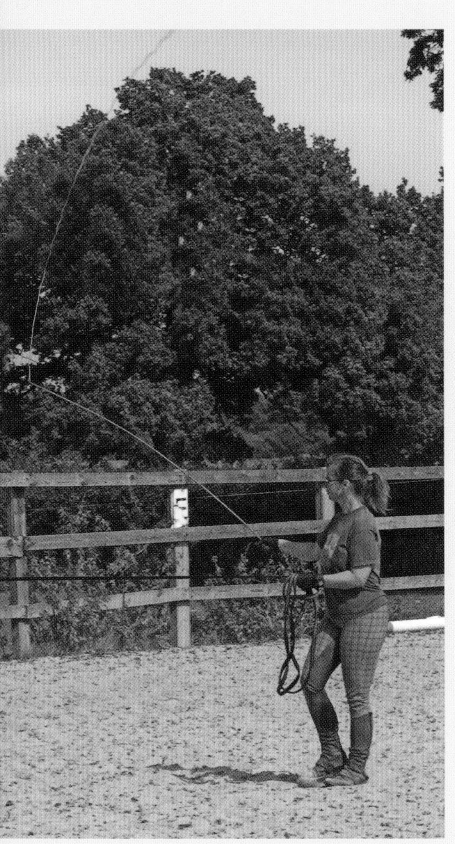

- Make many transitions between gaits. When he is more advanced this can include direct transitions, e.g. walk to canter.
- Decreasing and increasing the circle – the size of the smallest circle must be determined by how supple and strong he is, just as it will when you are mounted.
- Transitions within the gaits: reduce the trot until he is just about to walk and his croup has begun to lower, and then send him forward again. You want him to spring off his hind legs with a clear bending of the joints and an energetic muscle bunching, but not to run onto his forehand. This can also be done in canter.
- Working towards medium trot can be done by having a really active working trot on a circle, then moving off the circle onto a straight line for several strides along the long side of the school. This will encourage him to lengthen his strides. Also use your voice, repeating 'Trot-trot-trot' in exactly the same tempo as his working trot, to help him maintain the frequency of his steps rather than making them quicker.
- Trotting over ground poles and slightly raised poles: this encourages bending of the hind legs and stretching of the hamstrings.

To benefit from these exercises he must be working in a rounded outline so that his muscles are functioning correctly.

Alternative Lungeing Equipment

Other pieces of equipment can be used to target specific issues on the lunge. The most common and useful are as follows.

The Chambon

This teaches the horse how to stretch down to seek the contact. It works by applying pressure to his poll and mouth when his head is too high, and employs the ideal training technique – when he does as required (lowers his head and neck) all pressure is released. He will quickly learn that working with a lowered neck (and as a consequence, a lifted back) is comfortable.

The Chambon is particularly appropriate to a horse who tends

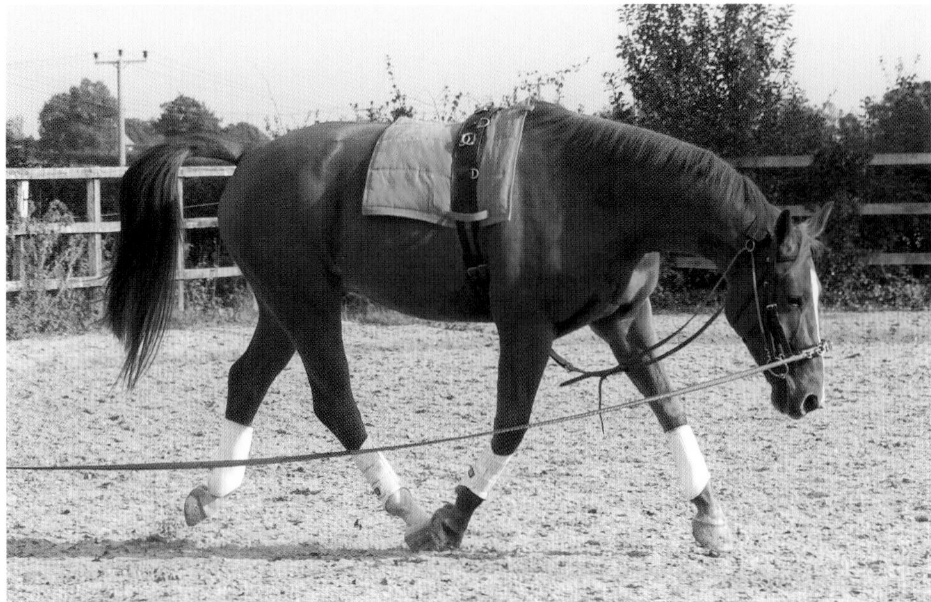

The Chambon – running from the girth between the forelegs, up to a padded head-piece (attached to the bridle), through running rings and down to clip onto the bit.

to duck behind the contact offered by side reins: keep him moving forward in his new outline and he will investigate the option of pushing his nose forward as there is no restriction offered in this direction by the Chambon. Praise him when he does this and you are on the way to teaching him to stretch forward and down to seek the contact.

The first time you use a Chambon, fit it *very* loosely so that the horse's first contact with it is only a mild pressure on his poll: strong or sudden poll pressure may cause him to panic, run backwards, rear, and/or fall over, none of which you want! Once he has accepted it you can tighten it *gradually* until it has the desired effect.

The Chambon *must not* be used when riding.

The Harbridge

The Harbridge has a similar effect to the Chambon, but it can also be used when riding. It works simply by limiting how far the horse can lift his head – bit and poll pressure result if he goes too high. It does not allow the total freedom to reach forward that the Chambon does, but it can be more quickly and easily fitted and removed. It can be useful to a less experienced rider as it prevents the horse from going above the bit yet, unlike draw reins, the rider cannot use it to manipulate the horse's head into contorted positions.

Elastic Bungee

The bungee has the rounding and lowering effect of the Chambon, but does not permit the nose to reach forward. As such it is not ideal, but it *can* be used when riding as well as lungeing. In fact its greatest application is with a horse who is too strong and wilful for his rider as it helps control his outline. It should not be used long-term as it may teach the horse to overbend, and may encourage him to stay on his forehand.

The harbridge attaches to a loop around the girth then splits into two branches that attach one to each bit ring. It has elasticated sections that would break under severe pressure in case the horse was to put a leg over it.

The Bungee: an elasticated cord runs from the girth, through each bit ring and up, over the top of the horse's head. A small leather triangle slips under the headpiece to keep it in place, and the loop on top can be altered to adjust the length of the bungee.

TROUBLESHOOTING

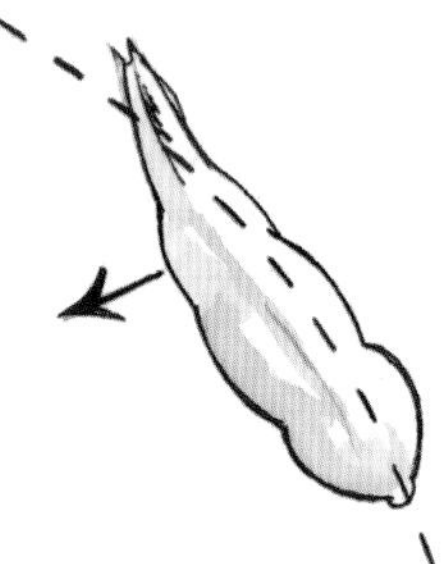

He falls in so the lunge line is constantly loose

You need to send him outward with the lunge whip. See p.60 for how to do this. Remember your goal is that he maintains a constant contact with your lunge line so, every time the line sags, use the whip towards his shoulder to send him out again. This problem is most likely to occur when you lunge him with his stiff side nearer to you.

He falls outward so the contact on my lunge line is really strong

This problem is most likely to happen when his soft side is nearer to you, as he will be bending too much to the inside, with his weight falling outward onto his outside shoulder. You need to make frequent half-halts (little jolts) on your lunge line so there are brief moments of slack in the line. Eventually, you want a constant, light contact but to get there you have to teach him not to use the rein as a prop for his balance.

The half-halt should make him hesitate in his stride, reducing speed and allowing him to balance better, and be followed by a stride or so when you have dropped the contact altogether and offer him no support – this will focus his mind on having to find his own balance. Repeat as often as necessary until he stops leaning – this may take several weeks, so be patient.

He is constantly too fast, ignoring my half-halts

First, go back and reinforce his leading lessons – he must start and stop to command. Next, practise starting and stopping in the same way but on the lunge circle. You may find initially that you need to keep the line shorter and walk closer to him to keep control. Gradually send him further away from you and keep making transitions between gaits.

If he ignores you when he is further out on the lunge circle try a strong jolt on the line – raise your hand slightly then give a good strong tug *downwards*. This should be sharp enough to startle him into taking notice. He may stop abruptly, in which case you should praise him – walk out to him and stroke him, then start him off again and make subsequent half-halts small and light. Alternatively, he may panic at the jolt on his nose and run. In this case you need to make repeated strong half-halts (always in conjunction with the appropriate voice aid), and/or reduce the circle until he stops, then make much of him. This procedure must be repeated every time he ignores your aid – this will teach him to take notice when you make a small half-halt. Remember it is all about demanding that his attention be on *you*.

In extreme cases you may find it easier to lunge him on two reins (double lunge) with at least one rein attached to his bit. This is best avoided if possible as you do not want to compromise his mouth, but it is an answer to a minority of horses. Take advice from a professional – this is not a technique for the inexperienced amateur.

He is slow/lazy, never really going forward on the lunge

He needs to have more respect for your lunge whip. If he ignores you when you flick the lash *towards* his quarters you should aim with your next flick to catch him with the tip of the lash somewhere between his hock and buttock. Practice will improve your accuracy!

Having touched him once with the lash you will almost certainly find him sharper to respond next time you flick it towards him. Your aim is not to frighten him into running forward, but to get a more energetic reaction. Each time he ignores you, touch him again more sharply until he believes you mean business.

He kicks out when I touch him with the whip, but ignores me if I don't

Either he has a poor attitude, or he has a physical reason for not wanting to go forward. Begin by checking his health/soundness so you are sure it is just a matter of temperament that you are dealing with.

Once you are *certain* it is just attitude, you need to deal with him firmly as this behaviour will surely recur under saddle.

- Review leading in hand, p.54. After a few start and stop transitions, during which you reinforce his obedience, go back to lungeing.

- Each time he kicks out when the whip touches him you must touch him again – it is essential he accept the forward-driving aid. *Be very sure that you are not in range of his hind legs*. You must have a whip with a long enough lash so that you can remain beyond his reach.

- If he runs forward at speed instead of kicking, let him; he needs to understand that your aid means *forward* and *any* response in this direction should be encouraged. In the (very) short term it does not matter *how* he goes forward (gait or outline), only that he does, as a means of developing forward *reactions* and as a consequence, a forward-thinking attitude.

  Once he has given you a forward reaction, praise him, then quietly ask for a downward transition.

- Now ask him to go forward without touching him. If the lesson has been learned he will go willingly. If not, repeat the process above.

- It is very important that this attitude is dealt with and not ignored as it has many implications further on in his training. If you feel he is dangerous (becoming more aggressive, or you are losing control of him), or you do not seem to be making progress quite quickly (in one session), *seek professional help.*

He is nervous of the whip and runs away from it

Review the procedure outlined above under Key Points of Control, p.59. It is important to gain his confidence in the whip and you should spend plenty of time on this phase.

If he still runs forward too fast or changes gait or speed when you lift the whip, use smaller movements of the whip or drop its point down to let the lash trail on the ground. Simply raising it slightly may give you all the response you need.

He bores down onto his forehand and leans on the line

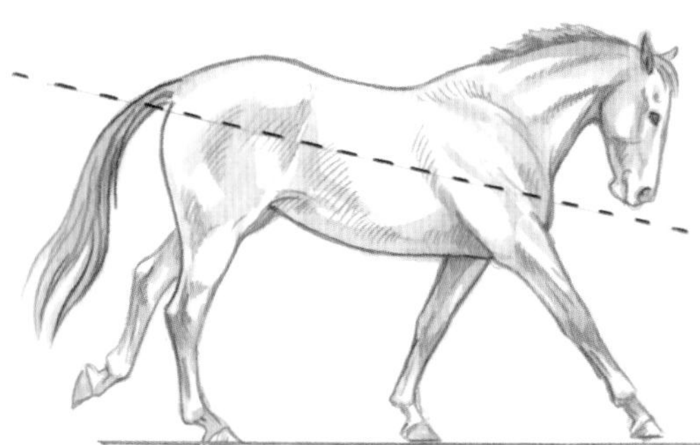

Try positioning his side reins higher. If he continues, you will also need to give upward half-halts. Drop your hand slightly down then give a sharp jerk upward, which should cause an upward jerk on his cavesson. This should be followed immediately by a brief moment with no contact at all to allow him to readjust his balance and learn that you will not hold him up with the line.

Now allow him to reconnect to your contact, but repeat the procedure every time he bores down.

He bends to the outside

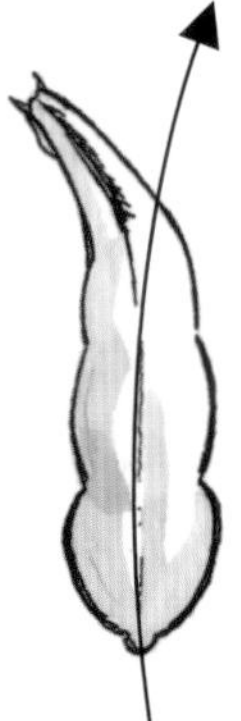

He does this as a result of his natural crookedness (see Chapter 3, p.23).
Shorten the side rein on the inside by two or three holes. This will encourage him to look towards the inside of your circle.

If his haunches swing out you may need to seek advice about how to use the double lunge (see above, under '*He is constantly too fast…*'), although it is likely that after a few sessions he will become more supple and the problem will resolve itself.

Do not forget to readjust the length of the side reins when you change direction. You will probably only need the inside rein shorter when he travels in one direction – although there is no harm in having the outside side rein one hole longer anyway, to allow him room to bend.

He fights the side reins, constantly hollowing

First, check that he is genuinely comfortable in his mouth: is the bit correctly sized/fitted? Is he teething? Discomfort may be the cause of such argument.

Next, have his back checked: you are asking him to stretch it by lowering his neck carriage and any discomfort will be magnified by this stretching.

Once you are sure that he is physically fine, but he still disputes the contact, lower your side reins until they are as far down the roller/girth as you can take them. In this position, so long as they are short enough he will be unable to hollow and should learn to accept their limiting influence.

Alternatively, you can try using a Chambon (see earlier this chapter).

He overarches his neck and won't take a contact with the side reins

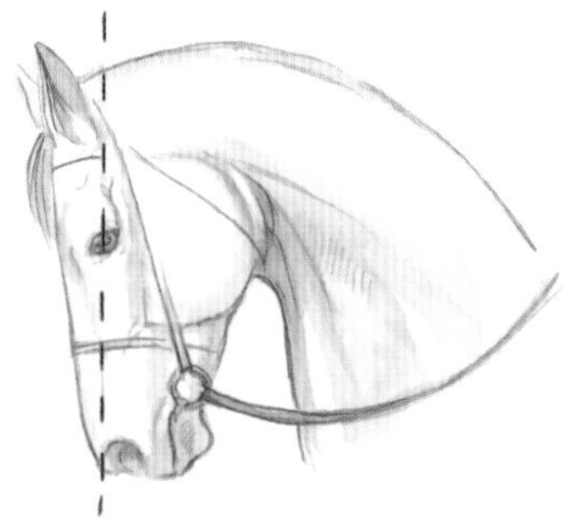

Start by checking his bit/teeth to ensure that he is comfortable in the mouth. If so, try using a Chambon instead of side reins until he has learned to both lower his neck and reach forward with his nose. Ensure that you send him forward actively (but without hurrying) to encourage forward thinking.

7 Transitions

As with everything in training, it will take time and patience to achieve your end goals, but it is important that you know exactly what you are trying to achieve. Ultimately you want transitions between gaits that:

- Are without hesitation.
- Are resistance-free.
- Have no loss of balance.
- Are in the same outline throughout.
- Have the first step of the new gait regular and of the required length of stride.

Introducing Transitions under Saddle on the Lunge

During backing, when you first sit on a horse on the lunge his attention will be to the person on the ground – the one who has given him all his instructions until now.

Once he is carrying you on board in relaxed fashion in walk and trot, with transition commands made by his handler on the ground, it is time to begin transferring his attention to you, his rider.

Start

Take over the verbal command to 'Walk on'. Your handler should still use the lunge whip in the normal way but your horse should now start listening to you, as his handler remains silent. (At first, the handler might need to back you up verbally once or twice, but only if the horse is truly confused.)

Once he is obedient to your voice, squeeze your lower legs gently against his sides at the same time as you say 'Walk on'. Always remember that movement on top may startle young horses, and using your legs too strongly might make him buck, so keep your aid *very* light until you are sure he is going to accept it. See text on use of legs in Chapter 3.

Once you are certain that he is not going to react in an explosive way, try the same voice and leg aid but without the lunge whip for back-up. Now you should find out how strong a leg aid you need to get a reaction. Every horse is different: where one may move off for a light squeeze, another will require a fairly hefty smack with the inside of your calf. Don't worry at this stage if he feels like hard work – things will change as he strengthens and increases in understanding and, to a degree, sensitivity to the aids can be taught later on, if necessary (see '*He won't walk on*', p.77).

Stop

Use the same logical progression as above: gradually replace the handler's instructions with your own, starting with the vocal command. *Always use the same words and inflection*. There are more ways of saying 'Whoa', or 'Stop', than there are for 'Walk on'. In Continental Europe a downward trill is a favoured way of indicating a downward change of gait. Always use the command with which your horse is familiar.

One of the main ways of indicating to the horse that he should stop is to cease following his movement.

Whilst in walk you will be allowing your seat to swing softly along with the saddle, your upper legs will be relaxed and your hands will be gently *but not excessively* following his head motion.

To stop:

1. With the muscles around your pelvis, hold your seat still (*without* clenching your buttock muscles). Also increase the tone of your inner thigh (adductor) muscles to hold the saddle more firmly, almost as if you were trying to prevent the saddle from moving. This must be accomplished by increasing the *tone* in individual muscles *without gripping* (tensing all the muscles of seat and leg), which would lift your seat upward.

2. Stop following with your hand. If he becomes anxious, strong or fussy in his mouth, add tiny vibrations (quicker movements than the 'sponging' that is often described) along both reins, as if you were trying to make the bit rings tremble. Do this with your fingers and minimal use of your wrists, never with a backward movement of your fist or whole arm. The closure of your fingers and the intensity of the vibrations can be adjusted until he understands that he should stop, *but they should never become a pulling back*.

3. Finally, lift your diaphragm away from your tummy so that your shoulders move slightly backward behind your seat. This must be accomplished without pushing your lower back forward into an arch, the effect being to drop more weight into the back of your seat.

above Diaphragm lift – weight dropped slightly more to the rear of the seat.

above right How not to do it! The arched back is not only uncomfortable (for both of you) – it can actually damage your back.

4. Later on you will add a lower leg component to help draw his hind legs forward under his body, but at this stage that would only serve to confuse him, so leave the lower legs hanging passively draped against his sides.

As with *start*, the horse may initially take some time to respond. This will, in part, be because of lack of understanding, but it also relates to lack of balance. To begin with, he is trying to come to terms with stopping the increased momentum of your weight added to his own. He is like a child running downhill – your combined weight is pulling him faster even when he is trying to stop. So be patient: pulling at him with the reins is only going to add to his problems.

At first your handler on the ground will also be giving half-halts (vibrations) along the lunge line (see Chapter 6, p.59). This additional aid should no longer be given once his attention is on you.

Next Steps

The next step is to try *start* and *stop* off the lunge.

Choosing when to introduce trot will largely be dictated by how relaxed and relatively well balanced the horse is with you on top. Asking for trot should follow the same principles as 'Walk on', although at first he is likely to need both more vocal encouragement and more leg aids, and possibly also the lunge whip. This is a matter of both confidence and balance and should be started under saddle on the lunge circle with which he is already familiar.

Canter should be left until later as the horse will not yet be sufficiently balanced under your weight to canter on a circle.

Transitions between Gaits

BUILDING BLOCKS

The building blocks for these transitions are:

- Attention to you.
- Basic understanding of the driving aids (legs).
- Basic understanding of the restraining aids (seat and rein).

In the earlier stages you will make your transitions between consecutive gaits (e.g. walk to trot; trot to canter) as distinct from later when you may wish to make direct transitions 'missing out' a gait, e.g. walk to canter.

Transitions should be taught starting with the slower gaits first, in the order:

Upward – halt to walk, walk to trot, trot to canter.

Downward – walk to halt, trot to walk, canter to trot.

The basic principles remain the same although there are some subtle differences according to which two gaits you are moving between.

Upward Transitions

Halt to Walk

1. Sit straight, looking forward with legs parallel and both reins the same length.
2. Squeeze with both lower legs at the girth (i.e. 'inside leg' position for both legs) and ease your rein contact *slightly*.
3. As the horse walks forward, relax your legs. If he slows or lacks purpose, pick up alternating leg aiding as described in Chapter 11 (p.129).
4. Maintain a soft, *slightly* following action with your reins – see Chapter 11, p.129.

Walk to Trot

1. Make sure the horse is walking with energy, but not hurrying.
2. Close both lower legs in the girth (inside leg) position. As he progresses it becomes very important that your legs are parallel or he may misinterpret your aid and canter.
3. Swing the front of your pelvis upward with the feeling of how your seat moves in sitting trot (see Chapter 11, p.132). This should be done with your deep stomach muscles, keeping your buttock muscles relaxed.
4. In the moment you ask, stop following with your contact and hold your hands still. This will help him understand that you don't just want him to walk faster.
5. If you are going to rise to the trot, wait until he has established his balance (usually 2–4 steps) before you begin.

Trot to Canter

In the earlier stages you should ask for canter strike-off on a curve – either a circle or a corner – to help the horse pick up the correct lead. Later on, when he understands your aiding clearly, you will be able to make the strike-off onto the lead of your choice, even on a straight line.

1. Ensure that his trot is energetic but not hurried.
2. Make sure he is clearly bent to the inside on a curved line by putting your own body into position left or right (see Techniques in Chapter 3) and following the aids outlined in Chapter 8 for turning (p.87). Be careful not to over-position his neck to the inside.
3. Make a half-halt to warn him you are about to ask for something (see p.37 for a full description of the half-halt.) You must decide how much of a half-halt you need – it may be as described and take place over many steps until he comes a little more off his forehand or, if he is fairly well balanced, it may be as little as a brief closure of your outside fingers. The important thing is that you *give him warning* of a change to come and do not startle him with your aid, or make it hard for him to respond by asking him when he is in a poor balance.
4. Slide your outside leg back into the 'outside leg' position and in the same moment step down onto your inside stirrup so that your inside calf pushes downward/forward against his belly. Do *not* pull your inside heel up and dig the heel of your boot into his ribs; not only does this destroy your leg position, it lifts you off your inside seat bone, which is the most crucial part of your aiding.
5. As your inside leg deepens, push your inside seat bone forward/down onto the saddle. Imagine your inside seat bone to be a match, then strike it along the

saddle – it is called a 'strike-off', after all! This seat component tells him the difference between going into canter, where you continually have one seat bone further forward than the other (see Chapter 11, p.135), and going into a bigger trot (where your seat bones are always parallel). On a more advanced horse, it is the difference between going into canter and doing travers or half-pass.

6. Maintain your rein contact or even make it slightly stronger (just by a closure of your fingers, *not* by pulling back) in the moment of transition as this will help to stop him from running into a bigger trot. As he establishes his canter, start following the motion of his head with your hands.

Downward Transitions

Walk to Halt

1. Start by moving both your legs slightly back towards the 'outside leg' position and close them gently onto the horse's sides with equal pressure – this tells both his hind legs to keep going as your other aids restrain and eventually stop his front end, resulting in a slightly shorter outline.

2. Now use the aids as described above, for stopping, but maintain your leg pressure until the halt is complete.

3. Once he is stationary, relax your aids, letting your legs move into girth position. Be careful to sit tall with your weight fully into your relaxed seat as any tendency to drop your bodyweight forward may suggest rein-back to him.

At this stage *do not* fiddle to try to make him stand square – that comes later. In the earlier stages it is most important that he learns to stand *still*. Have patience and keep him standing until you are happy that he understands not to move again until you tell him to do so.

Trot to Walk

1. Begin by taking sitting trot and then move your legs slightly back as described for walk to halt.

2. Continue with the same aids as halt to walk, simply relax your aiding as he moves into walk and pick up the alternating leg aids and slightly following hands required for the walk (see Chapter 11).

NOTE: The majority of riders know that they should use their legs in downward transitions – but most people begin to use them *as* the horse breaks into walk, not *during* the process of making the transition. Your goal is to have his hind legs further forward beneath his body following your transition – this can only be accomplished if you ask him to step them more forward *whilst* you restrain his front end with your other aids. Put simply, you want his back end closer to his front end, so as you restrain the front, keep the back end going.

Canter to Trot

This transition is slightly different because you will always have the horse slightly bent (positioned) towards his leading leg, even when moving on a straight line.

1. Do not move your inside leg back as you have for the other transitions, because this may cause him to swing his haunches or possibly change lead.
2. Keep your legs where they are and close them a little more strongly.
3. Ask him to reduce the size of his canter for three strides prior to the transition using small squeezes on the inside rein. A useful tactic when schooling is to ride a slightly smaller circle as this will also help bring his hind legs further under.
4. As in your other transitions, increase your body tone and hold your pelvis more still.
5. Straighten your shoulders so that you are no longer positioned to his leading leg – this brings your outside hand back. Finally, close your outside fingers on the rein.
6. As you feel him changing gait into the trot, bring your outside leg parallel to your inside leg and close both legs in the rhythmic pulsing that you use in sitting trot (see Chapter 11). This also brings your seat bones equally into the saddle, again confirming to him that he should be in trot, not canter.
7. Relax your aids and swing along with him, going rising after a few strides when he feels balanced and in a clear rhythm.

Training Value

Transitions are not just a method of changing gait – they are the main building blocks for developing:

- Obedience.
- Submission.
- Strength in the haunches.
- Flexibility of the hind legs.
- The half-halt.
- Engagement.

- Balance.
- Suspension in the gaits.
- Collection.
- The range of the gait variants from collection to extension.
- Many of the higher movements. For example, walk/trot/walk leads to piaffe, as does trot/walk/trot; canter strike-offs lead to flying changes.

Exercises

Trot/walk/trot is the first and most important. Ridden correctly, with the transitions not too progressive (each transition should take about three strides from start to finish), the horse will bend his hind legs and step under (engage and balance). Think of his hind legs like coiled springs – when you ask for trot again (after three or four steps of walk) he will have more energy available to spring upward, not just forward.

This exercise should be repeated frequently – try two or three repetitions to a long side, and one on each short side.

Later, do almost the same but without quite achieving walk. Your goals are the same – that the horse accepts your restraining aids softly in his mouth and back, and that he steps further under himself, so he goes forward again with a more 'uphill' feeling. When you can do this over no more than a stride or two, you have achieved your half-halt.

Trot/canter transitions are *suppling*; walk/canter transitions (see p.212) are *strengthening*. Both teach the horse to accept the control of the reins and not run through it, leading eventually to ease when teaching flying changes.

TROUBLESHOOTING

He won't walk on

First, check that when you asked him with your legs, you slightly relaxed the contact – you must not say 'Go' and 'Stop' at the same time.

If your aiding is correct, and you have asked him nicely with light leg aids, which he has ignored, you should work your way gradually up through a series of progressively stronger leg aids until he responds.

1. Ask again with a stronger lower leg squeeze. If he is recently backed, don't forget to continue using a voice command as well.

2. If you still get no response, next use a strong leg aid – a kick – made by moving your legs directly outward away from his sides, then smacking them back inward. Often the sound of your leg slapping his sides will help to startle him forward, so be ready if he lurches into motion so that you are not left behind and pull on his mouth. If in doubt, throw your hands forward and lose contact totally until he is in motion.

3. Apply your strong aid several times in quick succession, being careful that your contact remains light and 'forward'. Usually, by the third or fourth kick, he will get the message – as soon as he does, relax your legs and praise him. This should be a learning process, not a bullying session.

4. If he continues to ignore your legs (and you are sure he understands what they mean) then use a smack with a whip. Initially with a young horse this should be a short jumping whip. Choose one with a double flap on the end to make a clapping sound – the noise is often more important than the smack.

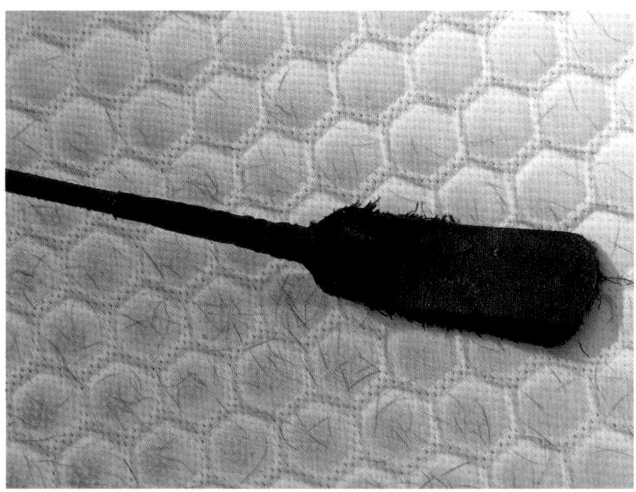

This type of double flap end is more suitable to a young or sensitive horse than a thinner, sharper schooling whip.

In the earliest stages, use the short whip on his shoulder – this makes him pick up a front leg and start into walk sequence.

When you are certain that he understands and is simply ignoring you, start using the whip directly behind your leg – this is to make him think that your leg has become sharper (with a short whip you will need to take your hand off the reins to achieve this). A schooling whip will come later in his education (after the first six months or so) and should also be used behind your leg for the purpose of sharpening his response to leg aids. Some horses react badly to a thin schooling whip and you may do best (at least to begin with) to choose one that has the type of end illustrated.

Once you have him walking freely forward, make a halt transition and try asking for walk again. Begin by asking nicely – if he fails to respond, immediately use the same level of aid that worked last time, skipping the intervening stages. Keep repeating walk, halt, walk, halt. He should begin to respond to the light aid fairly quickly because of anticipation of the stronger aid. Praise him every time he answers the light aid – this is how to improve his responsiveness.

If you are still having a problem after following the measures outlined, you need to backtrack and cover again the first lessons during which you took over from a handler on the ground (p.70–1), to ensure that he truly understands what you are asking.

He won't stop

Whilst it is comforting to know that you can stop when you want to, with a keen young horse it can be better to wait until the latter end of a schooling session to work on halts, when he is more relaxed and a bit tired. At this point you can explain things to him without entering into an argument, instilling in him obedience without stress. In later schooling sessions you will be able to halt earlier as his obedience will have become more automatic.

Apparent refusal to halt may also be caused by lack of balance – he simply cannot stop himself – so be patient.

Review your aids for halt. When you are certain you are asking clearly, add a pattern to help yourself:

1. Ride a small circle (about 10 m), and finish it back at the fence without quite completing the turn, so he ends up facing the fence.

2. Begin asking for your halt about halfway around the circle, and let him walk into the fence rather than pulling on the reins. You will need to be firm about keeping him straight as he comes towards the fence, but persist and he *will* stop once his face touches the rail!

3. Turn him (towards the same direction you were travelling before) and walk on, then repeat the pattern. You should find that he stops more willingly this time, just a little before touching the fence.

4. Repeat several times until he is stopping more easily from your aids.

5. Now ride a genuinely round circle and ask for the halt before you come back at the track.

6. Although he is no longer directly face-on to the fence, but at a slight angle, the psychological 'backing off' effect of the fence will still help.

7. This same exercise (the last part) will be used later to help teach other downward transitions, especially canter to walk, so it can be usefully started in this embryonic form now.

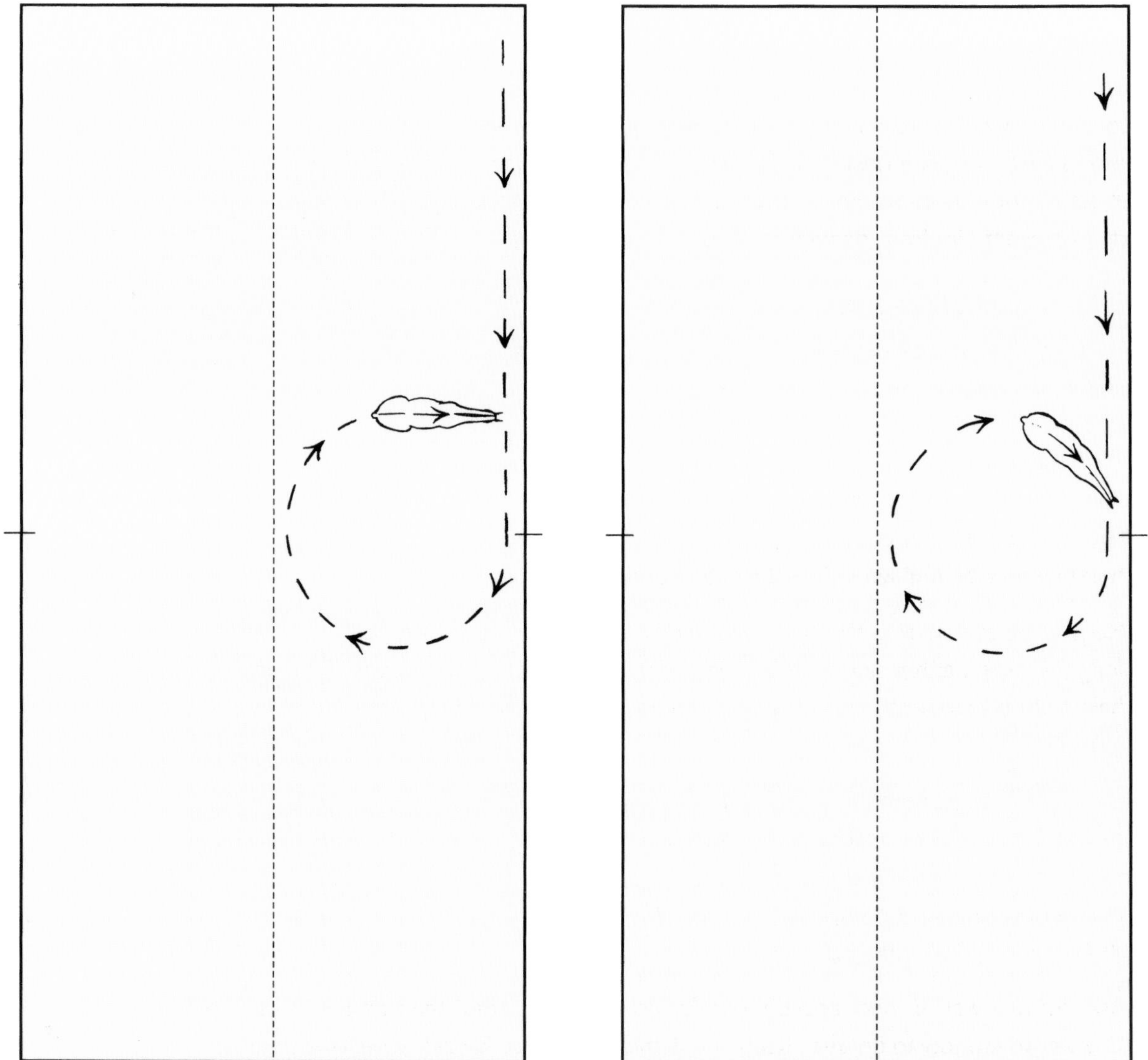

Using the fence to aid stopping – first phase.

Using the fence to aid stopping – second phase.

He hollows in transitions

Begin by checking out any possible causes of discomfort – teeth, back, lameness and saddle fitting. Sometimes a horse will tolerate discomfort to a degree whilst in motion, but the extra effort of a transition may show up a problem.

Having ruled these out, consider his physical strength: is he young and/or muscularly weak? Making a transition with the added weight of a rider is quite an effort and achieving it in correct posture even more so. In general, this does *not* mean that he must be allowed to hollow, as only by using his muscles correctly will he build them up. However, in the case of trot to canter transitions don't worry so much while he is still weak – he should be left alone to achieve these as best he can until his back is stronger.

He may have just cause for hollowing if your aids are too rough, abrupt or confusing, or he may be hollowing as an evasion such as unwillingness to go forward. Check your aiding, then set about educating him in the correct way of using his body to prevent him from damaging himself.

Halt to walk/walk to trot

There are several possibilities here and you may need to try each to find which is the right answer for your horse.

1. Review your aiding – are you absolutely clear how to ask for each transition?

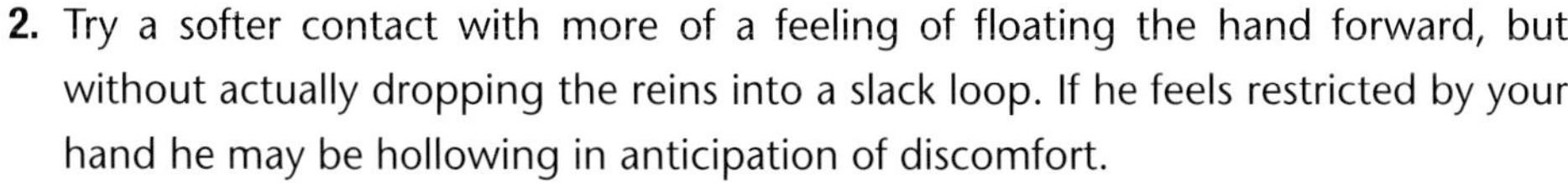

2. Try a softer contact with more of a feeling of floating the hand forward, but without actually dropping the reins into a slack loop. If he feels restricted by your hand he may be hollowing in anticipation of discomfort.
3. He may be too weak yet to lift your added weight without a struggle. Do more lunge work, on either side reins or Chambon, and use lots of transitions. This will help both his strength, and his understanding that he should stay round during transitions.
4. He may lack understanding of his required responses to the contact. See Chapter 10 for instructions on teaching him to chew down onto the bit. Once he understands that he should yield to your contact, you will have the tools to lower his head even during a transition with the smallest touch on the bit (even so little as a slight closure of your fingers).
5. Ask him to lower his neck and be rounder before you attempt the transition (see Chapter 10 for how to do this). Keep your hands low, possibly even lower than you will want them once the transition is achieved: use your hands and reins like a pair of side reins (see photograph, p.112). This does not mean pulling at his mouth. If he pulls against *you*, just keep your hands still with a passive resistance (see Techniques, p.35) but never use an actively backward pull. Now ask for the transition. By denying him the ability to lift his head whilst changing gait, you give him a new experience, and he learns that it is possible to make a transition without hollowing. After a few repetitions he will gradually lose the old habit.

Trot to canter

Again, there are several possibilities:

1. Does he hollow when you go to sitting trot in preparation for the transition? He may be stiffening his back either in reluctance to carry you sitting, or in anticipation of the canter (which young horses often find exciting or worrying). If so,

spend time alternating between rising and sitting trot *without* asking for a transition (see Chapter 11, p.141–2). When he accepts this, then quietly slip in a canter aid when you are in sitting trot, taking care not to startle him by being too abrupt with your aids. You will need to repeat this procedure many times until he loses the hollowing altogether.

2. Deepen his outline in trot (see Chapter 10) before asking for canter. Then if he moves his head up from the deep position he may only come up into a correct place instead of above the bit.

3. With a more educated horse who still produces this evasion, put him in shoulder-in on a circle (see Chapter 16) and make sure he is really bent around your inside leg (see Chapter 12) with a secure connection to your outside rein and a light inside contact. Only when this feels genuine should you ask for canter.

4. Try using a triangular rein position. The horse should be clearly connected to your outside rein, which remains in a normal position, while your inside rein (you will need to lengthen it) drops down and is anchored behind your leg so that he cannot shift it (be careful not to collapse your waist to the side). This acts like a side rein, disallowing any upward move of his head. As soon as you are in canter, move your hand into a normal position. This technique can help give him the experience of making the transition in a correct outline – he may have no idea he could use his body in this fashion as all his previous experiences have been to lift his shoulders by tossing his head up, not by using his back as a lever.

Triangular rein position – if you draw a line between my hands you can see the triangle, the reins being the other two sides. (NB this is not a correction *Stanley* actually needs and his disapproval is clear in his expression and his switching tail!

Downward transitions

Start by checking the usual potential problems: teeth, back, saddle, lameness.

Having eliminated these, the most likely cause is too much hand.

- Learn to use your legs and seat (p.32) to prepare and execute all your downward transitions, rather than relying on just your reins.
- Be sure to prepare: try to slightly slow the gait he is in, but keep your lower legs *on* to ask him to step more under himself with his hind legs, thereby taking weight off his forehand. This is not easy to do with an unbalanced youngster, but it will never happen unless you try.

Lack of balance may also be a reason for hollowing; the answer is the same as above.

He may also hollow because he is reluctant to make a downward transition at all. In this case you need to address his understanding of yielding to the bit (Chapter 10). It may also be valuable to review:

- The amount of exercise he gets.
- Feeding.
- Turnout.

A fresh horse is more likely to dispute your contact.

He becomes crooked in transitions, swinging either his shoulders or his quarters to the side

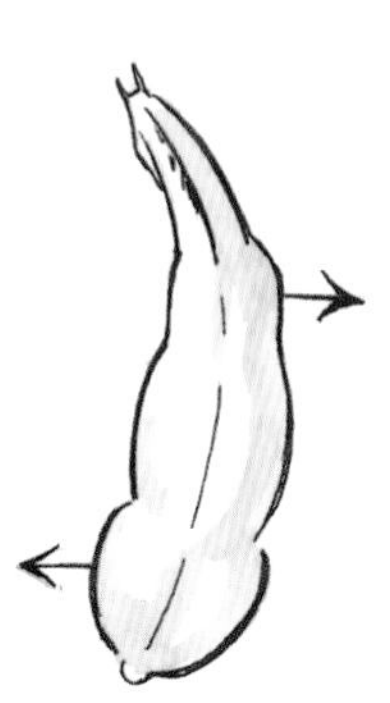

First ask yourself – does he always swing the same way? If so, this points to either you, sitting crooked, or an inequality (crookedness/weakness) in his muscles that needs addressing in all his work, not just in his transitions.

If you do not have access to mirrors, get someone experienced on the ground to check your position and/or his alignment, then work on appropriate corrections.

If he is not consistent in how he swings, you must decide (probably also with help from an expert on the ground) whether:

1. He is reluctant to stay *forward* (which would keep him straight), or
2. He is *stiff* in either back or hind leg joints, causing his body to twist awkwardly.

If (1), ride all your transitions for a while with a more positive forward attitude and tempo before asking. As he goes more forward with greater activity he will find it both less easy and less desirable to be crooked.

If (2), you must locate *where* the problem lies then begin suppling exercises to make his body more able to function in alignment.

He often strikes off on the wrong canter lead

This is common in young or crooked horses but may also be caused by incorrect riding:

- Unclear aids cause *misunderstanding* – review canter strike-off aids (p.74), paying particular attention to the placement of your weight in the saddle, and a clear difference between inside and outside leg positions.
- *Lack of preparation* may be a factor – you need to be in sitting trot with him accepting you, he must have an active enough trot, and you must make a half-halt to warn him. If you startle him by giving sudden aids without adequate preparation his response will be to run forward and fall into a fast canter, probably picking up his favoured lead, not necessarily the one you wanted.
- Approaching the strike-off from *too fast* a trot will also result in him striking his favoured lead. Horses can shift from standstill to canter quite easily – *speed is unnecessary*.
- Every horse favours one lead over the other because of the asymmetry in his body, with one hind leg weaker but more flexible, the other stronger but stiffer. All your early schooling work is designed to make him more equal on his two sides, but canter strike-off is where you are most likely to see the effects of his natural crookedness. He may also be looser in one shoulder than the other, the looser one being on the inside of his favoured lead where it will always be moving in advance of the other (see Definitions, p.19). More suppling and straightening work will lessen this problem.
- In the short term you can use this component of the sequence to help get a correct strike-off: try asking for the difficult lead with a slight *outside flexion* – young horses in the field do this naturally. This frees the inside shoulder and blocks the outside, encouraging him to step further forward with the leg on the inside and so strike-off with the inside lead. Once he understands (which may take one session or several weeks – patience), go back to correct flexion.
- Sometimes a tap on the inside shoulder with your whip will have the desired result. If you watch canter strike-off in slow motion you will see the first leg to move in the new sequence is the inside foreleg, breaking the diagonal pairing of trot by moving a little faster than its paired hind leg. A tap can just stimulate that little extra speed, thereby helping you get his legs into the sequence you want for your required lead.
- If he takes the wrong lead, *return to trot and ask again almost immediately* – often the best moment to get a successful strike-off is within two strides of him returning to trot.

He runs into canter

First, check your aiding. The most common cause of this problem is the rider who leans forward, putting her weight too much over the horse's shoulders and throwing away rein contact just when he most needs its support.

If this is your problem, you need to think beyond 'sit up' – you need to exaggerate in your mind and think 'lean back!' This should bring you upright.

If you are sitting correctly, then his problem may be panic – young horses can find canter with a rider unbalancing to the point of anxiety – or you may be frightening him with sudden aids. Alternatively, he may be having difficulty taking your combined centre of gravity far enough back to lift his shoulders into canter.

1. Think about your aids – do you warn him (half-halt) *before* you ask or do you just suddenly clamp your legs on? Make a point of warning him, then try with a less strong leg aid, and think more about your inside seat bone (p.74–5) – it is the feeling of one seat bone pushing in advance of the other that tells him to change to canter as opposed to just doing a bigger trot.

2. Prepare with a small circle that starts and finishes at the fence – not so small that he finds it hard, but small enough that you arrive back at the fence at an oblique angle (see right-hand diagram, p.30). Ask for your strike-off *as* you are facing the fence – this has a psychological 'backing-off' effect to help prevent him from running forward.

3. As soon as you achieve canter, put him on a big circle to help him balance, and praise him.

He jumps into canter

This may be a good or a bad thing depending on *how* exactly he is jumping.

If he springs enthusiastically into canter, clearly lifting his forehand by using his back as a lever with no head up, this is desirable (see photograph, p.213). If he leaps into canter, head up, back tight and possibly with a buck in mind, it is not!

In the latter case you should consider:

1. Your preparation – did you give him warning, or did you startle him?

2. The strength of your aids. Some horses are very sensitive and need only a minimal aid – even as little as a slight twitch of your inside seat bone.

3. His comfort – condition of back, fit of saddle, etc.

4. His acceptance of the bridle – is he afraid of the bit or might it be too sharp?

5. His fitness – a fresh horse on a cold day might be a touch sharp! In the winter use a quarter sheet – a blanket that covers his back – while you ride.

He makes abrupt downward transitions

Either you are using too much hand or he is dropping behind your leg.

1. Make your transitions with just the barest vibration produced by your fingers only – no closed fist, no backward movement of hand or arm at all.

2. If he habitually drops behind your leg in downward transitions you must take time to retrain him. Close your lower legs three strides before you intend to make a transition, then keep him going in his current gait for at least three strides longer than he wants to. Over a period of several weeks you should reach the stage where *you* control exactly how many steps there are in every transition you ride. Start with at least six then gradually reduce to the optimum of three – enough time for him to take weight back yet still maintain a forward attitude.

8 Steering

When you first remove the lunge line from a recently backed horse, he will be quite lost without its guidance. He will feel extremely wobbly because of his inadequate ability to balance the pair of you together, and he will never before have had to go in a specified direction without someone on the floor to lead him.

The aids – your building blocks for steering that you teach him now –apply just as much to the young horse taking his first solo steps as they do later to the sophisticated horse performing a half-pass.

Body Position and Weight Aids

On any horse, at any level of training, you must employ correct body positioning, either left or right (see Techniques, p.38) as you ask him to turn, and you must continue in this position until you want to travel straight once more. This puts your torso, your limbs and your *weight* exactly where you need them.

Your most basic, natural aid for steering is your weight. Horses have inbuilt mechanisms for balancing and righting their bodies. As we saw in Balance (Chapter 3, p.24–6) from the horse's viewpoint, falling over is one of the worst things that can happen to him, so his balance and ability to stay on his feet are precious to him.

A horse's centre of gravity is the point within him about which all his body parts balance exactly. In a moving horse this is never a static point; he is continually adjusting his body around it by:

1. Realigning his body parts (head and neck, shoulders, ribcage, haunches).
2. Moving his base of support (his legs) into position beneath it.
3. Adjusting muscle tone in individual muscles throughout his body.

So, by using your weight distribution on his back to temporarily displace your combined centre of gravity you can cause any horse to turn.

Put simply, if his centre of gravity is shifted to one side, he will step in that direction in an attempt to put it back where it belongs: in his middle!

You should achieve this adjustment by moving more of your weight to the side towards which you wish him to turn. Change your weight distribution by:

1. Dropping more weight into your inside seat bone. Do this by turning your body into position right (or left) – see p.38. Ensure that you draw your outside leg back *from the hip*, not just from the knee: you will feel your outside seat bone lift up inside your buttock muscle. As a consequence there will be more weight on your inside seat bone. At a more sophisticated level (when you have a greater degree of body control) you can also weight your inside seat bone by pushing your pelvis downward on the appropriate side: try lengthening the distance from your armpit to the top of your pelvis, but without lifting your shoulder upward. Alternatively, think about pushing your waist towards the side you wish to weight, still keeping your shoulders level.

2. Increasing the weight in your inside stirrup iron. This is done by lengthening your inside leg downward, taking care that, as the weight on the iron increases, you do not either push forward (straighten the knee) which would swing your lower leg forward and away from its correct inside leg position near the girth, nor brace onto the iron so, in effect, standing up and lightening your seat.

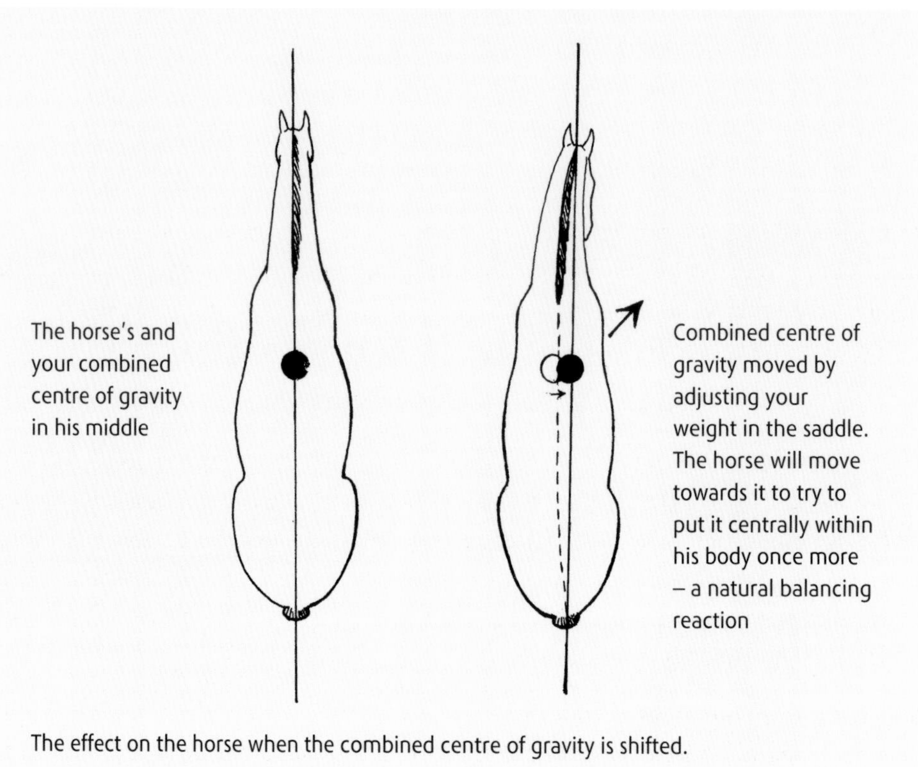

The horse's and your combined centre of gravity in his middle
Combined centre of gravity moved by adjusting your weight in the saddle. The horse will move towards it to try to put it centrally within his body once more – a natural balancing reaction

The effect on the horse when the combined centre of gravity is shifted.

Keep your head upright – it is surprisingly heavy and can influence weight distribution far more than you might think – and *beware of leaning over*. Trying to increase your weight to the inside by leaning onto your inside seat bone will have the opposite effect: as the inside of your waist and your hip fold over, your seat will slide to the *outside* of the saddle, lifting your inside seat bone up. The net result will be more weight to the *outside* of the saddle than to the *inside*: exactly opposite your aim.

The results of head tilting and leaning over.

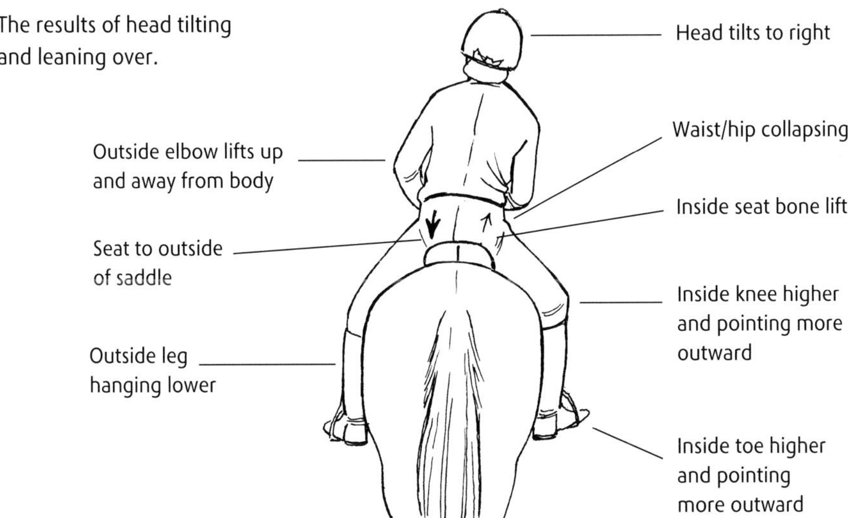

Rein Aids

The rein aids you give a horse in his earlier training differ from those you will use later on. This is because his balance is still so undeveloped that he cannot respond to the sophisticated aids you can employ with the more highly trained horse. There will, as in all things to do with training, be a gradual progression from one end of the scale towards the other as his body becomes more capable of answering your requests.

The *direct rein* (see Techniques, p.35) will be your aid at the beginning:

1. Turn your body into, let's say, position right.

2. If you have kept your upper arms closed and allowed your hands to move with your body, your right (inside) hand will now be slightly further back and your left (outside) hand slightly further forward. Your outside hand must not move more forward than this or you will encourage the horse to fall onto his outside shoulder. At the same time, it should have a feeling of *pushing inward and forward, towards his inside ear*.

3. Now move your right (inside) forearm away from your body to indicate right turn. This must be done *without* removing your elbow from your side – see photograph, p.36.

4. This will turn his head to one side and (so long as he is in motion) his body will follow as his natural body mechanisms try to realign his spine with his head.
5. As you do this, his hindquarters will try to swing outward. Use your outside leg behind the girth to keep his haunches aligned to your curve, so helping him develop lateral suppleness.

As his balance and suppleness improve, you will gradually keep your hands closer together, gaining greater control and finesse over the precise positioning of his shoulders and thereby of his straightness – see The Corridor of the Aids, p.40.

The 'Wheelbarrow Push'

In all steering, your hands should have a feeling of pushing forward, but *without* detaching your elbows from your sides. Imagine yourself pushing a heavy wheelbarrow: your hands are pushing forward but your elbows are well bent and kept at your sides to enable you to support the weight. This is exactly how steering should feel.

Leg Aids

Control of the horse's haunches is less important in the earliest days because of his body's inability to coordinate all your requests. It will, however, become increasingly important as he progresses in his training and you should begin asking him for alignment to the shape of your circle or curve (turn) within a few days of riding off the lunge.

To accomplish this lateral bend you must tackle two areas with your legs: his middle and his hindquarters. Your goal is to produce a mild 'banana shape' along the length of his body, which requires his ribcage to swing to the outside whilst his haunches move slightly inward.

Displacing the Ribcage

Your lower inside leg used at the girth (inside leg position) is your tool for this. However, in the earlier days or on an uneducated older horse (or a physically crooked horse), you may need to use your whole leg – thigh, knee and lower leg all at the same time to press his ribcage to the outside.

Increasing the pressure in your inside seat bone can also help, but if you have to push really hard with any or all of these aids beware of leaning over (collapsing your inside hip – see Weight Aids earlier this chapter) as this will have the opposite effect.

The outward movement of his ribcage will cause his neck and haunches to move slightly inwards in a natural automatic reaction to rebalance his body, which helps create the bend you want (see Chapter 12, p.149).

Controlling the Haunches

This is the responsibility of your outside leg. Draw you whole leg back from the hip and press with your lower leg to displace his haunches to the inside. Later on, when you have introduced him to turn around the forehand (Chapter 14) he will understand more clearly what you want, but if your groundwork has been done correctly he will know to move away from pressure – one of the earliest **building blocks** that needs to be firmly in place.

TROUBLESHOOTING

He doesn't turn when I ask

Physically, this is lack of control of his outside shoulder, but there is also a psychological component: young horses will often treat the school fence as a form of support and cling to it quite determinedly. Moving away into the open school where he must rely on his own balance can be either scary or too much effort, depending on his temperament.

It may also be a deliberate evasion of your aids to see to what extent he can dominate you.

Whatever the cause, deal with it in the same way. First check your aids:

1. Is your weight to the inside, or are you pulling him off balance?
2. Are you turning your upper body clearly into position left or right?
3. Are you using an open rein to guide him in the direction you wish to turn?
4. Are you pressing your outside hand inward/forward with the rein snug against his neck to help push his shoulder around?

If you have all these points in place and he is still not turning, then *exaggerate* your aids:

- Put more weight into your inside seat bone and stirrup (without leaning over).
- Increase the tone in your upper body muscles and close your outside elbow and upper arm tighter to your ribcage, pressing that outside rein inward/forward against his shoulder.
- Turn your shoulders more than you think you should for this angle of turn.
- *Open* your inside rein as far to the side as you can, but keep your elbow closed to your ribcage.

- Press your outside hand tight against his shoulder and *push* him round with the rein snug against his neck, your outside shoulder pushing forward with your elbow tight against your side.
- Use more *outside* leg to push him away from the fence and plenty of *inside* leg to keep him moving – the more forward he goes (without running) the better.
- Regulate his speed: if he travels either too fast or too slowly he can use his bodyweight more effectively against you – and he has a lot more of it than you do!
- If he persists, ride for a few sessions *off the track*. Try to be 3 or 4 m away from the fence and don't let him take you back to it. This will help to reduce his psychological dependence on the fence and teach him to listen more to you for guidance.

He turns his neck in the direction I want to go but his body doesn't follow.

This can also be described as *falling onto, out or through his outside shoulder*. Again, start by checking your weight distribution in the saddle – you may be pulling him off balance.

If you are positioned correctly, then he is either losing balance to his outside shoulder because of his natural crookedness (p.23), or deliberately leaning onto it as an evasion. The answer is largely as above (He doesn't turn when I ask), with very close attention to your upper body tone and closure of your outside elbow.

Also, review The Corridor of the Aids (p.40). Any gaps left between your upper body and that outside wall (defined by your elbow, forearm, hand and rein) give him room to escape by moving his shoulder out into the gap.

Sometimes a short-term (several sessions, or even several weeks) over-correction may be needed: keep your outside rein quite firm at the withers and disallow *any* bend in his neck as you move your inside hand into open rein position; you will find he can turn his shoulders quite successfully without the need to bend his neck. Only allow him to regain a little bend when you can turn his shoulders successfully with his neck straight.

He tilts his nose to the inside when he turns

This probably indicates that you are turning by pulling on his inside rein. You must turn him with your bodyweight clearly to the inside and with your *outside* hand pushing inward/forward towards his inside ear.

Remember to ride actively forward with your inside leg: he may also tilt his head as a result of a lack of hind leg support underneath his body – his *muzzle* will always move towards the side of the hind leg that is *not* supporting him. Lack of support may be a result of weakness or stiffness in that limb, or to your pulling on the inside rein which blocks his inside hind from moving forward.

He tilts his nose to the outside on turns

Your outside rein is too restrictive. While you should always maintain contact with your outside rein it must allow sufficiently forward in turns for him to be able to lengthen the outside of his body (see Positions Left and Right, in Chapter 3.)

He slows down when we turn

Think what happens to his body and legs relative to each other as he turns. If he is in a right bend, the right side of his body is shorter than the left side. This means that his right hind is further forward than his left hind, and thus is carrying more of his bodyweight. This is hard work!

Initially, he may slow simply because he lacks strength, but your goal must be to maintain the same speed before, during and after the turn – this will push him to make a little more effort, which will help him to build the strength to find it easy. Once it is easy, he will not try to slow down.

To maintain his speed:

1. First check that you are not turning him with your inside rein, blocking his inside hind from stepping forward and actually slowing him. It would then be unfair to correct him for a problem you are creating. See *He tilts his nose to the inside when he turns* (above) for how to turn without using your inside rein.
2. Keep aiding at the speed *you* want, not the one he wants. This means you will be closing your legs faster than he is stepping to encourage him to stay up to your speed.
3. If he is still a little behind you, use a light tap of your schooling whip to put your point more firmly.

He loses balance in his turns

Check:

1. That you are giving him clear warning of your intention to turn before you do it.
2. That you are not turning him too sharply.
3. That you are sitting quietly, with your weight and position correct for the turn.
4. That your contact is consistent. Young horses need a degree of support from your reins as they have not yet developed self-carriage.
5. The speed at which he is travelling – too fast and momentum will pull him off balance; too slow and he is likely not to be stepping his hind leg far enough under his body to support himself.

If all these check out then it is probably down to his natural crookedness and will improve as he becomes more equal on the two sides. Be sure to support him with a firm outside rein (closed elbow, fist pushing inward/forward against his withers) when his naturally longer side is on the outside, as he will invariably lose balance to his outside shoulder.

If he is falling inward, use more inside leg in the turn; upper leg and knee pushing his ribcage outward and lower leg to step his inside hind forward/under for support. Do *not* be tempted to hold him up with your inside hand against his withers – he will quickly learn to lean against it for support rather than relying on his own hind leg.

If he persists in falling in on corners, make a small circle in the corner until you have the bend and balance you want, then continue along the track to the next corner. If he falls in again, then circle again until he is organized before going straight on. Persist with this pattern, riding small circles in every corner, and he will soon anticipate the circle. Once he does this he will stay upright and bent in the corner and you can continue without the circles, but be ready to repeat them *every time* he loses balance.

His haunches swing out on turns

This suggests a lack of suppleness, crookedness (of horse and/or rider), an avoidance of correct alignment and thus engagement, or incorrect/lazy riding.

A horse's lack of suppleness and crookedness are longer-term issues that must be addressed, but there is no quick fix. Avoidance of alignment may be caused by a lack of strength (also a longer-term issue) or by laziness. All of these should be corrected in the same way, described below.

Rider crookedness, laziness or incorrectness is down to you! If you do not have access to mirrors, have your trainer check your straightness; if you are slipping to the outside your horse will have no choice but to swing his quarters out to stay beneath your weight.

1. Start by checking your weight in the saddle – it must be greater in your inside seat bone/stirrup. See p.38 for how to do this *without* leaning over.

2. Check your body position: are you truly in position left or right (see Techniques, p.38)? Is your outside leg in a genuine 'outside leg' position? If the rhythm of your seat is clearly telling him to trot, an outside leg position should not initiate a canter strike-off. It may, if he genuinely misinterprets your aids, but this must never be punished – just canter for a few strides then calmly return to trot and try again. He must learn to accept your leg in outside leg position and listen to your seat at the same time – a building block for future demands.

3. If he deliberately swings into/pushes against your outside leg, you need to return to walk and review/teach him turn around the forehand (Chapter 14) so that he understands better that he is to move away from leg pressure.

9 Balance and Outline – Why

A horse cannot be in good balance unless he is in a good outline.

Less experienced trainers may suggest not bothering about a correct outline in the earlier work, proposing instead that you 'get him going forward first'.

While it is true that the horse must react to your forward-driving aids, he can neither 'go forward' nor be in balance unless his outline allows his body to function in an efficient way.

An incorrect outline is also damaging to his spine, joints and muscles. Therefore, for his own welfare, a correct outline should be taught from the earliest stage, beginning with lungeing (see Chapter 6). If he forms a correct contact and outline with the side reins, when you first mount him he should already understand exactly the frame you wish him to adopt.

It would be unreasonable to expect him to sustain such a frame for more than a short time initially, as his muscles will not be up to the job, but this is the only functional position for him to work in and it should be expected right from the word go. If he does not do so, then he was insufficiently prepared (from the lunge work) when the rider was introduced.

A basic level of understanding of biomechanics will help you to see *why* you need to ask him to work in a specific outline – not just because it will get you better marks in a dressage competition! It will also help you with *how* you go about asking him to work in that outline.

Biomechanics in a Nutshell

Horses have within their bodies two separate muscle and ligament systems with two discrete functions:

A postural system – responsible for the shape in which he carries his body – his *outline.*

A locomotor system – which moves his legs to propel him forward.

There is a certain amount of overlap between the two systems, but for the sake of simplicity we need not discuss that here.

Problems occur when these two systems are not used for the purposes for which they are designed: particularly when locomotor muscles are used to support the horse's posture at the same time as moving his legs.

With double the demand on his locomotor muscles, which are trying to do a job for which they are not designed as well as the one for which they are, these muscles can do neither efficiently. Not only do you have an 'upside down' horse – a posture which is both uncomfortable to sit on and destructive to his body – but his gaits will deteriorate, becoming shorter-striding and choppier.

It is his postural system that you need to strengthen to enable him to carry your weight on his back and to develop *self-carriage*, freeing up his locomotor system to move his limbs in the best possible way that his make-up permits.

You can see that, with his head so high, this horse's hind leg joints show little bend, his croup is up, he has dropped at the withers and his rider is being pushed forward towards his shoulders.

The Postural Ring

Put simply, the postural ring consists of:

- The nuchal ligament, which runs along the top of the crest and has several points of attachment to the cervical (neck) vertebrae and is firmly attached to the withers.
- The supraspinous ligament, which starts at the withers and runs along the top of the spinal process (the bumps you can feel when you run your hand along your horse's spine), with attachments at the rear end to:

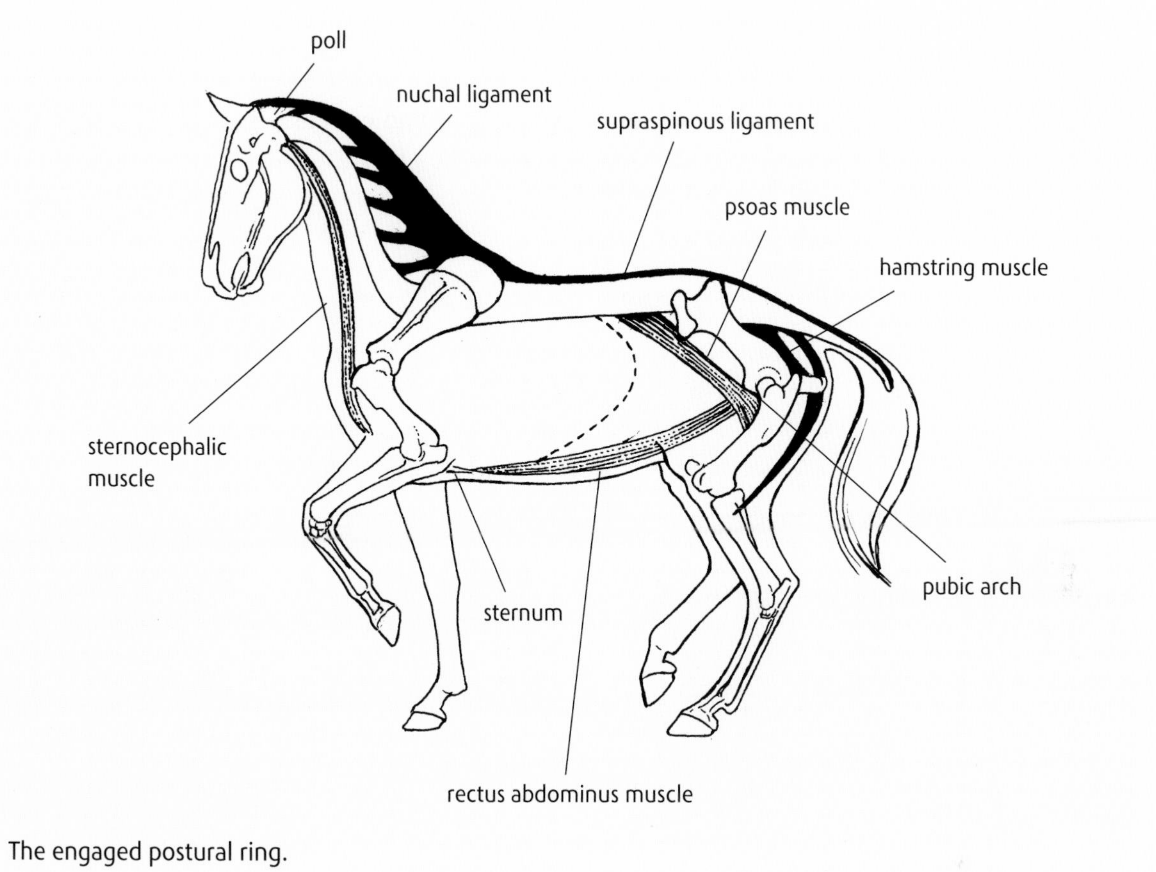

The engaged postural ring.

- the haunch muscles, which are attached to:
- the pelvic structure, the bottom front aspect of which (the pubic arch) is attached to:
- the abdominal muscles, which at the front end attach to:
- the sternum, which is attached to:
- the muscles on the underside of the neck, some of which attach to:
- the poll.

In short, a rounded outline is produced by shortening the underside of the ring (contraction of the buttock, stomach and underneck muscles), making the topside stretch longer.

Try it for yourself: get on your hands and knees on the floor, lower your head, tighten your stomach muscles and clench your buttocks. What happened: your back lifted and rounded (see photographs, p.32.) It is the same for your horse.

Next (so long as you don't have a bad back), try the same thing with a weight on your back – preferably something that moves, like a small child. First let your back sag down – it's not very comfortable, especially when the child bounces up and down!

Now lift your back as before – you will feel much stronger and more comfortable, even more capable of withstanding the bouncing in this position – and it's just the same for your horse.

Using the Postural System

The horse's postural system will not be fully active unless you ask it to do a job. Think about it: you can slouch along with your upper body quite limp and your head hanging, yet you will still cover ground. Alternatively, you can make an effort to hold yourself in an upright posture until eventually this becomes almost automatic and requires no thought – you have trained your body. You can do the same with your horse.

In addition to this very simplified description of the postural system, there are many tiny muscles throughout his body that the horse uses to regulate balance. Consider yourself standing still on a pavement, then doing the same thing on a moving bus. If you think about it, you will notice that you are making lots of small adjustments to your balance on the bus that you don't need on the pavement. Now imagine the same scenario with a heavy rucksack on your back – your muscular effort will be even greater. This is why you need your horse's entire postural system to be active to regulate his balance with you in the saddle.

Some horses never really awaken all their postural muscles – these are the horses who continually drift in one direction or the other, and are always on the forehand. Both of these postures are physically damaging as they overload and or/unevenly load his limbs, so it is your responsibility to get his entire body awake!

It takes effort to use the postural muscles fully: except for stallions displaying to mares, these muscles are not hugely important to the horse in his natural state. It is the addition of the rider's weight that requires this system to be strengthened: not only is there the very real danger of the tops of his spinal processes being compressed together painfully if the spine sags down because of inadequate strengthening of his top-line ligaments and muscles but, by default, he will tend to use his locomotor system for both postural and locomotive purposes, causing incorrect (damaging) movement of his limbs. Therefore, we need to persuade him to use his postural system until it becomes strong, after which he will use it automatically.

There are three aspects to this:

1. Lowering his neck.

2. Contracting his stomach muscles.

3. Contracting his buttock muscles.

These three combine to produce an outline often described as *long and low.*

As each end of his body is lowered, so the middle rises. Try it with a schooling whip – bend both ends downward and the centre bows upward.

With a horse, this is begun by putting the nuchal ligament into traction by lowering his neck. In nature, this occurs when he grazes; the 'S' shape his neck vertebrae form when his head is up (see picture, p.97), is straightened out when his head goes down to eat (a position a wild horse would be in for much of the day). This stretches the nuchal ligament, pulling on its attachment at the withers, which in turn puts his back (supraspinous) ligament into traction. If his hind legs are also brought for-ward underneath him at the same time by the contraction of his stomach muscles, his pelvis will tilt slightly (bottom forward, top back and downward), pulling on the other end of the back ligament and having the 'whip-bending' effect described above.

One important detail to note is the necessity of achieving the correct flexion at the poll to produce this effect: your horse must *seek forward* with his nose. *Poking* his nose will not cause the required traction on the nuchal ligament as there is no leverage on the front end of the ligament (where it attaches at the poll) without his head being drawn slightly inward, nor will dropping behind the vertical (*overbending or going deep*), when flexion tends to occur at the second vertebra back, not at the poll. *Hyperflexion* should also be avoided as this puts the top-line ligaments under extreme stress (not the gentle, progressive strengthening we should be seeking), and is most often achieved with the use of a backward hand or the leverage of physically and mentally damaging gadgets.

Lowering the neck might sound wrong when you know that, for dressage, you ultimately want a tall, 'uphill' carriage, but raising the forehand (as opposed to artificially lifting the neck) is only possible without damage to the horse's body *if it*

A long and low outline.

A 'deep' outline, face well behind the vertical, and a restless tail to display his discomfort.

is a consequence of the lowering of his hind end. It takes time and skill to strengthen all the right muscles to enable this to happen and it should not be asked for until the horse has been in consistent work for about two years in a long, low outline – around the time he begins Elementary level work.

The Horse's Neck is his Balancing Pole

You will often hear international trainers say that 'when you control his neck, you control the horse'. This must not be taken to mean that by manipulating his neck with rough hands you can get him to do what you want, but that his neck is the tool by which you can influence how he uses the rest of his body.

Watch youngsters playing in a field – their heads go down and forward when they gallop, and up and back when they brake sharply. These neck movements adjust the horse's centre of gravity, and so affect his balance.

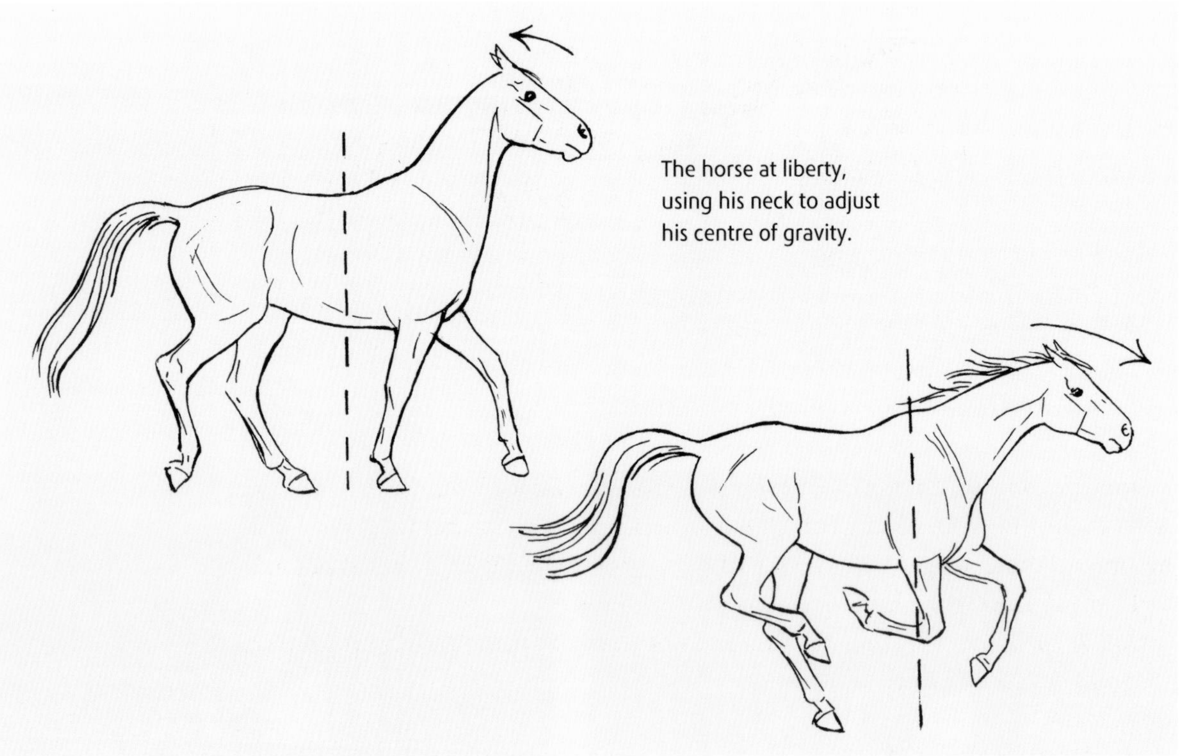

The horse at liberty, using his neck to adjust his centre of gravity.

In addition to using his neck, a horse has three other methods of adjusting his balance:

1. He can move a forefoot forward as he does when grazing, or when he runs out of balance.
2. He can bring his hindquarters further forward beneath him.
3. He can flex his hind leg joints, lowering his haunches.

These last two are what we want to encourage, leading eventually to what dressage judges describe as *engagement*. The tool we use to get there is his neck.

The Mechanism of Rounding

Muscles can contract in two different ways:

Isotonic – the muscle shortens but the tension remains relatively constant.

Isometric – the tension increases with little change in muscle length.

To produce a correct outline we need the horse's underneck and belly muscles to contract *isotonically* (shorten). His top-line muscles (the big muscles along his crest and the length of his back) will contract isometrically (increased tone without shortening) in opposition to the forces of gravity.

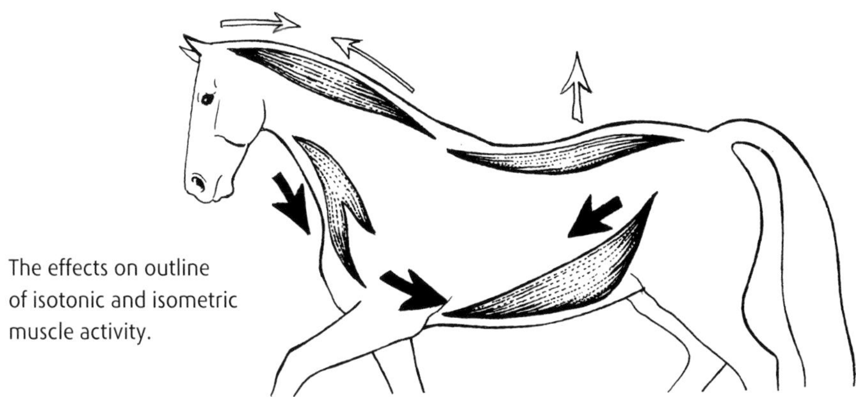

The effects on outline of isotonic and isometric muscle activity.

Isotonic contraction is relatively weak compared to *isometric* function and this is why his top-line muscles, when pitted in sustained action against gravity, will become so much bigger than the muscles underneath, despite the underneck and belly muscles being the initiators of the correct outline.

Riding 'long and low' puts the horse's neck nearly horizontal with the ground, causing maximum isometric strain on his top-line muscles, thereby building them up quickly.

WARNING: to build the horse up successfully requires that he spends more time in a correct outline than in an incorrect one: spending forty minutes battling to get an outline then five blissful minutes on a 'round' horse might seem like an achievement – but you have just spent forty minutes building the wrong muscles and only five on the right ones.

Also, remember that muscles *tire* quickly and need frequent rests. *Muscles are rested by stretching (relaxing)*. However, to stretch the neck down also requires effort, which is why some horses need to be taught to do this (see *Troubleshooting… He refuses to stretch down in free walk*, p.127). In a natural resting position, the neck is supported by the nuchal ligament, and requires no muscular effort to keep it there. (The shape and height of a horse's neck at rest will depend on the length and elastic-ity of his nuchal ligament, with some horses having a more naturally rounded outline than others – a short, tight ligament means a straighter neck.) However, to move the neck either up or down requires muscular contraction, which is why a young horse must be frequently reminded to stay in a working outline, and why he may have to be taught how to stretch after working in such an outline.

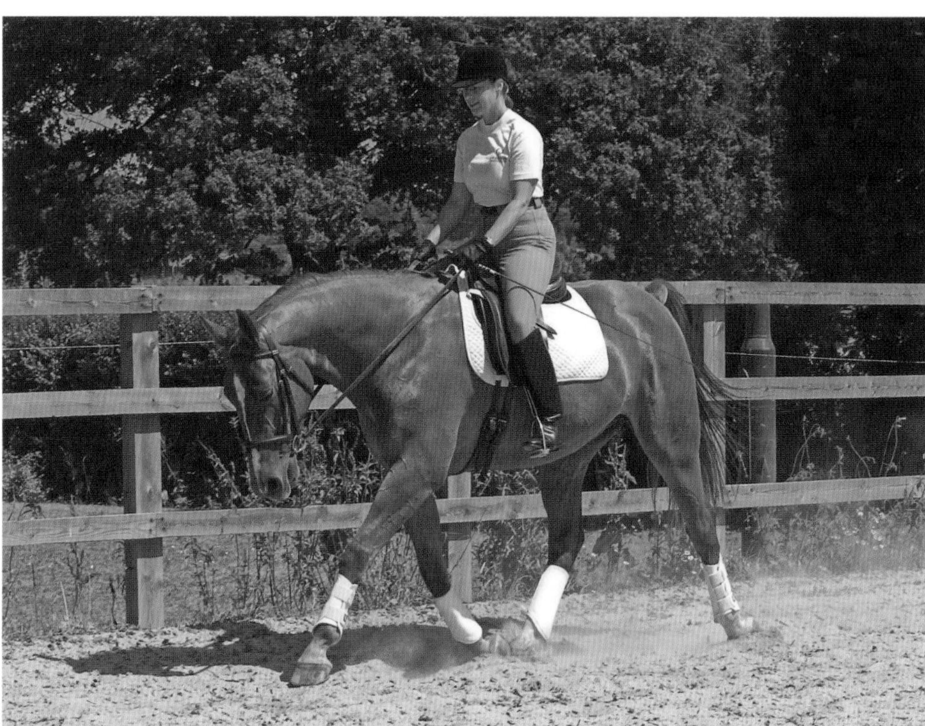

Stretching after work – lowering his neck until his poll is below his withers, and seeking forward to find the bit. This does not put him on his forehand.

Signs of a Correct Outline

- Jugular groove visible.
- Shadow between upper and lower neck muscles with upper neck muscle standing out (looks 'fat' when viewed from on top).
- Muscle along top of crest equally 'fat' all the way from poll to withers, not thinner towards either end.
- Triangular shape at base of neck bulging out.
- Heave line.
- Pelvic angle less horizontal than when resting or *not* working in correct outline.

Holme Grove Merlin and the author competing on the Sunshine Tour in Spain.

- A change in the horse's breathing pattern to become rhythmic with his trot – often preceded by some blowing (snorting) as his stomach muscles start contracting.

If these signs are not clearly visible *in the horse's neck*, yet he appears to be 'on the bit', then his neck muscles are under duress, either from your hands or in an effort to balance using only his neck as opposed to all the postural muscles throughout his body. In this case he contracts all his neck muscles *isotonically*, causing his neck to shorten and stiffen – see upper photograph p.104.

This results in a rigid contact and stiffening throughout his body with a consequent loss of freedom and elasticity of movement. This is most often seen when the rider 'holds the horse together' with the contact as opposed to developing his self-carriage (see Definitions in Chapter 3, p.21), and may also be caused by lack of preparation for movements or transitions, causing him to lose balance.

The *heave line* is evidence of the contraction of his stomach muscles. It is possible for the horse to achieve a correct neck shape *without* involving his abdominal muscles, but to get the rounded, lifted back you want, these are the muscles you must persuade him to contract to support his back (and you!).

Pelvic tuck is more difficult to see, but it becomes easier with practice – it is more open (flatter) when pushing out behind, and is most obviously tucked in piaffe.

Whilst clearly not 'above' the bit, the signs of correct outline are missing: there is no delineation between upper and lower neck muscles, the windpipe is not clearly visible, the triangle at the base of the neck is depressed rather than standing out, and the heave line is absent.

In piaffe, you can see the pelvic tuck by the position of *Merlin's* supporting hind leg – forward underneath his body – and compared with the previous photograph, the steeper angle from croup to tail.

Balance

As mentioned earlier, the postural system is responsible for regulating the horse's balance and it involves many small muscles which he may use to a greater or lesser degree, often depending on his disposition: lazy or laid-back horses use them less than excitable horses. However, regardless of your horse's disposition, you want him to use these muscles all the time, otherwise he will never develop the self-carriage that will enable *you* to have an easier and more comfortable ride.

When we ride the horse in a consistent outline, we remove his ability to use his head and neck to balance himself in the way that he would when free in the field. As already discussed, this outline is essential if he is to remain healthy and sound *as a riding horse*, as opposed to a pasture ornament. Therefore we need to teach him to use all his small postural muscles actively all the time we are in the saddle. As with the rest of his postural system, once they are strengthened he will use them automatically.

The young/uneducated horse will display his weakness in this area in several ways:

- Acceleration not resulting from enthusiasm!
- Leaning on the bit, threatening to disturb your balance and/or seat.
- Frequent deviations from the track on which you are trying to ride, be it a straight line or circle.
- Loss of correct outline during transitions.
- Spooking.

Unwanted *acceleration* and *leaning* indicate that the horse is 'on the forehand'. If he only had two feet and his centre of gravity was that far forward, he would fall flat on his face! As he has four feet he won't actually fall over, but he will speed up ('run away with himself') and also try to use your hands to help balance himself. In these cases you must *slow him down* using your legs and seat (see Techniques, p.32) until he (and you!) can find a better balance before you ask him for more impulsion. This does not mean that he should lack *activity* (see Definitions, p.19), therefore, as you slow him, insist with your leg aids that he keeps bending his hind leg joints so that he lowers his haunches, but with your restraining aids do not allow him to push himself faster.

Deviations from the track are dealt with simply by constant corrections to his alignment until he starts to take care of this for himself. Again, consistency is essential – he must *never* be allowed to believe that wandering off line is acceptable.

Variations in *outline* during transitions in the earlier stages of his training must *not* be dealt with by forcing him to remain in an outline with your hands – this will make him stiffen other muscles in his body to cope with his inadequate ability to do what you want. Instead, you should work to improve his balance immediately before and after the transition until he is able to manage his balance for himself.

Gradually, as he becomes stronger, you will be able to start insisting that he maintains his outline during all transitions, but you must always be aware of any stiffening in his frame and not do so until he can stay fully relaxed through changes of gait.

Spooking happens as a result of anxiety caused by loss of balance (see Definitions, pp.24–6) or by a lack of attention to you (see Submission, p.21). *Startling* can never be fully eliminated as it is a natural survival mechanism, but spooking can be largely eradicated or controlled by improving the horse's balance (giving him less excuse to spook) and his submission, which includes a lowered head carriage (produced by correct training, *not* by strong hands and gadgets), whereby he has to trust you to keep an eye out for predators!

10 Balance and Outline – How

Achieving the desired balance and outline entails activating the horse's postural ring (described in the previous chapter).

BUILDING BLOCKS

The building blocks for this are are:

- Obtaining the horse's acceptance of the bit.
- His response to your forward-driving aids.

Acceptance of the Bit

There are a number of techniques to teach acceptance of the bit and you may need to experiment to discover which is appropriate to your horse.

Chewing Down onto the Inside Bit

This is his first education in what you expect him to do in response to a slight increase in contact on one side of his mouth. He should do three things:

1. *Flex* (laterally – see Definitions p.22) to the inside.
2. *Chew* the bit softly, thus relaxing his jaw muscles and consequently his poll.
3. *Lower* his head and neck – also a sign of submission (see Definitions p.21). The added bonus to this lowering with inside flexion is that it lifts and stretches his outside back muscles – a necessity for correct carriage within bend.

These three responses are the basis for the other techniques that follow.

To teach him to yield to the increased pressure of your contact, start on his stiffer (harder to bend) side on a 20 m circle in walk (if he is inclined to become anxious) or rising trot (if lazy).

1. Check your body position – ensure that your weight is slightly to the inside without leaning over (p.88).
2. Make sure that he travels forward actively but without hurrying.
3. Take up a contact that is definite without being too tight. Move your inside hand inward, put it against his withers and keep it there. If he tugs at it you can take hold of the pommel or the front of your saddlecloth to help stabilize it.
4. Ease your outside hand forward until you release the contact on that side.
5. Now just keep on riding with good rhythm and activity, making sure that you keep a clear contact on that inside rein until he gives you the three answers listed above. If it takes time or he argues, don't lose your confidence, just stick with it; have plenty of patience as he will probably try out a variety of options, but if you persist he *will* give you what you want.
6. Do not be tempted to tug at the inside rein – the passive resistance offered by the still hand is correct; he must never feel you pulling backward.
7. If he becomes anxious, stroke him on the neck with your *outside* hand – the one you are giving forward.
8. When he gives you the correct *flexion*, *chews* the bit and *lowers* his head, move your inside hand forward immediately and allow the two rein lengths to equalize.

Tormenta, (8-year-old Spanish x Warmblood) chewing down onto the inside bit. The outside rein could be even slacker than seen here.

Don't worry that you are giving away the outside rein. Riding from inside leg to outside rein comes later. First, he must understand how to chew onto the *inside* contact.

When you can achieve this on his stiff side you can try on his softer side. This is more difficult as he will want to bend his neck too much this way, and lean onto his outside shoulder. You must try to counteract this by using a strong outside leg (rhythmic squeezes) to push his body more to the inside so that he cannot lose connection with your inside hand. Most horses respond more quickly on this side so long as you succeed in keeping this connection.

To repeat: always ensure you are *instant* in your response (giving the inside rein forward) the moment he gives you the correct answers. If you are even one step too late he will get the wrong feedback.

Alternating Rein Contact

This technique depends on the horse yielding to the rein contact first on one side then on the other to achieve the desired lowering and rounding of his neck. Some horses will respond without going through the previous process, but many will need to be taught that technique first so that they understand what you are asking them to do.

- Start at halt or walk. Move your left shoulder slightly back – so long as your upper arm stays against your ribcage you will have increased the contact to the left side of his mouth. If he understands correctly he will respond by flexing *slightly* to the left, chewing the bit and lowering his neck.
- Once you have this response, move your right shoulder slightly back. This moves your left shoulder forward, which releases (rewards) his response to your left contact, whilst at the same time asking him to do the same thing to the right.
- Once you have the correct response on the right, straighten your shoulders and soften both contacts forward by pushing both hands slightly towards his mouth. He should now be straight and resting lightly onto a soft contact with an arched and slightly lowered neck.
- If he does not respond first time, or he raises his head as soon as you soften the contact, you will need to repeat the procedure – it may take a number of repetitions before he is convinced you mean him to stay put.
- When you do this at walk (and later, in trot), try to *match the speed of your shoulder movements to the speed of his steps*, so that his left shoulder and yours move back simultaneously, then your right shoulders together. This means that your right contact lightens as his right foreleg steps forward, allowing him to feel freedom at each step, helping him to relax and to *want* to seek the contact.

- Make sure that your upper body movements are from your *waist*, so it is only your upper body that moves. This action causes a slight alternation of weight into your seat bones but you should not swing your hips from side to side or you will both be unbalanced.

- Using an alternating upper body movement means that your horse never feels an unsupported backward pull on his mouth – as you move your left shoulder back, so your left seat bone will press into the saddle with a corresponding forward drive to match the 'take back' on the rein. If you alternate the contact merely by moving your arms backward and forward, you are pulling (sawing) at his mouth.

- As he becomes more easily responsive you can reduce the size of your movements, refining down until they become near enough invisible, and eventually just a tiny alternating closure of your fingers.

- As before, it is crucial that the *instant* he responds by lowering his head, you *stop asking*. This means that you sit straight and square, and soften both hands slightly forward. If you continue to ask after he has responded, he will assume he has given the wrong answer and will try something else.

Vibrating the Inside Rein

This is usually the next step, after having used the first two techniques so that he understands clearly what his response should be to a slight increase in rein pressure.

- On a circle (any gait) keep a steady inward/forward contact on your *outside rein* (see Chapter 8, p.89) and press him with your *inside* leg both to bend, and to move actively forward.

- Vibrate the inside rein with your fingers. The feeling you want is as if you are shaking his bit ring – quick little actions of the fingers, several to each of his strides (not a strong rhythmic squeezing, often described as 'sponging' the reins). You may need to use a *little* movement of your wrist as well, but *never* your whole arm. Your forearm and wrist should be utterly relaxed, whilst your upper arm and elbow hang close to your ribcage.

- Circles are by far the easiest place to induce a round outline: if the horse is bent correctly to the inside, his inside hind leg will be further forward (engaged) under his body than if he were moving on a straight line. Combine this with a vibrating contact on his inside bit ring to request *flex, chew* and *lower the neck,* and you have the simplest way to achieve a correct outline. The two techniques described previously are how you teach him to understand what you want before you can reach this point, although some horses achieve this more naturally than others.

- As always, confirm to him that he has answered you correctly by releasing the inside rein pressure – either hold a soft but still contact, or move your inside hand forward in a full release.
- This is your first step towards confirming inside leg to outside rein connection.

Inside rein release – nothing alters in his way of going.

Passive Resistance: the Side Rein Effect

This technique is appropriate to horses who have a problem or an already confirmed resistance to the techniques just described (especially those who swing their noses from side to side), and should be a last resort. It also requires strong legs and good feel for even the slightest response.

- At trot, take a fairly short, firm (not pulling) contact with both sides of his mouth.
- Press both hands *slightly* down (keep some bend in your elbows) so that your reins approximate to the feel of a pair of side reins.
- Ride positively forward with both legs *into* this contact – you must always use sufficient leg to match the strength of your contact.
- One of two things may happen:
    1. He yields to the pressure and drops his head. So long as your contact is a passive resistance (see Techniques, p.35) and not a backward pull, as he lowers and rounds his neck he releases the pressure on his jaw for himself. You may reward him further by exaggeration – push your hands forward until the

Here I am demonstrating the passive resistance technique on *Stanley*, who does not need it, and as a consequence he has dropped behind the vertical.

reins slacken to further confirm to him that he has given a correct answer (see photograph, p.22).

2. He resists even more strongly – this may take the form of extreme hollowing, overbending, running away or even rearing. Be aware of the possible consequences and if you think you may be in danger go back to the technique of getting him chewing down onto the inside bit described earlier instead, and also seek professional advice.

   However, if he is not dangerous, then continue and wait him out, but this must *never* deteriorate into a pulling match – ensure that you always have enough leg pressure to match your contact, and that your contact is truly passive.

   At even the slightest *hint* of yielding, reward him by releasing the contact forward. He has got to *want* to do this – it must be education, not coercion. You will almost certainly need to repeat the procedure almost immediately as he will probably take advantage of the respite and stick his head up again, but it is *essential* that you reward him every time he yields, no matter how little. Each subsequent yielding should then come a little quicker. Eventually he will get the idea but, as always with horses, great patience is of utmost importance, as is the consistency and speed of your actions and reactions.

He will still need to develop enough strength in his neck muscles to remain in this outline for long periods.

NOTE: genuine 'mouth problems' are rare – they are usually an indicator for another problem: riders' hands, uncomfortable bit, general tension, or a problem in the hind end. You should always try to discover the *cause* of an acceptance problem, not just resort to a tighter noseband, which may well exacerbate the problem.

Contracting the Horse's Stomach Muscles

The horse may do this naturally when you push him forward, or he may need to be taught. When he uses his stomach muscles you should feel as if the saddle is supporting you with an upward push, as opposed to feeling as if you are sitting in a hammock! From the ground, his heave line will show clearly when he is supporting himself correctly (see photograph, p.103).

Waking Up the Stomach Muscles

1. Start in walk. Sit tall and wrap your lower legs around his belly in a steady, consistent squeeze. Keep them there!
2. If he speeds up, close your upper leg as well and restrain slightly with your contact (see Passive Resistance, p.35). Your goal is to prevent the energy generated from going into propulsion, directing it instead into carriage – the contraction of his stomach muscles to lift his back and to pull the bottom of his pelvis forward, bringing his hind legs further forward under his body.
3. Keep your legs closed in that steady squeeze until you feel the saddle lift up underneath you. If you find it hard to feel this, have someone on the ground confirm the appearance of the heave line, but this is an area of feel you can develop fairly easily, and is essential if you are to make instant responses to him.
4. Once he lifts you up, relax your legs. He will probably drop you straight down again, in which case you must repeat the procedure but, as in all other things with horse training, if he answers you, you must respond by releasing the pressure – this is the only way he can learn. Repetition, repetition, repetition.
5. When he understands to use himself like this at walk he can be easily persuaded to do so at trot and canter just by riding with stronger (not quicker) leg aids into a passively restraining contact. In other words, a prolonged half-halt (see Techniques p.37).

The Pelvic Tuck

This will occur as a result of him contracting his stomach muscles – shortening the underside of his postural ring (pp.96–8). It can be developed further by more sophisticated use of transitions and half-halts, but this takes a lot more strength and comes at a more advanced level of training.

The Three Bascules

These were mentioned in Chapter 3 (p.27) under Correct Posture, and describe the rounding/arching of the neck, the back and the haunches, which are achieved by accepting the bit, contracting the stomach muscles and developing the pelvic tuck.

We know we must always ride a horse from the rear towards the front, so it may seem wrong to discuss the production of these bascules in this order (front to rear). However, it is only in this order that you can *teach* each of these interdependent components. The young horse, whilst always being urged to stay active and forward-thinking, must first be taught acceptance of the contact, or you will be unable to send him from your legs *into* your hands to access the middle bascule – his back. Only once you have acceptance of the bridle and a consistently rounded back can you begin to ask for the hind bascule – the pelvic tuck – otherwise known as *engagement of the hindquarters.*

Putting the Horse on the Aids

A full description of what it means to be 'on the aids' was given in Definitions, p.26. A certain degree of balance, strength and suppleness are needed before a horse can be truly 'on your aids', but this is the starting point for taking him beyond the most basic training, towards developing his skills for whatever discipline you are aiming at.

You should begin every riding session by putting him on your aids within the limits of his experience. This involves:

1. Getting him relaxed – walk and trot on a loose/long rein, with his top-line stretched by lowering his head and neck.
2. Making him as loose as possible by riding curved lines and circles, paying close attention to any deviations from correct alignment to your figures and correcting him without making him stiffen – in other words, don't be too sharp with your aids.
3. Getting his attention by riding transitions.
4. Making sure that he is obedient and willing, reacting to your aids without tension or tardiness – again, through transitions.
5. Gradually working into a shorter outline, using transitions and circles to help bring his hind legs further underneath him and taking your reins gradually shorter *as his body shortens.* Always bear in mind that the length of his body in front of you should equal the length behind you – in other words, you must not pull his front shorter with your hands, but persuade his body to shorten itself by bringing his hind legs further forward, and taking up the slack in the reins when his neck shortens as a consequence of this.

This procedure should be run through at the beginning of *every* ride, and should be the basis of your warm-up, taking about twenty minutes. It is likely that when he first comes onto your aids he will feel lazy – this is natural as he is starting to use *all* his muscles and that is hard work. As he becomes stronger over months and years of work this 'laziness' will vanish, so do not think of it as a problem, merely as a sign of progress.

In the earlier stages of training you should be able to achieve a feeling of harmony and coordination (on the aids) in trot, then in canter. Getting this feeling at walk and halt will come later and the walk, in particular, should be largely left alone when he is young, never taking him on too short a rein as this gait is easily spoiled by tension and is almost impossible to recover once damaged (p.136).

Putting the horse on your aids is also the point to which you must always return if he is disobedient, tense or has any bad habits. Trying to further his training without doing so is a pointless waste of time.

This all sounds very simple, but it is really the most difficult skill you, as a rider, will ever learn. It is also the most important. Few horses are ever put correctly on the aids; you and he will enjoy so much more comfort, ease, safety and success in all spheres of riding if you take the time to learn this skill.

TROUBLESHOOTING

He goes above the bit/hollows

Aside from physical pain associated with a health problem (sore back/lameness), poorly fitting tack or an over-heavy rider – all of which should be checked first – there are several reasons why he might go above the bit:

- He is uncomfortable because you are pulling at his mouth or bumping on his back.
- His bit is uncomfortable.
- He is losing balance.
- He has never been taught to answer the aids correctly.

Address things in this order:

1. Check the corners of his mouth – are there any signs of soreness on his lips or bruising on the bars (gums)? Does he draw his tongue up inside his mouth or stick it out to the side? If so, he may need a different bit. Bear in mind that, just because no marks are evident, this may not mean that he finds the bit comfortable: it may be too thin, too fat or the wrong shape for his mouth. X-ray studies have shown

the interior of horses' mouths to be much smaller in volume that previously believed, so a fat bit may not be the most comfortable. If you are unsure, take professional advice. If you plan to compete, bear in mind that it is best to stick with a bit that is permitted under the rules of your chosen sport or you may have problems later.

2. Have someone assess your riding – if you are stiff and/or out of balance your best option is to take some lunge lessons. You cannot expect him to work in a correctly rounded outline if you are bumping on his back.

3. Pulling at his mouth can take several forms: direct backward pulling (using your biceps muscles), upward or downward pulling, pulling alternately at each side of his mouth, or fixed, rigid hands (usually associated with rigid elbows, wrists and/or forearms). Check the correctness of your arm position and function:

   - Your *upper* arms should be closed against your body with a feeling of downward weight into your *elbows*, as if someone has hold of your elbows and is pulling them downward. When you employ passive resistance, as in a half-halt, your upper arm may be held quite tightly against your ribcage using the *triceps* muscle (the one down the back of your arm), *never the biceps* (front of the arm).
   - Your *forearm and wrist* should always be relaxed – try waggling your wrists to check looseness.
   - Your *fists* should be closed around the reins – open fingers do *not* make a light contact – they simply allow the reins to slip. The reins should be held firmly between thumb and forefinger with the lower fingers more relaxed – this permits the finger movements you need to vibrate the rein (see photograph, p.10).
   - If *he* pulls at *you* that is quite a different matter. So long as your contact is a passive resistance (see Techniques, p.35), if he chooses to pull you must not give way, but equally *you must not pull back against him.* Always remember: *it takes two to pull.* Trite though that sounds, it is *always* true and pulling is *always wrong.*

     This is not just an ethical point – though welfare must always be important – but a practical one also: pulling at his mouth induces him to use incorrect muscles in his effort to get away from discomfort, so it can never be justified as a means of getting him 'on the bit', as in reality it can never do so.

4. An unbalanced horse will try to use his head and neck to rebalance himself as described earlier (p.100). Ride him at a slower speed than you will eventually want, to enable him to find his balance more easily. At the same time encourage him to work in a round outline using one of the techniques already described, together with positive but slow and rhythmical leg aids that encourage him to draw his hind legs further forward under his body to assist his balance. Do *not* run him forward

(i.e. confuse speed with impulsion, see Definitions, p.20), or his hind legs will be left further behind and the problem made worse.

5. If you think the problem may be lack of understanding, you need to check both his response to your driving aids and his reaction to the bit.

   - Send him more forward into your contact by closing your lower legs in stronger, rhythmic squeezes – to support a round outline he must contract his stomach muscles (in response to your leg aids) and move his hind legs further forward under his belly. You may find that you were simply not asking him for enough energy, but if he fails to respond when you use your legs, review Chapter 7 *Troubleshooting 'He won't walk on'*, and use this technique to improve his responsiveness.
   - If he responds to your legs but does not yield softly when you send him more forward, try asking him to chew down onto the inside bit (p.107). It is quite likely that you will find he does not understand this demand, or offers you one or two of the three responses you need (flex, chew, lower), but not all three. Go through the procedure outlined until he understands what you require, then proceed to an alternating rein contact (p.109). If, when you alternate the contact, you find that he swings his nose from side to side, then use the passive resistance technique (p.111).

He won't stay on the bit: he goes there when I ask but then hollows as soon as I stop asking

As usual, there are a number of possibilities:

1. He may be too weak as yet in his postural muscles to sustain an outline without constant prompting. Lungeing and hill work (so long as he is in a long, round outline) can both help to build up strength in his back and hindquarters, as can pole work and small jumps.

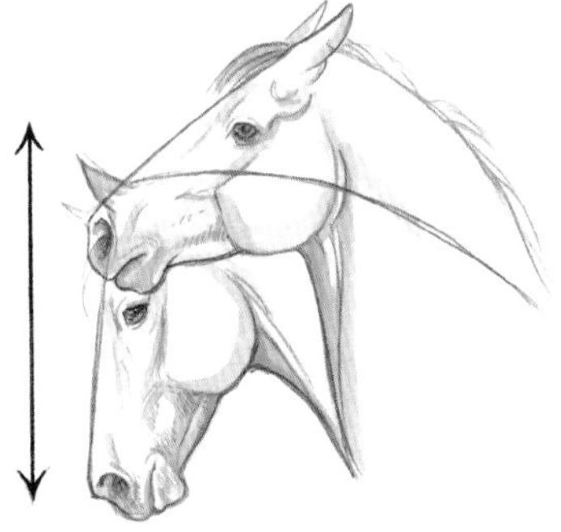

2. His hind legs may not be stepping far enough under his body to support him (not enough stomach muscle contraction). This can be through lack of strength but could also be laziness or lack of understanding. Use stronger (but not quicker) leg aids to ask him to step more energetically forward. *Do not* allow him to speed up – if he tries use passive resistance (see Techniques, p.35).

   Try holding a schooling whip with one hand at each end. Keep one end still and push the other slightly down and towards the still end – what happened: the middle of the whip bowed upward. This is what you want his back to do, but if you let the front end run away from the back end you will never achieve this effect (called 'riding from leg into hand'). Also, to be successful, you need him to accept the bit, so if he stiffens his neck and/or pokes his nose, review the techniques described for teaching acceptance, then try again.

3. He may not be genuinely 'through'. Read the definition of 'throughness' on p.20 and consider if any of those factors are missing: is he tense or stiff anywhere, or resisting or using incorrect muscles? An observer on the ground may be able to help you pinpoint where the problem is. Mental tension can usually be seen in the horse's expression (though it may take an experienced trainer to see it) or a restless tail. Physical tension/resistance may be a physical problem/tack issue. You will need to locate where the problem originates and deal with that before you can achieve genuine 'throughness' and expect him to stay happily in a consistent outline.

4. You may not trust him enough! It is essential that *every* time he responds to your aids and comes into a correct outline, you reward him by harmonizing (ceasing to ask), and you must do this even if you know that two strides later he will lift his head again! If you keep asking, even when he is round, in the belief that you can 'keep him there', he will assume he has not given you the right response and will try something else. *Huge amounts of patience* are needed here – it may take months before he begins to stay put on his own, but if you do not give him the opportunity it will *never* happen.

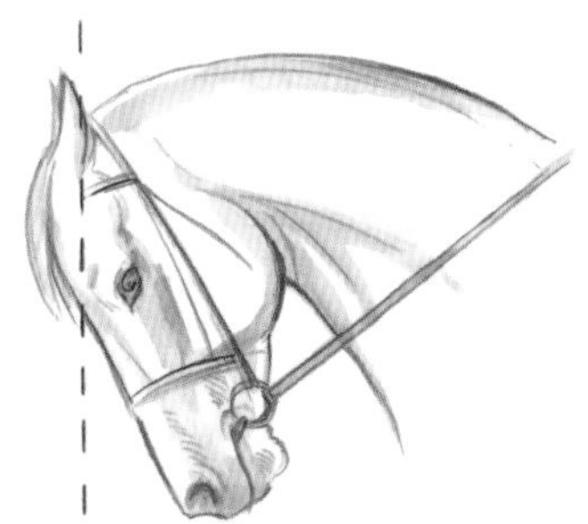

He goes over-deep and leans on my hands

If he is young and/or it is early in his training, *don't panic!* His back muscles may still be too weak to support his posture against the pull of gravity, so he is using your hand to help him. Initially you must permit this although your goal will be to strengthen him – hill work, trotting poles and lungeing are all good for this. It may be some weeks or even months before he can begin to support himself without your help, so be patient.

If he is actively leaning onto your hand because he is *lazy*, you need to remove his prop! Use positive, rhythmic lower leg aids to ask him to step further under from behind, and make frequent, unexpected (to him!) releases of the contact by pushing your hands forward suddenly and letting the reins go into loops. He will either support himself or fall flat on his nose! For safety, do this in a school with a good, level surface and sit very upright – you don't want to go over his head if he stumbles. Your giving of the reins must be sudden, or he will follow your hands by dropping even further down. You should find that he quickly loses the inclination to lean on a contact that suddenly disappears without warning.

He overbends, dropping behind the bridle

This is a tough one that needs nipping in the bud as early as possible, but it should not be confused with the situation described above (over-deep). The horse who is

genuinely *behind* the bridle over-flexes at the poll, tucking his nose back to avoid contact even as far as placing his chin on his chest.

Overbending is often accompanied by running, so first slow him using your seat and legs (see Techniques, p.32). This allows him to rebalance.

Next, you must persuade him to take his nose forward. First try to push his nose forward by keeping a contact and imagining your reins are like a pair of metal rods with which you can push his mouth forward away from you. As these 'metal rods' are rigid, your reins cannot sag into loops (when you would lose the contact altogether), but you are pushing forward with your hands as much as you can to invite him to take the bit forward. Always support this forward offering with your legs asking him to step forward and under without hurrying.

In more extreme cases, where this technique fails, try using a forward/upward half-halt - a 'flick' forward of the reins (a bit like a cowboy in a B-movie Western going 'Yah'!), to startle him into lifting his head up and out. *Be careful* – use only as much action as you need to achieve this result; you do not want to frighten him or he might react badly, bolting or rearing, neither of which you want!

If you are riding a more established horse in a double bridle you must first make sure that it is fitted correctly and that you are not using too much curb rein, as you may find this is causing the problem in the first place. Then, if you still need to make this corrective action, ensure that your curb rein is really loose when you do it, or it will only serve to winch his head further in and down.

Immediately you have his head up, even if he is above the bit, use your lower legs more strongly (not more quickly) to encourage him to step forward more actively under himself with his hind legs.

Your goal is to connect him to the contact by sending him forward (lower legs and positive seat swing) towards the bit, but if he runs you will need to slow down and repeat the procedure. You may also need to repeat the 'flicking' action many times before he will stay with his head up and out and in more confirmed cases this is less likely to work. At that stage it becomes a job for a very experienced rider with strong legs and seat.

He won't settle on my contact; is sometimes against it, sometimes behind it, with his neck constantly changing length

This is usually an issue of balance, but may be a deliberate evasion. Either way the answer is the same: slow him until he finds a better balance, even if he is crawling along, and use a *floating contact* (see Techniques, p.33). There are two ways to achieve this:

1. By allowing your hands to follow his head wherever it goes, so you keep a constant weight in your hands. This requires a great deal of skill to anticipate where his head is going next, and to react extremely quickly.

2. By widening and narrowing your hand position either side of his withers to (a) absorb the slack (hands wide) when he draws back, and (b) follow him forward (hands together) yet not lose your upper arm position. This last is crucial to you being in position to move instantly into passive resistance if he pulls against you.

Whichever technique you use, your goal is to keep a constant weight in your contact to either help him with his balance, or to teach him that no matter what he does, he cannot evade your hand. As he begins to settle into a steadier outline, reintroduce a more forward gait.

left The right way to widen your hand position – with your elbows still closed against your ribcage.

right The wrong way!

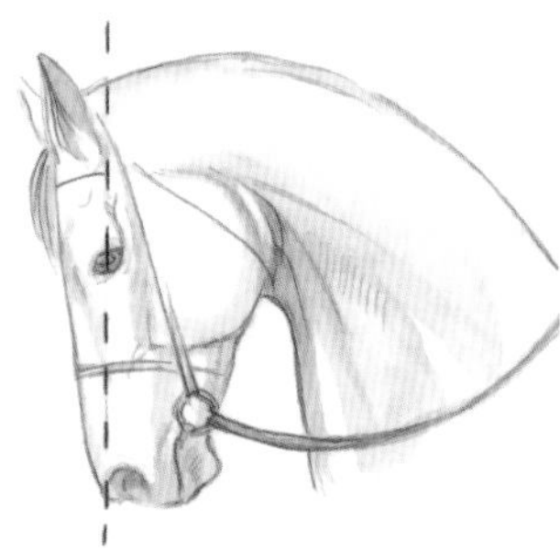

He hangs behind the bridle

This describes a contact that is 'too' light, or non-existent, and in most cases it is a product of anxiety – too sharp a bit, sharp teeth, a rider with over-strong or rough hands. Also, it may be a consequence of the *memory* of one of these as opposed to the problem being current. (It may also occur in a young horse yet to find his balance and confidence, in which case it should gradually resolve itself without intervention.)

First eliminate any mouth problems and *never* give the horse cause to doubt your hands – they must always be stable and relaxed (trustworthy).

To address the issue directly, take up a contact by widening your hand position (see previous problem). He must learn to accept your hands, knowing you will never pull backward. Now ride him forward more actively (you may need to *slow* him first to achieve a better balance, then ask for more activity). If this is an evasion as opposed to an anxiety, you will find out now, as he will be unwilling to accept your driving aids. Whatever the cause, you must calmly insist (slow, strong leg aids and longer swing of your seat) that he responds by stepping more forward with a longer stride to encourage a lengthening of his frame and the craning forward towards the bit that you need.

Be patient but persistent – this will take time to resolve.

He is strong/feels rigid in the contact

First ensure that it is not you who is taking the strong contact! Consciously relax your forearms and wrists and try a crest release – first with one rein, then the other (see photograph, p.111) – taking the contact back with less weight in your hand.

If this is not successful then you must identify *why* your contact is not soft/light:

1. Does he accept your contact?

2. Is he flexing at the poll?

3. Are his neck muscles tense?

4. Is he comfortable with his bit?

5. Is he in balance? He may be leaning on your hand for support.

6. Is he sufficiently engaged?

The first three points can all be addressed by showing him how to chew down onto his inside bit (p.107) – this teaches him to relax his jaw (accept the contact), flex at his poll and lower his neck.

You can try changing bit type/thickness to find one more suited to the shape of his mouth.

Balance and engagement are dependent upon each other – if he is using your hands for support he is not engaging his hind legs under his body to support himself. You will need to use half-halts (see Techniques, p.37) and contact (crest) releases (photograph, p.22) to teach him to step under, rebalance and carry himself instead of relying on you.

He feels harder on the right side of his mouth than the left (or vice versa)

This is common and is *very rarely* a genuine mouth problem – it is more often a symptom of a stiffly braced hind leg. This causes the whole of one side of his body to be braced, resulting in the heaviness you feel in one hand. To solve it you must encourage him to be yielding and supple throughout the whole of his body on this side, not just address his contact.

Review Natural Crookedness and the Soft/Hard Sides in Chapter 3 (p.23), and start by having an equine physiotherapist check him over – he may have developed tight/sore muscles as a result of his bracing. After this, begin improving the feel in your hand on the stiff side:

1. Put him on a 20 m circle to the stiff side.
2. Ask him to chew down onto his inside bit (p.107).
3. Press your upper inside leg (knee and thigh) inward to push his ribcage to the outside and use your lower leg in rhythmic squeezes to ask him to step his inside hind leg further forward.
4. When you feel the contact in your inside hand become lighter, briefly push the hand forward in a mini release of contact (even touch your knuckles to his neck as a little pat) and praise him with your voice.
5. Take the contact back as lightly as you can.
6. If, when you release your contact, he swings his head to the outside, check that your outside hand has a forward enough feeling to allow the bend. If that is not the problem, you need to repeat the above process using a stronger (but not quicker) lower leg aid, making sure his gait does not become bigger (use seat and leg control – see Techniques p.32), then try the release again. He needs to have his inside hind leg far enough forward under his body to support his balance for you to achieve this fully, so frequent repetitions will be needed.

He tilts his head

If you are certain that he has no mouth (teeth) or musculo-skeletal problems, likely reasons are: an unequal contact, a tight neck frame created by strong hands, an unequal push with his hind legs, or general stiffness to one bend. You can see tilting easily by checking the levelness or otherwise of his ears.

1. Check your contact: if you are pulling on one rein, his muzzle will tilt to that side (muzzle right, left ear down and vice versa). This may happen if you are asking him to yield on that side but do not notice that instead of relaxing his jaw he tilted his head. Always ensure that you feel for his yielding to your contact and answer (reward) it by yielding back to him. That way you do not end up in a pulling contest. (Remember: *it takes two to pull!*)
2. Check the relaxation of your forearms, including your wrists, and ensure that you are not pulling his neck into shape with your hands alone – he may be twisting his head/neck in an attempt to relieve the discomfort in his neck muscles.

3. He will tilt his muzzle towards the side of the hind leg that is not supporting him. Push your hand forward on this side and lose the contact (even if it is the outside rein – a horse cannot be ridden into the outside rein until he is straight and evenly load-bearing over his two hind legs). Now use a stronger leg aid on that side to push that hind leg further under him and his head will straighten. Take the contact back carefully, keeping it lighter than the other side until he maintains (in several weeks time) level ears even when you take equal weight in both hands. Repeat the rein yielding and stronger leg as often as you need to, i.e. every time he tilts.

4. If you are asking for more bend on his stiff side than he is physically capable of giving as yet, he may tilt in an effort to answer your bending aids. While you must push him constantly to stretch his short (out)side muscles a little more each session, don't demand more than his body is capable of.

He never settles in his mouth, constantly fiddling with the bit and opening his jaws/pulling his tongue up

- Start by having his teeth checked – horses develop rough edges at different rates to each other, some need rasping as often as three-monthly, others annually.
- If he is young he may still be teething – either stop riding until his mouth is no longer sore, or use one of the gels available from the chemist for teething babies and apply it to his gums just before riding.
- Try him in a different bit – see p.115. Different thicknesses, shapes of mouthpiece, a central lozenge and different metal compounds should all be considered – he is an individual and should be treated as one. Bit 'banks' now exist from where you can hire bits to try before buying.
- Check his noseband – one that is too tight, or leather that is too narrow around his nose can cause stress.
- Check the stability of your hands: hold your saddlecloth/pommel of your saddle/neck strap, or rest the heels of your hands against the saddle. Does he become more settled? If so, he has discovered that by playing with the bit he can move your hands without you realizing it, and thus avoid a true contact. Focus on keeping your hands at the 'contact point' (see Techniques, p.33), not permitting *him* to move them.
- Make sure that your contact is not too strong: discomfort is a major reason for opening the mouth.
- *If* everything else checks out, and especially if he is drawing his tongue back up because of an old habit, you should consider using a Flash noseband, tightening both straps until his mouth is less able to open. If he cannot open his jaws it is

harder for him to draw his tongue up. This should be considered a temporary measure until the habit is forgotten, as a tight noseband will also restrict how much he can chew the bit, and therefore how much he can relax his jaw.

He puts his tongue out/over the bit

Follow the procedure above (*He never settles in his mouth...*):

- Check teeth and gums.
- Check the fit of his bit/noseband.
- Check that your hands are not at fault, moving too much or being too strong.
- If all these check out, try a Flash noseband, doing it up firmly so that he cannot draw his tongue far enough up to get it over the bit.

  In cases where he habitually puts the tongue over the bit you may need to raise the bit higher than you would ideally wish for a period of a few weeks (always checking for sore spots in the corners of his mouth after riding) in an attempt to break the habit – if he cannot succeed for several consecutive rides, he should stop trying.

  Tight nosebands and high bits should only be used in the short term. Your ultimate goal is to teach him to accept the contact correctly so, as soon as possible (when his tongue is under the bit), use the procedures outlined on p.107–110 to help him understand how to relax his jaw (chew the bit) and yield softly to your contact.

He tosses his head/yanks at the bit

Tossing and yanking usually arise from pain or anxiety. These actions prevent the hind legs from stepping forward and can escalate to rearing in the worst cases.

Pain may occur if you have had him in a particular outline for longer than his neck muscles can take and he will try to stretch his muscles to relieve the discomfort. Always be on the lookout for the first signs of muscle stress: small twistings of his neck or a little unsteadiness in your contact. Once these occur, insist that he maintains his outline for only a little longer (a circle or two) before allowing him to stretch.

If there is no excessive muscle stress, you have not been unsteady, over-strong or aggressive with your hands, and he has no other reason to be anxious, then he is just being rude and each yank should be met with passive resistance (p.35). This will stabilize your hands and his head, and increase the drive of your seat to bring his hocks forward. If he continues, meet each toss/yank with a sharp kick. *Never* yank back at him – *your hands must always be trustworthy.* Teach him that every time he pulls at you he will have to step more actively with his hind legs and he will pretty soon lose the habit.

He drops his poll / the highest point of his neck is several vertebrae back from his poll ('crest high')

- This can be a result of youth and/or weakness and may improve as he gains strength.
- It may be evidence of an outline created by coercion – strong hands or draw reins – and, if so, may be hard to correct. You must maintain constantly forward-offering hands and ride positively forward from your legs *into* your hands to encourage him to stretch forward and lift his poll. You may need to use lots of little forward/upward half-halts as described in *He overbends...* p.118 (note accompanying warnings), repeating them every time he drops his poll, then riding forward to connect him from your legs into your hands in this higher position.
- *A stallion will often give this appearance without actually dropping his poll, because of the size and height of his crest.*
- *Certain breeds (particularly Trakehners) also give this impression by their conformation.*

He arches his neck but his back is dropped

If he is not sway-backed (through conformation or age), then his neck has been shaped without his stomach muscles being engaged. Revue Waking up his Stomach Muscles, p.113 and use this technique to lift his back. You will probably find that, in doing so, his neck and poll will drop. Do not worry about this in the short term – when he is strong enough in his belly muscles to keep his back lifted continuously, then you can encourage him towards a taller posture.

His outline is round but he is heavy on his forehand

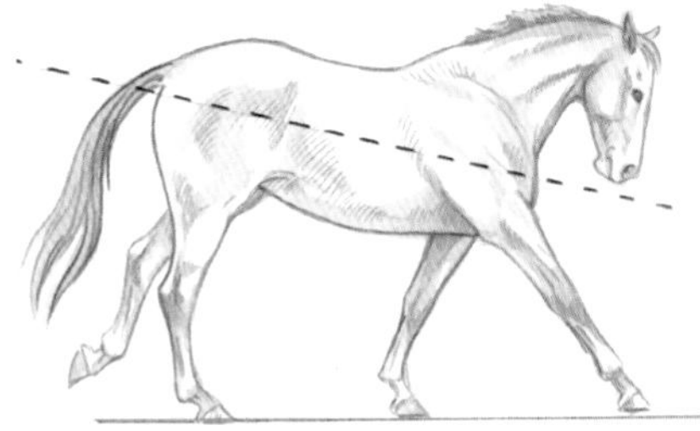

Don't worry – round is a good place to start!

Until he is strong over his top-line (two years of consistent rounding and stretching work), simply work on asking his hind legs to step more actively forward, using lots of transitions, especially *within* the gaits (see Chapter 19). Changing his balance (taking more weight back on his haunches) comes later, as it involves him using his back as a lever to lift his *withers*, and it must be well strengthened before this is possible.

His head and neck will rise as a consequence of his croup going down and *must not* be lifted artificially with your hands.

To produce more *engagement*, which is extra bending of his hind leg joints and increased pelvic tuck (p.113), you need to use a combination of patterns (leg-yielding,

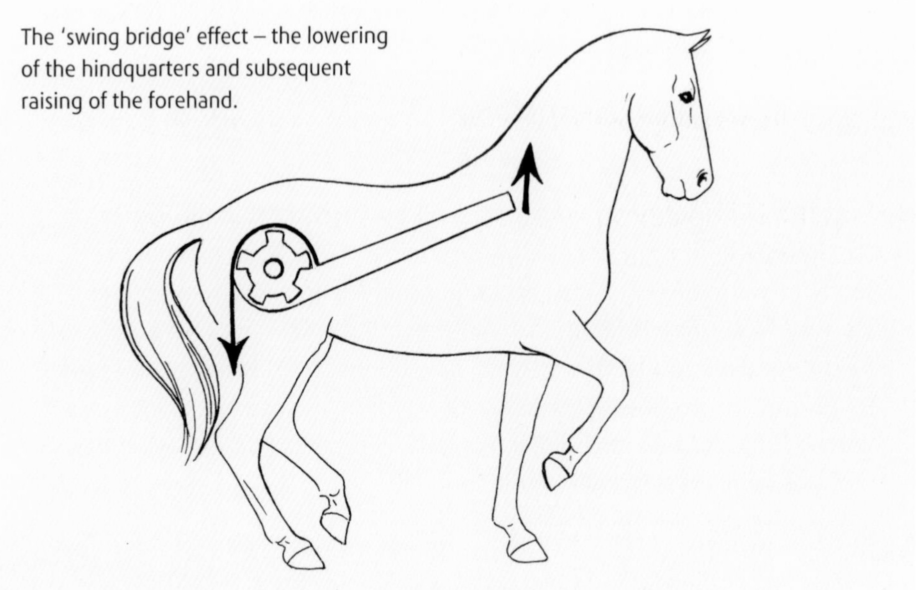

The 'swing bridge' effect – the lowering of the hindquarters and subsequent raising of the forehand.

spirals, shoulder-in, haunches-in – see later chapters), transitions (ridden correctly!) and aids, particularly half-halts.

Once you begin this work you will never finish: engagement is something you can never have enough of – dressage judges will always ask for more, so never take this as a criticism.

He hollows and runs away

1. Review: *He goes above the bit*, p.115.
2. Put him on a circle in trot, making it as small as you need to, to help slow him down.
3. Use your seat and upper legs to slow him (see Techniques, p.32).
4. Make sure you are sitting upright, not leaning forward – trying to lighten your weight off his back will only encourage more speed, not more stepping under. You need to sit very quietly and very *adhesively* to your saddle.
5. Do *not* pull at the reins – use them only to guide him around the circle.
6. Stay on this circle, however long it takes, until you can quietly close your lower legs and he accepts them without rushing faster – *you cannot school him until you can drive him.*
7. Once you can put your legs on him, begin teaching him to chew down onto his inside bit (p.107).

8. Once you can lower his neck, use your lower legs to ride him forward into the contact to find a secure connection from your legs into your hands.

With 'fizzy' horses always use frequent circles – straight lines only encourage speed!

His outline is fine during work, but he refuses to stretch down in free walk

Try first on a circle – asking him to chew down onto his inside bit (p.107), and opening your fingers to allow him to continue to take the rein down once he begins to lower his neck.

Once this is successful, use an alternating contact (p.109) whilst walking in a straight line. As he begins to lower his head in response, open your fingers and allow him to take the reins down. If he stops taking the rein, or raises his head again, close your fingers without shortening the reins then *widen* and *lower* your hand position – this allows you to take up the slack in the contact without moving your hands backward. Repeat your aids with your hands in this new position, always allowing him to take the reins when he lowers his head, even if only by a little. In the early stages, you may, in this case, even need to lean forward a little to lower your hands sufficiently for him to understand.

Keep repeating this process, remembering to keep enough leg on so that he steps actively (but without hurrying) and his hind legs are far enough beneath his body to support him as his outline changes. It may take two or three sessions for him to really grasp the concept, but then it should be with him for life.

Encouraging stretching in free walk. Inclining slightly forward from my hips (without rounding my back), and slightly straight-ening my elbows, I have lowered my hands either side of his withers to encourage him to drop his neck. As he does so, I will open my fingers and let the reins slide out steadily.

He is round in walk and trot but hollows in canter

Sometimes a young horse will take longer to find his balance in canter than in walk and trot, so do not try to pull his head into place. Instead, ride canter in a light seat (see photograph, p.134), and hack him out on hills and do gridwork and small jumps to strengthen him and improve his balance under saddle.

If he is not so young, or not so inexperienced, you may need to address this directly.

1. Review 'alternating rein contact' (p.109) so that you understand clearly *how* to move your body from the waist.

2. Sit very upright to assist his balance and to put your seat bones firmly in the saddle.

3. In canter, move your left shoulder (and contact) forward in one stride, followed by your right shoulder in the next. This may feel quite slow, but it is the right rhythm for this gait, where the biggest influence is from your alternating seat bones in the saddle, which encourage him to relax and raise his back. If you feel this is not giving you a sufficiently positive result, make the movement bigger, not quicker.

4. As soon as you feel him lowering his neck, harmonize with his canter (i.e. *stop* alternating), and praise him with your voice and a pat on the neck.

The lifted and rounded back and neck will bring him into a correct outline, as opposed to him just arching his neck with a stiff back.

11 Riding the Gaits

First, review the definitions of correct sequence for each gait on pp.17–19.

To achieve harmony and effectiveness, each gait requires you to move your seat and apply aids in a different way.

Walk

- Your seat must follow the motion, not 'shove'. So long as the walk is purposeful, allow the saddle to 'pull your seat along'. Your *upper body* should be tall and not swaying backwards and forwards, or side-to-side; all motion should be from your waist downward.
- If necessary to motivate the strides, your *legs* should close alternately, left and right, as if you were marching. Initially, just try to find this rhythm. Later on you should match your leg closure to the movement of the horse's hind legs: your right leg closing as his right hind lifts into the air and vice versa. In order to know when each hind lifts, feel what his belly is doing beneath your legs – it swings from side to side as he walks. His *left* hind is in the air as his belly swings *away* from your left leg, so this is the moment to close your left leg, and vice versa. It can help to get someone on the ground to call 'left – right – left – right' as each hind lifts to help you find this coordination. *You can only influence his hind legs to step longer/more actively when they are in the air.*
- In the earlier stages of training you should keep a fairly long rein with a light, slightly following *contact*. As mentioned earlier, walk is the gait most likely to be damaged (loss of sequence) by restriction from the hands. Initially, the horse uses his head and neck to balance himself. As his balance develops, his head and neck will move less – you can then take the rein a little shorter and move your hands less. Beware of 'rowing' with your hands: this causes exaggerated nodding of his head, which is not only unnecessary (wasteful of energy for both of you) but also encourages excessive motion in his neck, which *discourages* movement

further back in the loin area where we want a soft, swinging back. Eventually, the advanced horse will carry his head on a highly arched and raised neck with a supple poll and you will see little head movement and the barest minimum of hand motion, but this takes years of work.

Free Walk

Free walk on a loose rein is performed with no contact at all, allowing the horse total freedom to lower and stretch his head and neck. He should remain active and straight.

Free walk on a long rein requires you to allow the horse enough rein to stretch forward and down, but to keep a light contact – i.e. the rein must not become totally slack as it does in loose-rein walk.

Variations of the Walk

Walk can be collected, medium or extended in length. Medium walk is what you will use exclusively with a young horse and is best defined as a comfortable, natural length of stride, neither sluggish nor hurried, and in a relaxed and rounded but not shortened outline. Extended walk is ridden much like free walk on a long rein, but with a little more contact (still in a stretched frame) and is the maximum stride length you can encourage the horse to produce without hurrying. Collected walk should only be attempted once he is sufficiently strong and supple (about three years into consistent work), and demands a shorter, taller frame with his hind-quarters lowered and with an increased activity, producing shorter, taller steps.

Trot

Of the three basic gaits, trot is the one that can be most easily altered to improve quality. Many people are impressed by a gorgeous trot and pay less attention (when purchasing) to the other gaits – this is not the best procedure as much can be done to improve the trot whilst very little can be done with the walk and only a limited amount with the canter.

A young horse should be ridden actively forward in trot but never hurried – you need to find his natural tempo in which he can most easily maintain his balance. If you feel that he is accepting your hand and leg aids without resistance, and that you could jump a small fence out of his trot, you probably have it. If you are not sure, ask someone experienced to watch and help you find the correct tempo for him. Then it is up to you to maintain that tempo wherever he goes.

The elasticity and swing that ultimately produce greater suspension will develop gradually out of a relaxed top-line combined with this active trot rhythm. The bonus is that larger movement produced this way (as opposed to those superficially 'impressive' trots produced by tension and a tight back) is supremely comfortable to sit on.

Rising Trot

Initially all your work with a young horse should be done rising as his back muscles are not yet strong enough to carry you sitting. It is also easier with the young horse to encourage a clear rhythm by rising at a regular tempo, not just following what he offers you.

Some young horses have good natural rhythm and these are the easiest to train. More often, the trot of a young horse will vary, with losses of balance and accompanying stiffening as they try to manage their carriage. For these horses, a well-defined rhythm will develop later as consistent schooling helps them to maintain balance more easily.

Seat

In rising trot you must incline *very slightly* forward with your upper body and swing your hips *up and forward*, not just up. Because the horse is in motion, by the time you come back down again his body has moved forward; if you have not also swung forward you will land at the back of the saddle when you come down – not comfortable for either of you! Your swing up and down should be as a result of alternately straightening then bending your knees: you should *not* attempt to stand onto your stirrup irons to achieve this, but rise from your knees as if you had no stirrups. This does not mean you need to grip with your knees, merely that you tone your inner thigh muscles sufficiently to close your knees to the saddle (practise rising trot without stirrups to get the hang of this). If you press onto your irons, your feet will be pushed forward each time you rise, so putting your lower legs too far forward and leaving you behind the movement.

You must ride on the correct *diagonal* to develop the horse's back muscles equally. Initially you may need to check by looking down at his shoulders: you should be sitting as his *outside* shoulder is coming back, i.e. as his outside forefoot comes to the ground – which is also the moment his inside hind comes down. Later on you should try to develop a feel for this timing – notice that when you rise on the wrong diagonal, your hips twist towards the outside. Change diagonal by sitting for one extra beat. This should be done every time you change the rein.

Legs

We sit as the inside hind is on the ground for the horse's ease of weight-bearing. You should also time the closure of your lower legs to the moment you sit down – not as you rise. Your combined weight and leg aid can influence him to deepen the bend of his inside hind leg joints – desirable both in terms of shock absorbency (elasticity) and engagement.

Hands

Your hands must stay still, not go up and down as you rise. This is achieved by flexing your elbows slightly. Try pushing your hands down as you rise, then bend your elbows (or push your fists up) as you sit. Try doing this off the horse, with your hands in rein position, and your knuckles touching a wall. Bend and straighten your knees to simulate rising – you will soon feel your elbows flexing.

Sitting Trot

You should only begin to introduce sitting trot for long periods when the horse's back muscles are developed enough to support you – probably many months into his training. Even then, periods of sitting trot should be interspersed with bouts of rising trot to rest his back muscles.

At an earlier stage, do not avoid sitting trot totally, as you need it to make transitions both up and down – just limit how much you do.

Seat

You must be sufficiently developed as a rider in terms of your posture and muscle control to ride successfully in sitting trot. Your seat must remain glued to the saddle during every phase of the trot, not bouncing out of it at any time. To achieve this you must be:

- Balanced.
- Capable of holding a fair degree of muscle tone in your upper body without becoming tense.
- Supple in your waist and hips.
- Able to swing your pelvis, using your deep stomach muscles and your back muscles to tilt the front of your pelvis (your crotch) slightly upward in every stride.
- Able to ensure that your buttock muscles remain relaxed – these are your contact area with the saddle and should be spread over as wide an area as your anatomy permits!

Riders are often advised to 'let the back swing with the horse'. This suggests a passive following; in reality, an adhesive seat can only be produced by positive muscular action.

Remember what it felt like to sit on a swing as a child. Call up the feeling as the swing reaches its highest point on the backward swing and you want to urge it to greater effort. That feeling of combined stomach and back muscle action that pushes the swing is exactly the same as you need to sit with the trot. You will find later that increasing or decreasing the effort you put into this swing is the key to lengthening and shortening his strides.

Legs

Your legs should lie quietly against the horse's sides, moving gently in and out in every stride but never totally leaving his sides. If you need to use them for motivation, you should close your calves tighter, then less tight – not put them on then off (leaving his sides). Especially on a nervous horse, even one who tends to run away, you must not take your legs off – not knowing where your legs are or when they might touch him suddenly is more worrisome to him than having them lying against his sides.

Hands

Your hands must be totally still. A sound horse has no head movement in trot and your hand position must reflect this. You must keep relaxed wrists and forearms, and supple elbows, to allow your hands to remain motionless while the rest of your body absorbs the motion of his gait. If you need help, try resting the heels of your hands onto the pommel of your saddle until you can feel how to flex your elbows gently to absorb your body's motion, then raise them just slightly away from the saddle and focus on keeping them still.

Variations of the Trot

Trot can be collected, working, medium or extended in length. Always remember that the variations are a difference in *length* of stride, not of tempo. In fact, because the longer-striding trots spend a greater amount of time in the air, they should *feel* slower, not faster.

As mentioned above, the length of stride is determined by the action of your *seat* making a longer stroke along the saddle, (or a larger swing up and forward in rising trot) for extension, or a more vertical 'sucking upward' feel for collection. Your *legs* are responsible for the *amount of impulsion*, but not for the *length of stride* – kicking harder will only make him run faster.

Canter

Canter is often considered the most challenging gait to sit well as it has the greatest amount of movement in terms of length and height, plus the added challenge of a lateral rock. This last is caused by the sequence, with both legs on the inside (side of the leading leg) moving in advance of both legs on the outside. (See Definitions p.19 for the canter sequence, and watch horses cantering – you will soon see that the inside foreleg always steps further forward than the outside foreleg, and the same applies for the hind legs.)

This sequence affects the horse's straightness (see Functional straightness, p.23), causing a slight curve in his spine and inviting his haunches to move to the inside. This is further exacerbated in the young horse who does not yet bend his hock and stifle joints (these are his supporting joints and are yet to be strengthened) and so deviates with his hip to compensate, causing him to canter with his haunches to the inside. Straightness has to be achieved by encouraging his shoulders inward in front of his haunches, the correct position being with his two inside legs aligned and the slight bend of his spine placing his nose directly above his inside knee.

Little canter work should be done in the earlier stages of training – the horse should be developing his balance and strength in walk and mostly in trot in the arena. He should not even be asked to canter in the arena until he is accepting the bridle correctly at walk and trot, as the canter can only be improved if his outline is correct.

Cantering out in the country in straight lines, preferably on gentle uphill slopes to help his balance (and brakes!) is often the best place to start and you should be balanced enough to ride him in a light seat to take your weight off his back.

On a horse with an established canter you should sit fully in the saddle, paying attention to the following points.

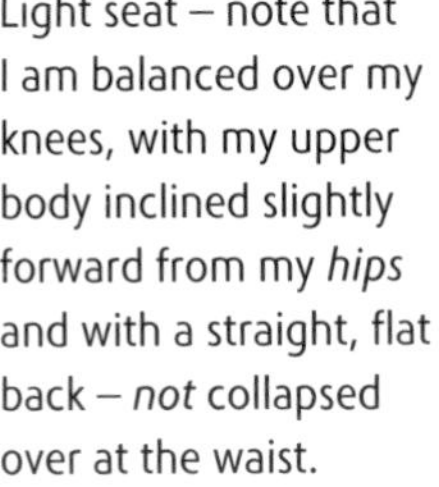

Light seat – note that I am balanced over my knees, with my upper body inclined slightly forward from my *hips* and with a straight, flat back – *not* collapsed over at the waist.

Upper Body

This should be still – all movement should be from your waist down, with your hips pushing in front of your shoulders then back beneath them. Watching other riders, you will see much rocking backward and forward of the upper body – this shows a lack of muscular control or stiffness through waist and lower back. Picture a rider cantering along behind a hedge that hides everything from their waist down: you should simply see their body gliding along as if on wheels – no rocking, no up and down motion.

Seat

Your seat will be slightly angled across the saddle, with your inside seat bone continually in front of your outside one, mirroring the horse's hips. Your seat must move in harmony with his back – the action of your pelvis should be almost circular: forward/downward – forward/upward – return to starting position – begin sequence again. Obviously the horse has moved forward during this sequence, so your return to the starting position is relative only to his saddle, not to the ground!

Another way to picture this is to think of polishing the saddle from the back to the front in every stride, *but without rocking your upper body.*

Legs

Your legs should remain in position – inside leg at the girth, outside leg behind – to achieve the correct position of your pelvis in the saddle (see above), and to drop more weight into your inside seat bone and stirrup. This helps absorb the lateral roll of the gait, as your inside leg should alternately stretch deeper then relax in every stride. Think consciously of deepening your heel (or pushing a little onto the inside stirrup iron – though not enough to lighten your seat) at every stride.

Hands

Your hands need to follow the motion of the horse's head – slightly forward and back. There may also be a small downward component, depending on the height of his head carriage – this will vary with his stage of training. Put simply, your hands should move slightly towards his mouth, then return to the contact point (see Techniques, p.33) in each stride, never letting the reins go into a slack loop. This is done with a slight straightening then flexing of your elbows.

The variations of the canter are as for trot.

TROUBLESHOOTING

His walk sequence is not always clear

In less extreme cases this would be called 'loss of rhythm'; at its worst, he may be 'pacing' – when the two legs on the near side move almost simultaneously, followed by the two legs on the off side (also described as a 'camel walk' as this is how camels actually move).

A walk in incorrect sequence is sometimes, though rarely, natural. More often it is created by a rider either hurrying the walk or being too strong with the hands – often in an effort to create a short outline too early in the training. It may also be a product of tension or excitement.

If the habit of moving in this fashion becomes too ingrained it may prove impossible to recover the true sequence. However, if it is caught early enough it should be possible to manage it by controlling the causes mentioned above:

- Slow the walk with your legs and seat (see Techniques, pp.30–2), *not* with your reins.
- Use small circles (and later, lateral work) to help contain his speed.
- Ensure that your rein contact is not so strong as to be restricting, as this will make him tense. Allow your reins to be slightly longer and follow his head a little more with softly flexing elbows.
- Use anything you know that will help him relax: for example, play music, work him in company, etc.
- Walk him over ground poles (at least four in a row) set at about 1 m (3ft 3in) apart, adjusting the distance to suit his stride length so that he is in a comfortable medium walk, neither shortening his strides nor stretching to reach the poles. He will be obliged to lift his legs in the correct sequence to negotiate the poles. Distribute sets of poles at various places around the arena, including around corners, so that he has to walk in correct sequence frequently as he travels around the school.
- Walk him in water – deep puddles, shallow streams or ponds (where you are certain of the security of the footing), or in the sea. The effort of walking through the resistance offered by water encourages more evenly distributed footfalls.

He doesn't stride out in walk/ his steps are too short/ restricted in the shoulder

Assuming that his conformation is not a limiting factor, then consider the following:

1. Check that your rein contact is not restricting him. While you should not 'row' him along with your hands, you must follow the movement of his head with flexible

elbows and an appropriate length of rein for his level of training: long enough in the earlier days so as not to interfere with his natural movement, only becoming shorter as he progresses in terms of balance, suppleness and strength.

2. Check that your seat muscles are relaxed – any tension in your seat will transfer through the saddle to his back, making him tense up. Tight back muscles cause tight shoulders and this restricts his strides.
3. If his body, especially his back, is tight because of mental tension, try pressing alternating seat bones into the saddle (as opposed to using leg aids) to encourage him to relax his back muscles.
4. Check that your legs are not clamped too tightly around his ribcage; again, your tension will make him tense and you may even restrict his breathing by disallowing the full expansion of his ribcage – a sure cause for anxiety and tense muscles producing short, choppy steps.
5. Check that he is not hurrying. The more he hurries, the shorter his stride will be. This might sound strange, but if you think about his balance you will realize that to save himself from falling forward he feels the need to put his forefeet down more quickly; in other words, after covering less ground.
6. Check that he is working with a rounded top-line (see Chapter 9). If his back is dropped he will be physically unable to stride forward with his hind legs – see photographs p.32.
7. If he is simply lacking energy, first review his fitness and diet, then encourage him to walk with more purpose by using alternating leg aids. Do *not* shove more with your seat – this is likely to cause him to drop his back.

He tends to jog

Jogging arises from tension or anticipation, often of a transition. General attention to relaxation is essential – make sure he is happy in his working environment as far as you are able: time of day (near feed time/turnout time) can affect him adversely, as can working with others turned out beside the school, working in the school with a horse he dislikes, etc. Many factors can have a bearing on relaxation and you should try to control as many as possible.

Jogging may also be caused by a restricting rein contact that either makes his top-line too short and tight, or makes him anxious because you have taken away his ability to rebalance himself using his natural balancing pole – his head and neck. So check that your contact is not too strong.

You may also cause jogging by over-riding his walk. This may be because you feel he is not carrying you forward with enough enthusiasm, but bear in mind that a really good walk with a big overtrack *feels* slow. Whatever the reason, you must learn not to push his walk to the point where he jogs, so learn to live with a slow walk for a while – as he strengthens and progresses you will be able to gain more activity (see Definitions, p.19) without him hurrying and jogging. If you push him to gain those extra marks in lower level competitions you could ruin his walk for the future.

If he threatens to, or begins to jog, turn him onto a small circle and stay there until he walks again. Do *not* be tempted to take your legs off his sides – this will only add to his anxiety (see p.133) and he must learn to accept them if his training is to progress. Use the small circle to:

- Help relax his top-line muscles by using the lateral flexion to bring him into a rounder outline (chewing down onto his inside bit – p.107).
- Demand that he gives his attention fully to you by focusing him inward onto the circle, thus removing his attention from his external environment.
- Deliberately bore him until he relaxes.

Do not use walk only in your rest period: practise it every day. This must not be done on a short contact until much later in his training, but spend time even whilst out hacking lengthening his contact and retaking it until it does not *always* mean a return to work.

His walk has a strange foreleg action – almost like 'goose-stepping'

This stiff-legged action with the forelimbs is caused by tension in his back. To correct or reduce it you need to tackle the causes: general tension and tightness over the back. Ask him to work with his neck in a lower, rounder outline (see Chapter 10), especially when he is in a tense situation such as a competition arena.

He doesn't lower his head and neck enough in free walk on a long rein

The lowering required should happen as a consequence of his need to relax and stretch his top-line muscles after a period of holding them in tone, i.e. in a correct outline. If he is spending insufficient time in this correct outline then he will not feel the need to stretch, so this should be your first consideration: is he in a good outline in the rest of his work? (See Chapter 9 for more detail). He may also need to be *taught* how to lower his head – see Chapter 10, p.127.

I get left behind in rising trot, often landing on the back of my saddle with a bump

First, have the balance of your saddle checked. If the front is too high you will be thrown backward at every step. This is likely to occur as he muscles up – his shoulders become wider and lift the pommel. It is possible that the saddle is also pinching his shoulders and he needs a wider fit – you cannot correct this simply by putting a rear riser pad under the saddle as this may put even more pressure onto his shoulders.

If the saddle is okay then your lower leg position is at fault: it swings forward as you rise so it is not beneath you to support your weight when you sit back down – you land too heavily and too far to the back of the saddle.

Check your leg position at the halt: do you have the straight line ear-shoulder-hip-heel, at right angles to the ground – see photograph p.9. Another guide is that your stirrup leathers should be perpendicular to the ground.

An easy self-check is to stand up and stay up – first at halt, then walk. Can you do this without hanging onto the reins or his mane, and with no wobbling? If not, bend your knee more to bring your lower leg further back and try again. You should be balanced over your knees, not your stirrup irons. Don't grip with your knees; just close them snugly against your saddle. Imagine yourself kneeling on a stool: your toes will be on the ground but your weight rests onto your knees – this is the feeling you need.

Now try standing up at trot – you will find you can only do this with bent knees as this is where you absorb up and down movement – any time your lower leg swings forward you will lose balance and crash down. Finally go back to rising with this feeling of keeping your lower leg drawn back beneath you, rising by alternately straightening then *flexing* your knees. It is the flexion that keeps the lower legs drawn back beneath you.

Also, do rising trot without stirrups. This will help you discover how to rise off your knees. Don't worry, it doesn't teach you to grip (gripping is a tensing of all the leg and seat muscles which pushes you out of the saddle) – this exercise teaches you to use individual muscles independently.

His trot rhythm/speed varies

This usually arises from variations in his balance, sometimes also in his attention, and is only to be expected in a young horse. It is your job to help him become more regular – this is one of the main tasks of training.

In *rising trot* make sure that you are in balance (see The Rider in Chapter 2), and check that you are rising *from your knees*, not your stirrup irons, as just described above. Rise determinedly at the speed and rhythm *you* require, regardless of what the horse offers. This will mean that, at times, you will be slightly out of synchronization with his steps, but if you are persistent he will begin to conform to you. If he is too fast, you can also tighten your knees slightly onto the saddle – this will help slow him by inhibiting his shoulder muscles. If he is too slow, use slightly quicker squeezes of your lower leg to encourage him to speed up to match your rising.

In *sitting trot* use the same technique, but this involves using the muscles around your pelvis to hold the speed of your seat swing to the rhythm *you* want. It takes practice, but it is possible to move your seat to your own command, not just to follow the horse's movement. Use your legs as described for rising trot.

As his attention and balance improve, so his rhythm will become more clearly defined. As his rhythm improves, he will be more relaxed and so more attentive. It is up to you to influence this situation.

He hurries in trot

Use the technique described above to help regulate his speed. Also use patterns such as circles – these can help you harness his energy by placing his inside hind further forward under his body, provided his bend is correct (Chapter 12). Facing a horse at a long straight line can be an invitation to run and gain speed, so ride only short straight lines, or avoid them altogether, sticking to continual curves.

His trot steps are short and choppy

Assuming that this is not a result of some injury, or his conformation – 'short pasterns' (p.16) or 'upright shoulders' (p.14) – then he is tight in his muscles because of tension or stiffness.

Tension may have many causes, but aside from external factors they can include an unbalanced rider bumping on his back, or too tight a rein contact. Start checking in order:

1. Physical problems – lameness, sore back, saddle fit.
2. Rider balance.
3. Contact.
4. His speed – too fast and his stride will necessarily shorten to maintain his balance.
5. His outline. As described above for walk, a hollow outline will tighten his body and shorten his strides.

Once you have found and eliminated the cause, you can encourage him to take longer strides by rising with a bigger, longer swing of your seat or, if sitting, a longer swing of your pelvis. Be careful not to increase the speed of your seat action as this would ask him to speed up – one of the causes of a short stride!

His trot lacks suspension

Causes are similar to those of the short and choppy trot described above, so start by going through the same checklist.

Speed is very important – too fast and he will not have sufficient time in the air between footfalls.

In sitting trot:

- Slow him by closing your upper legs.

- 'Spring' more with your seat. This is a more vertical motion as described in Techniques, p.30. The feeling is one of holding the saddle with your thighs and 'sucking it upward' with your swinging seat in every stride.
- Pester him with your legs for impulsion, squeezing with your lower legs and/or tapping with your whip even as you slow him.

He will also lack suspension if he is on the forehand. This will need tackling gradually as you strengthen his back and haunches and enable him to carry his shoulders higher. At this point suspension may well appear of its own accord.

Trotting in water (puddles, or on the edge of the sea) can give him the experience of using himself this way, so don't become a fair-weather rider!

He trots lazily

- If he is young, unschooled or unfit, this may be a result of weakness. You will need to address it, but limit yourself to short bits of work only.
- Review his feeding – does he have sufficient nutrients to support his level of work?
- If he is genuinely lazy you would do best to tackle his responses by riding short, sharp transitions.
- Within the trot itself, use stronger lower leg squeezes, at the speed at which you want him to trot. If he ignores your leg aids, back them up with a sharp tap with your schooling whip just behind your leg to make him think your leg has suddenly become sharper. When he responds by going more forward, let him, even if it is more than you want (take care not to catch him in the mouth if he lurches forward), and reward him with a touch on the neck and praise with your voice. Repeat this sequence several times and he will be keener to go.
- Often working at a strong canter first, possibly in a forward seat, then returning to trot work will give you a more forward-thinking horse.

The lazy horse should be worked in straight lines as much as possible, such as going large around the arena, but also out hacking or around fields. You want him to find enjoyment in going forward, not to be sullen about it.

He tenses his back when I change from rising to sitting trot in preparation for a transition

First check that you are not bouncing in the saddle when you sit. If you are, you may need to work on developing your sitting trot, preferably by taking some lunge lessons.

If you are not the cause, then he is either tense (you are doing something different and this makes him anxious, or he is anticipating a transition), or his back muscles are weak and he is having trouble carrying you when you sit. Particularly if he is still in his first two years of ridden work he may need longer (rising trot, hacking, hill work, etc.) before you can safely start sitting trot work.

If you are sure that he is strong enough, you need to expose him to the change from rising to sitting more often. In the short term, allow him to trot more slowly (which will make the process more comfortable for both of you), then change to sitting and stick with it until he relaxes and allows you to sit comfortably, then immediately rise as a reward. Keep repeating this, only making transitions occasionally. Gradually he will learn to accept the change.

Once you have achieved this acceptance, build his back muscles up by going large around the school; sit for the short sides, rise on the long sides. When he manages this more easily (which could take several weeks), change to sitting for the long sides, rising on the short sides. Eventually you will be able to sit for longer periods.

He bounces me out of the saddle in canter

It could be that you have not yet mastered the seat movement required by canter, or he may be ejecting you involuntarily because of stiffness in his back or hind limbs, or deliberately to stop you from engaging him. Whatever the cause, you must refuse to be bounced out as you need your weight firmly in the saddle to help compress his hind legs down until he bends the joints more acutely and makes things more comfortable for both of you. Try the following:

1. Lean your upper body back – this will not put you behind the movement, merely help you wedge your whole seat into the saddle more securely. Once your seat stays put, sit tall again, but keep your lower back relaxed enough to allow your seat to move with the saddle.
2. Without collapsing your upper body, try to find a feeling of pressing your seat down and forward into the saddle at every stride. Imagine you are trying to polish the saddle, wiping your seat firmly from the back to the front in every stride.
3. If you struggle to find this feeling, try putting your reins into your outside hand and sit on your inside hand, palm upward – this can help you feel how much you are leaving the saddle. Then find the correct motion as you squash your own hand down onto the saddle. (Always use your inside hand – this turns your shoulders the correct way).

His canter is fast and unbalanced

This is quite normal for a young or unschooled horse. The first thing to consider is how he gets into canter, i.e. the transition. If this is achieved by running faster in trot until he falls into canter, then he has little or no hope of balancing himself – see *He runs into canter*, p.85.

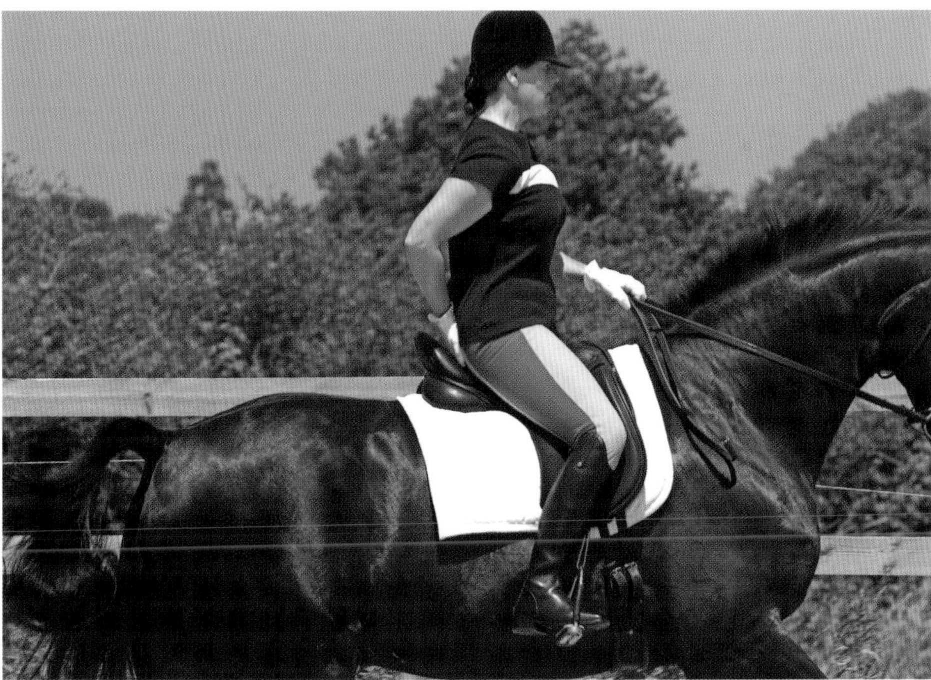

Putting a hand under your seat can help you feel how to sit closer to the saddle in canter.

To help develop his balance in canter, you should stick initially to riding circles – this brings his inside hind leg further forward under his body than it will be when on a straight line. You must also pay attention to his *bend* – for more detail, see Chapter 12. If he lacks bend he will lean over like a bicycle and gain speed until he is performing the wall of death! Rather, insist that he bends.

You may find he will balance more easily if you ride him in a light seat because he will be more able to lift his back and come rounder without your added weight in his saddle – see photograph, p.134. Be careful not to lean forward too much as this would put more weight over his shoulders, making the problem worse.

Once he slows and balances a little, gently regain your seat in the saddle a little at a time – it may be several weeks until he can carry you sitting fully upright.

If he is hollow this will also make it impossible for him to balance. In this case see Chapter 10, p.128.

As he gains both a rounder outline (more relaxed back) and a bit more balance, you will be able to slow the hurried canter more with the use of half-halts – in the canter just a brief moment of increased tone in your upper body, lower back and legs, and your inside fingers, holding it no longer than the length of one stride, then relax again and repeat as necessary. You will need to keep your lower legs on, or back them up with a small tap with the whip if he tries to break, but be aware that he may genuinely misread your aid to mean 'make a downward transition' and if this happens you must not tell him off or you will make him anxious. Simply reorganize his balance in trot, put him quietly back into canter and try again, this time with more leg.

He often falls out of canter

Breaking is usually a consequence either of loss of balance (hind legs too far behind his body to support him/ rider out of balance), or laziness. Always start by checking that your balance/position is not the cause.

If you feel him about to break, use a sharp tap of your schooling whip to liven up his hind legs and make them jump more quickly. Beware of shoving with your seat – this will only serve to push him into a bigger canter that will almost certainly leave his hind legs behind.

He may also break if his outline is hollow, as this disallows the forward movement of the hind leg (see p.32). See Chapter 10 p.128 for the technique of producing a round outline in canter.

His canter is slow/laboured/lacks jump/loses clear three-beat

You may be causing this with too strong a rein contact in relation to his level of impulsion. Check this out by making frequent small releases of your rein contact – push both hands forward briefly until you lose contact (see photograph, p.22) then re-take it but with less weight in your hands. The duration of release should be one stride or less.

If your contact is okay, this canter needs to be speeded up. You will need to use stronger leg aids (possibly rhythmic kicks – see Techniques, p.31) in a quicker speed than he wants to travel. Remember *he takes the speed of his stride from the speed of your aids.*

Do not use your seat to push his stride bigger – this will only make the problem worse.

Do ride him in straight lines, as an open long side (or field) in front of him will encourage him to go forward more.

If he is able to do so, ride lots of changes between working canter and medium canter – the frequent transitions will make his hind legs react quicker.

Do lots of hill work and jumping.

He bucks when I use my legs in canter

As ever, start by considering the condition of his back, his soundness, and the fit of his saddle. The most frequent cause of bucking is a poorly fitted saddle causing back pain.

Bucking *can* simply be high spirits, or it may be resistance to your leg aids that must be corrected before it becomes a habit:

- Keep his head up – he can only buck if he gets it down.
- Use more leg, not less! He is trying to intimidate you into removing your legs and he must not win.

- Try riding in a light seat (p.134) – he will be likely to go forward more willingly with less weight on his back – just be careful not to tip too far forward where he might catch you off balance!
- If he also bucks/kicks out against the whip, try swishing it alongside him (like a jockey scrubbing with his whip in the last few furlongs), or turning it up in front of your face and whistling it from side to side (be careful the first time – he might over-react). See Techniques, p.42.

He goes disunited in canter

This is often seen in young horses trying not to take the weight onto the inside hind leg; they change behind to bring the outside hind leg forward. Lameness and back problems can also be a cause, as can loss of balance (of horse or rider). The problem is often seen in Arabs as they have relatively tall/straight hind legs that are hard to bend sufficiently to step under easily.

Once the horse has changed behind you must return to trot and start the canter again.

He makes the change behind by swinging his quarters out, so as you gain more control of his haunches you will be able to prevent him from doing this. Work on lateral suppleness in trot, and response to your sideways-pressing leg (see Chapter 14) so that you can keep his haunches aligned.

Once you are into canter you need to keep him well bent around your inside leg, so keep your outside leg drawn well back and pressing rhythmically in each stride to move his haunches inward. Be careful that your inside leg does not creep backwards as you aid the canter – in fact, think about keeping the canter going with your outside leg and inside seat bone. This work is best done on large circles to help facilitate the bend.

It is also possible for him to stiffen his hind legs and push his croup up to throw you out of the saddle so that he can change behind more easily. You need to sit firm and deep, even leaning back to help you press more weight into the saddle – use the image of yourself sitting on his croup and compressing his hind legs down.

Part Two

The Building Blocks

12 Bend and Straightness – Circles

Do Horses Really Bend?

When talking about bend, many old textbooks will tell you that your horse should 'have a uniform bend throughout the length of his body'.

In the light of more modern scientific investigation, we know the equine spine is not uniformly flexible – in fact many parts of it are quite inflexible, so we need to start this chapter with an understanding of how we can create within our horses the *illusion* of a uniform bend and why we should do so.

Starting from the front:

- The horse's neck (cervical vertebrae) is the most flexible portion of his spine, being able to move both up and down, and from side to side.
- The next set of vertebrae – the thoracic – are those we sit above. They have the ribcage attached to them and are almost entirely *inflexible*.
- Next along are the lumbar vertebrae – the loin area. These have a limited ability to flex up and down, and side to side.
- His pelvis and his sacral vertebrae (which are fused together, so have no movement whatsoever) are joined via the sacroiliac joint, which has very limited lateral movement.
- The vertebrae of his tail are, as you know from watching him swat a fly, very flexible in all directions.

The Illusion of Bend

This is created by a number of components that together give the illusion that the horse is bending along the length of his frame. We already know he can bend his neck a great deal – often more than we want when he is using it as an evasion – but a major tool we have to help us is his ribcage.

There is no bony attachment between the ribcage and the shoulder girdle, allowing the ribcage freedom to swing from side to side between the forelegs.

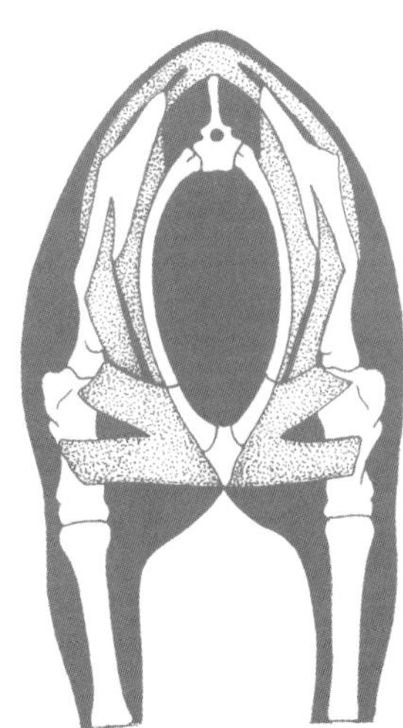

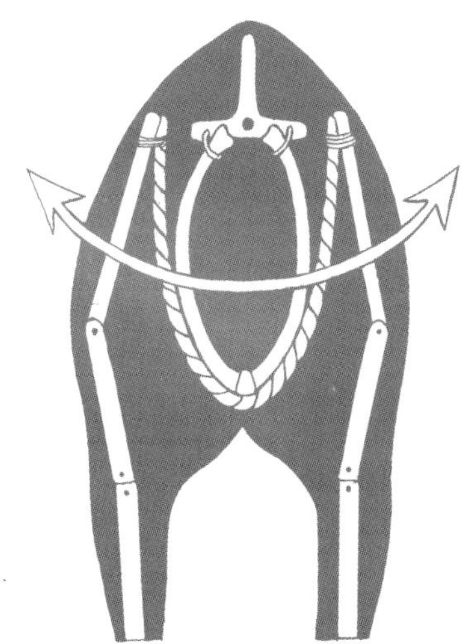

His shoulder girdle is attached to his spine only by ligaments, tendons and muscles. This relatively flexible connection is what allows the strong advanced horse to literally raise his withers up between his shoulders.

In terms of bend, this allows the displacement of his middle section to either side – in other words his ribcage can swing quite extensively from one side to the other. This is further assisted by his intercostal muscles, which primarily move his ribcage in and out for breathing. When they contract on just one side they pull the ribs on that side closer together, so making one side of his body shorter than the other.

His legs also play a major part in his apparent ability to bend as, in addition to their ability to move backwards and forwards, they possess quite a range of movement to either side.

If you stand on the floor beside the his girth area and, with your hands, push his ribcage away from you, you will see the natural result: as his ribs move away so the hind leg nearer you will move forward and towards you, the foreleg nearer will move back and towards you, and his neck will bend to your side. This is the reaction you want to your inside leg when you are on his back.

Why is Bend Important?

This might seem like a silly question, but a horse can produce what looks like a circle without bending at all – he just leans over like a bicycle. What this fails to achieve is any form of physical value to his body. In fact, it will have been damaging, putting excess strain on the joints of his inside legs as he carries extra weight on joints that are leaning at odd angles.

Horses can travel round circles and turns either by bending or leaning – *the two are mutually exclusive.* In other words, if you succeed in producing the desired bend in his body, he will not lean over. This in turn achieves correct tracking (see

Definitions, p.24) which encourages correct and active bending of his joints with his limbs remaining upright.

Study the flight of your horse's limbs (on video, or with another rider on him) to check the correctness of his tracking – sometimes the inside hind leg will cross outward even when he feels correctly bent; this is an evasion of activity by swinging his leg from the hip joint only, avoiding bending his stifle, hock and fetlock joints. This must be corrected by first displacing his hindquarters slightly inward (with your outside leg), then using your inside leg to demand that he bend his inside hind joints. You will need to repeat this correction often, as this is part of his natural crookedness – and thus a long-term project.

In summary, only if he is bent to the path he is travelling and tracking correctly with his limbs will he be developing both sides of his body equally in terms of suppleness and muscular strength.

Circles

BUILDING BLOCKS

The building blocks for circles are:

- Forward reaction to your legs to enable you to maintain a consistent rhythm.
- An understanding of basic steering.

Circles themselves are the most basic building block for many other movements; they will be your first useful school figure, and the one you will ride more than any other throughout the training of any horse.

They can be ridden at any size the horse is capable of, but the sizes most commonly used in training (and related to competition) are 20 m (the largest size possible in a standard-width arena), then later 15 m, 10 m, 8 m and down to 6 m.

Those of 10 m and below are known as *voltes* and should only be ridden on horses at quite advanced levels of training, as they demand great suppleness, balance and engagement.

Take a quick look back to the Basic Principle relating to accurate riding of figures in Chapter 1 (pp.4–5). Obviously a young or unschooled horse will be far more difficult to ride in correct alignment on an accurately shaped figure, but that must be your goal – whether by the end of a schooling session or in several weeks.

Requirements

1. The horse travels forward with as consistent a rhythm as he is capable of, meaning that:
2. He maintains the same energy level and consequently:
3. Keeps the same quality of gait before, during and after the circle.
4. His outline should stay round, with a continuous soft contact which may feel lighter in your inside hand than your outside.
5. He remains upright and bends his body to conform to the arc of the circle and so:
6. His hind feet track into or over the prints of his forefeet, but never to the side.

Aids

1. Vibrate the inside rein (p.110) as you approach your circle. This will serve both to warn him you are about to ask him to leave the track, and to ask for a slight flexion to the inside.
2. Turn your body into either position right or left as appropriate (see Techniques, p.38). The *amount* you turn will determine the size of the circle.
3. The more you turn, the smaller the circle, so experiment until you know how much you need to turn for a 20 m circle (tip – it's not very much!).
4. Increase the weight in your inside seat bone and stirrup (p.88) and take care that your seat does not slip to the outside of the saddle. A crooked horse may push you outward and you must be aware of this possibility and not allow him to displace you.
5. On a young or uneducated horse you may need to use an opening rein to guide him (see Techniques p.35).
6. Use your inside leg at the girth with rhythmic squeezes (in time with the speed of his gait) to (a) keep his energy levels constant and (b) push his ribcage to the outside which, as discussed above, will cause both ends of his body to move inward as his ribcage moves to the outside.
7. Always look ahead round your circle – you need to see where you are heading and this will also help you find the correct amount of body turn for your size of circle.
8. As you approach the track (or wherever you intend to leave your circle), begin to straighten your position so that, as you finish your circle, you are facing your line of departure. This will also equalize the weight in your seat bones and stirrups.

9. The act of straightening your body will have brought your hands parallel to each other, resulting in his neck straightening and pointing straight forward. There is no need to take more outside rein to straighten his neck; this will only bend him to the outside and cause both a wobble and a loss of the impulsion you have gained by performing the circle.

10. Ride straight on with the same speed and energy as you had on your circle.

Patterns

20 m Circles

These can be ridden in three places in a 20 x 40 m arena, or 5 places in a 20 x 60 m arena.

Practise visualizing how your circle should look if you were watching from outside the arena, but beware of looking down as if you could see the circle drawn on the school floor – this will distort your position and pull your horse off balance.

Riding accurately shaped circles takes practice. The easiest starting position in the school for accuracy is at either C or A in the 40 m school, where you must also

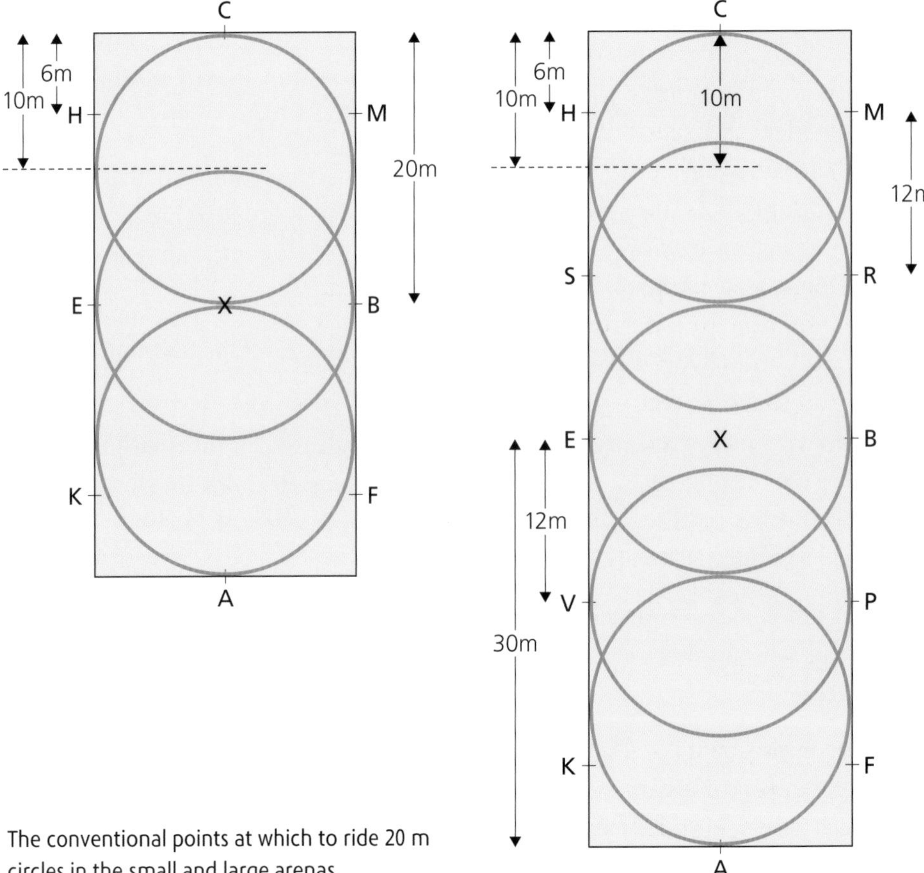

The conventional points at which to ride 20 m circles in the small and large arenas.

pass through X in the dead centre. Note: the points at which you touch the long sides are not the quarter markers – these are only 6 m from the corners. You need to touch the track 10 m from each corner – halfway between the corner and the half markers (see dimensions on the accompanying diagrams). The extra markers of the long arena are 18 m from the corner, so they cannot be used in the same way – you must judge a point on the wall 10 m from the corner.

Make sure that you touch each point every time, keeping the lines between the points as quarters of a true circle. Try to remember how this shape *feels* in terms of how you needed to position your body to achieve the consistent curve. When you ride a circle in the centre of the arena you will only have two clear reference points (E and B) so you will need this muscle memory even more to give your figure two symmetrical halves.

15 m Circles

You can, of course, ride circles of other sizes between 20 m and 15 m, and with your horse at an early training stage you should begin by simply riding circles that do not quite touch the track so that he (and you) become used to not relying on the support of the fence.

However, once you can manage 20 m with relative ease, riding accurate 15 m circles is your next clear goal. To reduce the circle size requires that you have more control of his shoulders and haunches. He needs greater suppleness, balance and impulsion. Always remember that the quality of his gait must not be lost.

15 m circles can be ridden at all markers except the quarter markers. Riding them from the long sides is easiest as you ride from the track to the opposite quarter line. From A and C you require more judgement to get the size and shape perfect – guidance from your trainer and practice will be needed.

At this stage, 15 m is about the smallest size you should attempt. Smaller than this and you may find problems maintaining rhythm and quality of movement – your horse will need greater suppleness and balance which will come later.

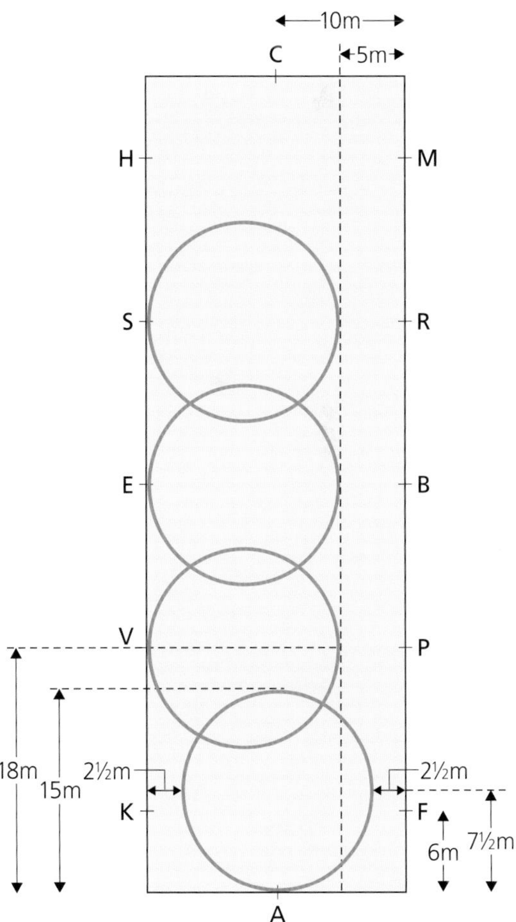

Various positions for riding 15 m circles.

Spirals

These involve a gradual reduction of your 20 m circle around a central point (say, around X) until you are on a circle of about 15 m centred around X (later on you can take it down to 10 m). You then stay on this smaller figure for two or three circuits, then gradually increase it back to your 20 m circle.

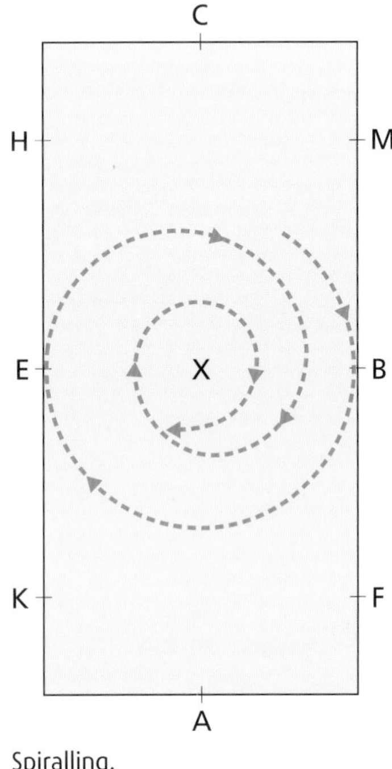

Spiralling.

It is imperative that *you* remain in charge of exactly how quickly you increase or decrease the size of the figure, as this determines whether the horse is tracking (see Definitions, p.24) correctly along the figure. If he tries to take over, then simply stop moving inward or outward and instead go round a constant circle (size dependent on where you are within your spiral) a time or two before resuming the pattern you wanted.

In the earlier stages of training you should introduce spirals that are slow to change size. Later on you will ask for lateral steps within them, but for now keep it simple and undemanding – just introduce the idea of the figure.

Training Value

1. To address suppleness. As you progress, the horse's body will need greater suppleness to perform more complicated work, especially lateral movements. Even if you do not wish to progress that far, the more supple his body and joints, the better his shock absorbency (longer life for his joints), the more easily he will make tight turns (e.g. in a jump-off) and the more comfortable you will find him to sit on.

2. As strengthening tools. On a circle his hind legs, particularly his hocks, work harder – even more so when riding spirals. His joints will become more supple and his muscles stronger as he contracts those on the inside of his body and stretches those on the outside. If he is working correctly he will also lift the muscles on the outside of his back slightly more than those on the inside. This is why work must be done equally in both directions.

3. Circles are the most effective solution to shying. Most shying is an attempt to get out of work; the harder the work, the more likely the horse is to be spooky. Circles allow you to use half the shape for relaxation (away from his 'spook area'), and half where you can drive him forward towards and past the problem site whilst keeping his face turned away from it. Keeping control of a bent horse is easier because you can make a stronger connection from inside leg to outside rein (see Techniques p.41) than on a straight horse. At the same time you are using reverse psychology on him: spooking results in *harder* work.

TROUBLESHOOTING

He falls in

Check first that your weight is not too far to the inside – *you* could be pulling him off balance.

If your position is correct, review Natural Crookedness (p.23).

If his body is finding it hard – or impossible – to bend to the line of your circle because you have his naturally longer side on the inside of your figure, his bodyweight will be leaning onto his inside shoulder. This is made worse by his shorter side (on the outside of your figure) trying to pull his body into an outside bend, also pushing his weight towards his inside shoulder. The result is that he falls inward towards the middle of your circle, often also leaning in like a bicycle.

As an example: he falls inward on a circle right. To fix this, you need to persuade the long muscles on the right side of his body to contract, and the short ones on the left side to stretch.

This is likely to be a long-term project over months of work, but it is a hugely important step towards the eventual equality of both sides of his body.

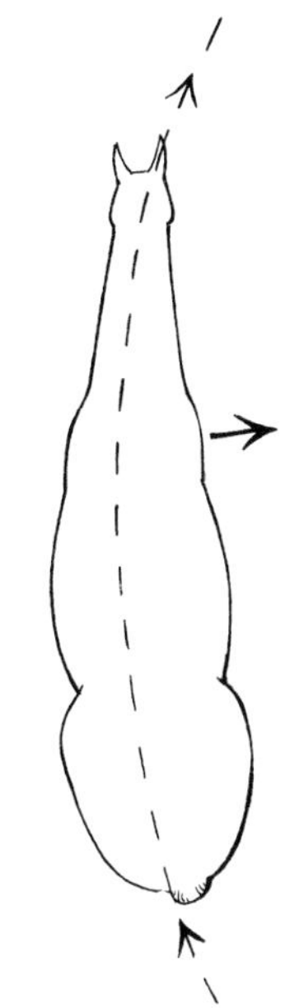

Falling inward on a circle to the right.

- First check your own position – are you in position right (p.38)? You cannot expect him to align himself correctly if you are not creating the correct shape on top of him.
- Be more demanding in terms of inside bend. Can you see his right eye? If not, you must ask, using rhythmic squeezes on your right rein, until you can persuade him to contract the muscles on the right side of his neck and so turn his head. Remember: if he is bending, he cannot lean – review Why is Bend Important?, earlier this chapter.
- Keep your right hand slightly away from his neck (opening rein – see Techniques, p.35), towards the inside of the circle. *Do not* hold it against his withers, or take it across his neck to the outside – both of these give him a prop to lean against and he *will* use it, given the chance. You have to make him stand up and balance on his own legs, not use your hand for support. (But see below for extreme cases).
- Make sure you have some weight in your outside hand, but with a forward feeling to *allow* him to turn his head to the right. Keeping too strong an outside rein (disallowing the bend) will only compound the problem.
- Stimulate his right side intercostals to contract to shorten his ribcage on the right and so swing his belly towards the left. Do this with stronger (but still rhythmic) squeezes of your lower right leg.
- If he does not move his belly outward, also use your thigh and knee to push his ribcage to the outside. As soon as he has responded, relax your upper leg.

- Ride around your circle with a feeling of leg-yielding (see Chapter 15) towards the outside, especially where you know he is likely to fall in. Horses will usually repeat a pattern of falling in more strongly at one particular spot on a circle. Notice where this is and start pushing more strongly with your inside leg *before* you get there.
- If he does not understand the requirement to move away from your leg, you must teach him or review the turn around the forehand. Although this is covered later (Chapter 14), you will be teaching him this around the same time as you begin to tackle his body's inequality. Use it to teach/remind him that he must move sideways away from your inside leg, then go back to your circle and ride with a feeling of leg-yielding outward whenever he tries to fall in.
- In extreme cases you may, in the short term, need to use an indirect rein (see Techniques, p.35) to reposition his shoulder to the outside. *The moment* his shoulder moves out – his neck will bend to the inside in the same moment – you *must* return your hand to its normal position. If you leave it crossed over his withers he *will* learn to lean on it and soon you will be supporting the weight of his shoulder with your hand!

He leans on my inside hand

This is a consequence of the above, so will be solved by following the procedures outlined.

He leans/pushes against my inside leg

Again, as above, with particular attention to teaching him to yield away from your leg. See Turn Around the Forehand (Chapter 14) and Leg-yielding (Chapter 15). You will need to teach him both of these to address this problem, with the work from Chapter 14 and the earlier work from Chapter 15 being tackled concurrently. Check out the timeline outlined in Chapter 22.

He bends to the outside of my circle/ he doesn't bend enough

As above.

He falls to the outside

This is often noticed only when you pay close attention to the precise shape of your circle – are you returning to the school fence at exactly the same place you left it?

Falling out occurs when you have his longer body side on the outside of the circle, so his weight is falling outward onto his outside shoulder. This will be manifest as either a physical drift away from the shape of the circle, or as *too much neck bend*. In extreme cases he may use this natural crookedness as an evasion, throwing all his weight to the outside shoulder and running sideways, (napping), often in the direction of the exit!

Corrections below are in increasing order of extremity – if the first doesn't work, move on to the next, then the next:

- Have someone on the ground check the straightness of both you and your saddle – if either/both have slipped to the outside, your weight will be pulling him outward. Crooked horses often push their riders to one side, so frequent corrections may be required over several months – see: *He pushes me to the outside on circles*, later this chapter.

- Review your steering aids – are you trying to turn him by pulling on the inside rein? If so, you may be causing or exacerbating the problem. Try softening your inside rein forward and see what happens. If this is not the answer, go on to the next point.

- Check your body position. You may even need to exaggerate your body turn to the inside, putting extra weight into your inside seat/stirrup (p.88) to counteract his weight going outward. Make sure that your outside elbow is snug against your ribcage (any gapping gives him room to escape), your outside shoulder is well forward and your outside hand is pushing inward/forward against his crest with a direction towards his inside ear. Your outside rein should be pushing against his neck but must *not* cross over his withers (this asks for the opposite bend). Make sure you are turning from your waist – your inside hip and seat bone must be forward compared to your outside hip to ensure that your weight distribution is correct (in your inside seat bone and stirrup) and your inside hand should be leading him round in an open rein position.

- Try riding the circle with no bend at all – take more outside rein to straighten his neck and control his outside shoulder. Keep steering in the usual way (inside hand towards the inside of the circle and outside hand pushing inward/forward) but disallow any bend by having a shorter outside rein. This will teach him how to keep his shoulders in front of his haunches around the curve of the figure. Only when he can do this should you *allow* the tiniest bit of inside bend.

- If the above is still not working, try riding him around the circle with an *outside* (counter) bend. This is hard, especially with an unbalanced youngster, but it can teach both of you a lot about steering. On, for example, a circle right, take both hands even more towards the inside of the circle, use vibrations on the left rein to flex him to the outside, and press your left hand close in to the withers, and even slightly across if necessary. Keep your weight central above him. Use an opening right rein to lead him around the circle and you will find that, even though it is hard, it is possible to steer him around the figure whilst bent to the outside. The result will be to position his shoulders more towards the inside of the circle, just where you want them when you are ready to allow him to recover a slight inside bend.

He leans on my outside hand

Cause, as above: too much weight on his outside shoulder.

Corrections: as above, moving in order through the corrective exercises until you find the lighter contact you desire.

Don't forget – you *should* have more weight in your outside hand than your inside – this is a sign of connection from inside leg to outside rein, but it should not be excessive.

He goes above the bit

Provided you are certain of his health (back/teeth) and the fit of bit and saddle there are a number of possibilities to consider.

Loss of balance/lack of strength. In a young horse, hollowness is often caused by loss of balance. Watch young horses race around a field – as they turn, they throw their heads up. Their head and neck unit is their natural balancing pole. Under saddle this is compounded by lack of strength. As already discussed, we know that once we add the weight of a rider we need to change the horse's manner of carrying himself to prevent damage to his body. This means strengthening his postural muscles until he is able to balance our combined weights, which means initially persuading him to use them!

If he is too weak to carry you on a circle without coming above the bit you may need to do:

1. More lungeing in side reins to help build his top-line.

2. Hacking in straight lines, preferably up and down hills to help build him up – *in a round outline*, or you will build the wrong muscles.

Your rein contact. Your hands may be causing him to hollow by being too strong, or by being unsteady.

1. Think about *pushing* him forward round your circle. Review the description of the 'Wheelbarrow Push', (p.90), and try to press your contact forward in this manner.

2. Unsteady hands or an over-strong contact (helping you maintain your own balance) are often the result of a weak seat. Lunge lessons will help you develop more depth and stability in your position so that you can gain control of your hands without setting them.

He may not yet be accepting your contact. Review Chapter 10 for techniques for teaching him to accept the contact, starting with chewing down onto his inside bit. This involves both acceptance and bend together and should be your starting point if he hollows when you try to bend him.

Insufficient impulsion. If he is not stepping his hind legs forward sufficiently under his body to support his posture, his back will sag downward and he will become hollow.

Review the section on biomechanics in Chapter 9. If he is willing to accept the contact then all you need to do is ride more positively forward *into* your hands. (If not, review Chapter 10).

Keep a soft contact (forearms and wrists relaxed with closed, but not clenched fists), and squeeze with your legs at the same speed, but with more strength. As he steps more energetically forward he will begin to contract his stomach muscles and his back will rise, producing a rounder outline.

His head is unsteady

It is most likely that your hands are unsteady. See the point about your rein contact above.

Unsteadiness can also be a symptom of discomfort and this possibility must be investigated.

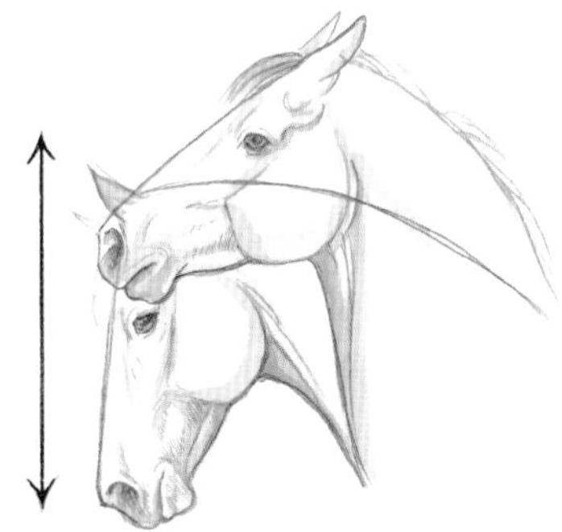

- Have his teeth and his back/saddle checked.
- Check his bit for fit and wear.
- If he is young, he may be teething.
- Lameness can also be a cause.

If you have eliminated all these, then it may be that he is not accepting your contact correctly – review that point above.

Alternatively, he may lack *balance*. Check your own *straightness* – you may be disturbing his ability to balance – and/or slow him down until he is able to find a better balance. Refrain from re-introducing more forward power until you can lengthen his steps without loss of balance or outline.

He steps unequally with his hind legs

You will see either that he takes shorter strides with one hind leg or that his rhythm is lost, compromising the sequence of his trot so that he appears to be trying to break into canter.

These symptoms may be caused by:

- Lameness behind.
- Weakness, most often in a young horse or one in poor physical condition.
- Stiffness in one hind limb – this may have a physical cause such as spavin, or could simply be a schooling issue.
- You being too strong in one hand, so blocking the corresponding hind leg from stepping through.
- You sitting crooked.
- Lack of balance (yours or his).

You need to decide *why* he is unequal before you can tackle it, ruling out conditions requiring veterinary investigation before anything else. Next, check your contact and position and if these are not at fault then the other issues can be addressed with the same approach:

1. If the short-stepping hind is the left, keep your contact exaggeratedly light (forward) on the left (and vice versa for the right) *regardless of the direction of travel.* This will give the stiffer/weaker hind more room to step forward under his body.
2. Use your leg on that side with a little more strength – enough to encourage his hind to step forward, but not enough to displace his quarters and upset his alignment.
3. Ensure that you do not rush him. Lack of balance causes stiffening and anxiety and his steps will become shorter rather than longer.
4. Vary the size of your circles and ride spirals to strengthen and supple his hind limbs.

It is then just a matter of time and repetition before he begins to step equally.

Do not fret about giving away the outside rein if he is not stepping through with the hind leg on the outside. The oft-repeated instruction to ride from inside leg into outside hand (suggesting that you should always keep a firm outside rein) is certainly valid – *but only once your horse is straight and equal.* A crooked horse *must* be straightened *before* it is possible to do this.

He loses rhythm/becomes irregular on circles

If there is no underlying physical reason, then:

1. You are probably asking him to perform too small a circle for his level of suppleness and balance. Go back to larger circles and work gradually down to smaller ones on a spiral to improve his physical ability to cope with the increased demand of the smaller circle. You are probably looking at several weeks of work, not a single schooling session.

2. He may be losing impulsion. If you are sure he is capable of the size of circle you are asking, then try to ride him more energetically forward by using stronger squeezes with your lower legs, *but in the same tempo – remember he takes the tempo of his steps from the speed of your aiding.*

3. Speeding up can have the effect of making him lose balance and, as a consequence, stiffening his body, thereby causing loss of rhythm. If he has become tense and stiff, encourage him to relax. This may entail taking some pressure off him (e.g. enlarging the circle), slowing down (if too quick) or talking to him and stroking him (a little) on the shoulder.

4. Hollowing/resisting the contact may also cause irregularity because of the stiffening effect of dropping his back. Review contact issues in *He goes above the bit*, earlier this section.

He loses impulsion on circles

He is lacking strength, or he is lazy. Whichever is the cause, it is down to you to maintain his impulsion by using stronger lower leg squeezes whilst maintaining the timing of your aids at the speed at which *you* wish to travel – not the one he wants.

If lack of strength is the issue, always be aware of him becoming tired and once you have made your point (i.e. achieved a circle or two with good impulsion), quit and put him away for the day.

He speeds up on circles

This is caused by a loss of balance or anxiety – often both. Slow him down by closing your upper legs tighter onto the saddle (blocking his shoulder action) and rising more slowly, or hold your seat to a slower rhythm (keep those buttock muscles relaxed) if sitting at trot, or cantering. Increase the muscle tone of your upper body and whatever you do, *sit tall* – allowing your weight to go forward will only make the problem worse by overloading his shoulders.

He pushes me to the outside on circles

This is most often noticed by the observer on the ground and is a consequence of the natural inequality of the horse's two sides – one having bigger, bulkier muscles than the other, with the consequence that the saddle and you are pushed towards the less well-muscled side of his back, perpetuating his crookedness.

- Readjust your seat position (and saddle) to the inside very frequently, possibly as much as twice every circle.
- Step exaggeratedly onto your inside stirrup to help keep your weight to the inside and indicate to him that you will not be pushed back out.
- Think about pressing down with your inside seat bone (p.88) – imagine your seat compressing his inside hind leg down. Be careful not to lean over in your effort to do this or you will slide out again.
- Motivate him more with your *outside* leg to persuade him to lift his outside back muscles, giving you a more level area to sit on.
- Use the straightening and counter-flexion exercises described in *He falls to the outside* p.157 to help develop more equality between his two sides.

You will need to persist with these corrections for some time – weeks or even months, as you are trying to make a physical change to his body. Be patient and persist – it is truly essential work in developing the equality of his two sides.

13 Bend and Straightness – Straight Lines and Changes of Direction

Straight Lines

BUILDING BLOCKS

The building blocks for going straight and changing direction are:

- Reaction to the forward-driving aids.
- Response to the turning and straightening aids.
- A degree of balance.

Initially, try to avoid riding too many long straight lines with the young horse as he will find it hard to stay balanced and will often run onto his forehand. Intersperse short straight lines with large circles to help him regain/maintain his balance.

Straight lines can only be truly achieved when your horse is equally supple on both sides. In the earlier stages, straightness will be your *goal* even though you will know that you are not going to be totally successful.

Horses of certain conformation, particularly cob types, find apparent straightness easier than most because of an equal *lack* of flexibility to both sides and they can gain higher marks for centre lines in competition than for anything else! The most difficult horse to ride straight will be the loose, big-moving young Warmblood. Only time and work will eventually give the required result – much patience is needed.

Requirements

Horse

- That his spine is absolutely straight and aligned along the line you are riding.
- Sufficient balance, so that he can turn onto your chosen line without falling to one side or the other.
- That he moves his limbs straight forward (conformation allowing), hind feet in the same tracks as the forefeet.
- That he lifts both hind limbs the same height as each other.
- That he moves forward with energy and purpose. Good reaction to your forward-driving aids is essential as the more positively you ride and channel his energy into forward motion, the straighter your line will be.

Rider

- You need good basic steering aids for the turns (Chapter 8) at start and finish.
- A good straight body position and a centrally situated saddle are necessary to prevent you from pulling the horse off balance.

Riding a Centre Line

1. Start thinking about your turn as you approach the first corner of the short side (i.e. the one before the centre line).
2. If your horse is still in the earlier stages of developing suppleness *do not* try to ride a corner then a turn, instead ride half a 10 m circle that begins just past the quarter marker and ends facing down the centre line (see aids for starting and finishing a circle, p.151).
3. Start to straighten when his *nose* touches the centre line. Horses are quite long and it takes time for the whole body to respond, especially when they are young or inexperienced.
4. Look up throughout your turn and fix your eyes on the far end of your centre line, A or C.
5. Now keep your eyes glued on the marker and ride as positively and energetically as you can towards that marker without hurrying him.
6. As you approach the end of the centre line you will need to be on the correct diagonal for your turn. If you are changing direction, change your diagonal just before D or G, *not* over X in the middle of the school as this may cause him to wobble.
7. Begin vibrating your inside rein to warn him you are going to turn that way.

8. As you pass over D or G begin to turn your body into position left or right, remembering to allow your weight to drop into your inside stirrup (no leaning over!).
9. Ride the turn off your centre line also as half a 10 m circle. When he is further through his training you will ride two discrete turns, but he will not be ready for this at an earlier stage.

In addition to centre lines, straight lines can be ridden along the track, the inner track, quarter lines, diagonals, the half-school line (p.17) and other lines parallel to the half-school.

Training Value

1. Riding a straight line is the best opportunity you have to assess the horse's physical straightness. A tendency to deviate with any part of his body (head, neck, shoulders, ribs or haunches) will become apparent, especially if you can ride towards a mirror.
2. It is also a good chance to test out your own ability to control these various parts of his anatomy, and align him between your aids – he must answer both legs equally and take equal contact on both sides for a truly straight line.
3. As a rider you can learn a valuable lesson here: that positive forward riding is one of the main ingredients of straightness.
4. They are the most common means of changing rein.
5. Straight lines will become more necessary as you begin to work on variations within the gaits – shortening and lengthening the strides.
6. A straight centre line is your first opportunity to impress a judge!

Turns and Corners

BUILDING BLOCKS

The building blocks for turns and corners are:

- The basic steering aids.
- Circles.

A turn through a corner is simply a quarter of a circle.

Requirements

1. That the horse stays upright throughout turns.
2. That he maintains his rhythm and quality of gait before, during and after turns.
3. That he remains correctly aligned throughout.
4. That his impulsion and speed stay the same.
5. That his balance is maintained.

Riding Turns and Corners

Prepare by making a small half-halt (see Techniques, p.37) as you approach your corner or turn to let the horse know that you are about to do something different. Then, as for circles, use position left and right with an amount of body turn that defines for him how much to bend his body, followed by straightening your body position as you finish your turn.

Like circles, turns should be ridden to a precise size:

1. In the earliest stages you should not ride deep into your corners; to begin with you will treat the short sides like 20 m half-circles.
2. As you progress you should begin to ride slightly deeper, eventually riding each corner as a quarter of a 10 m circle with a straight section on the track past A or C.
3. Turns onto a long diagonal out of a corner will be about one third of a 10 m circle.
4. A turn onto the half-school line E–B should be a quarter of a circle: about 15 m diameter to start with, progressing to 10 m as suppleness improves.
5. A turn onto the centre line is best ridden as half a 10 m circle until much later in training.

Ultimately, with the advanced horse, corners are ridden as a quarter of a 6 m circle, but you should only ask your horse to go as deep into the corners as he can manage and still keep the requirements listed above.

Training Value

1. Corners and turns are necessary to link one movement to another.
2. They can be used as preparation, giving you the opportunity to engage his inside hind more and so correct/improve his balance.
3. If you make a point of *always* riding a half-halt prior to every corner, when you start riding lengthening (both trot and canter), he will anticipate the half-halt as he approaches the corner (whether from the long side or the diagonal) and will make the transition back to working gait almost on his own.

Changing Direction

BUILDING BLOCKS

The building blocks for changing direction are:

- Forward reaction to your legs.
- Basic steering.

Requirements

1. That the horse maintains the rhythm and quality of his gait.
2. That he keeps the same speed and impulsion throughout.
3. That he stays upright during the turns.
4. That he maintains correct alignment (tracking).
5. That he remains balanced throughout.

Aids

Changing direction obviously requires you to change your body from, for example, position left to position right. The speed with which you need to accomplish this change will depend on the pattern you use – with the young horse you want to take your time, so use long straight lines between your changes of bend e.g. the long diagonals of the school.

In a nutshell, you will follow the sequence: position left – straighten your body – turn to position right (or vice versa). Do not change your body position rapidly or you may upset his balance and make him tense. Use the following order:

1. As you finish your turn from the direction you have been travelling (left, in this example) and come onto, say, the long diagonal, turn your body smoothly until you are facing straight forward. Also move your legs until they are parallel. The horse should now be travelling straight towards the opposite quarter marker.
2. As you approach the marker (8–10 m before, so he has plenty of time to react) begin to press your new inside (right) calf against his side to encourage his ribcage to move away, thereby initiating the natural balancing and alignment responses of his body. Also, slide your new outside leg (left) back but keep it passive (off his side) or you may cause him to swing his hindquarters.
3. If you are in rising trot, now is the moment to change your diagonal. You may have been taught to do this as you cross the middle of the school, but this can

cause him to stiffen and/or vary his rhythm so it is better practice to make your change of diagonal when approaching your change of bend, near the end of the school diagonal.

4. Drop more weight into your inside seat and stirrup and begin to turn your upper body to the right, allowing his neck to curve into right bend whilst your outside (left) hand brings the rein close against his neck and outside shoulder to prevent him losing his balance by falling outward.

Patterns

In ascending order of difficulty these are as follows.

Long Diagonals

These are ridden from quarter marker to quarter marker: H to F; M to K. In other words, always from the quarter marker *after* a short side – this allows you to ride a smooth and easy continuation of your corner before straightening onto the diagonal.

In the large school, in addition to the true long diagonals, e.g. M to K, you have other choices of diagonals, e.g. M to V; M to E; S to P, etc., all of which entail turns that are gentle enough for young horses.

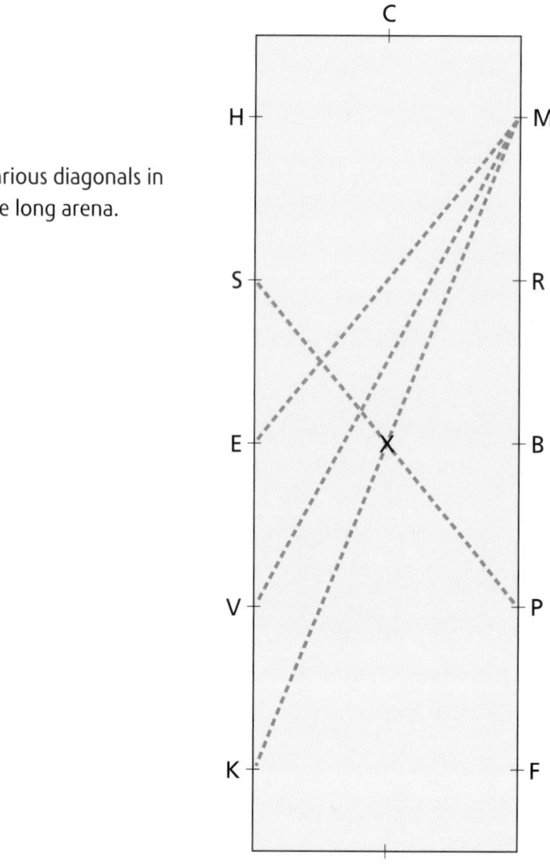

Various diagonals in the long arena.

From one half 20 m Circle to Another

This will be your first attempt at riding more directly from one bend to the other without a long straight section between the two curves.

1. Ride as if you were going to do a 20 m circle from C.
2. When you approach X (say, two or three strides before) begin to change your aids as described above.
3. If at rising trot, aim to make your change of diagonal one stride *before* X so your horse has time to react and adjust his balance. This means that you should pass over X with an absolutely straight horse, facing directly towards either E or B.
4. By one stride *after* X you should be completing your changes of position and weight so he moves onto the new half circle which will finish at A.

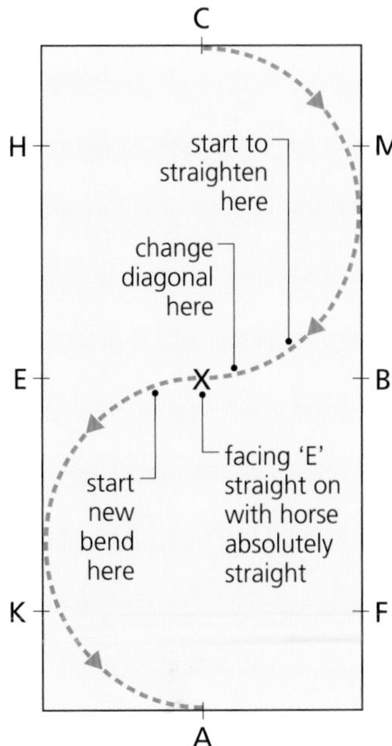

Changing direction in the short arena via two 20 m half-circles.

Via a 15 m half-circle

Ride a 15 m half-circle near the end of your arena: this will begin just before the quarter marker and should touch the short side, finishing with you facing the three-quarter line of the school. Continue a step or two further on your circle line then straighten: you will now be aiming diagonally across the school. Straighten onto this line and continue as you would for a change of rein on a long diagonal.

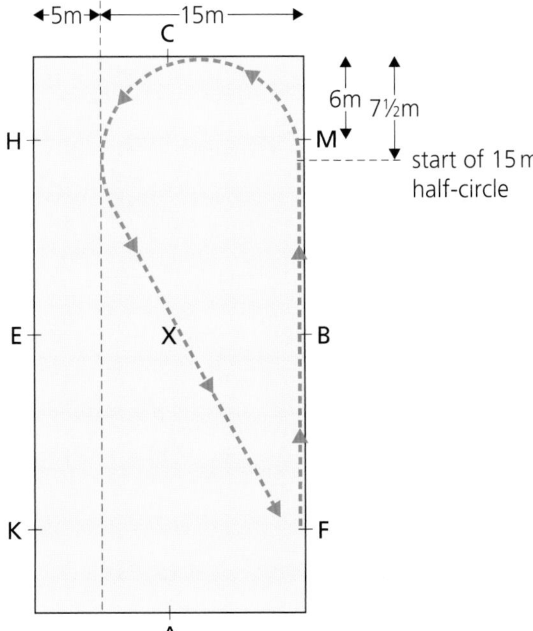

15 m half-circle to change direction.

Via 10 m half-circles

These smaller half-circles are necessary both for turning onto the centre line and for changing rein. Because the smaller arc is only required for half a circle even the young horse can be asked for a turn this tight – obviously not immediately, but within a few months of beginning ridden work.

You can use 10 m half-circles in several ways (again, in order of increasing difficulty):

1. Turn onto the centre line followed by turning in the other direction at the opposite end.

2. Turn onto the centre line and incline back to the track. The steeper (shorter) the incline (return to the track) the more demanding this is in terms of balance.

3. From the corner after the short side, ride a diagonal line to the centre line, aiming to meet it just before D or G (whichever is towards the other end of the school). At the end of the centre line turn in the opposite direction from the way you were travelling before.

4. Ride a half-circle onto the centre line followed almost immediately by half-circle the other way e.g. from B to X then X to E. This demands much quicker changing of your position and the horse's bend and is quite challenging to his suppleness and balance, so he should be able to accomplish it with ease in walk before attempting it in trot. This pattern can be ridden at any marker or any point between markers but it must include three straight strides on the centre line: one to finish the old bend, one absolutely straight and one to begin the new bend.

Figure of Eight

Unlike showing (where a figure of eight consists of two straight lines with part circles at each end), the figure of eight in schoolwork is ridden as two 20 m circles joined through X.

Review the preceding text relating to half-circles and simply ride full circles that start and finish at X, making the changes of direction as described.

Serpentines

Serpentines demand more than one change of bend in a pattern and they will be your next step after accomplishing the figure of eight. Ridden in a large school three-loop serpentines consist of three linked 20 m half-circles, and they are much easier, and can be attempted earlier, than if you are restricted to the smaller size of school.

Serpentines consist of three (or more) half-circles linked by short straight sections during which you make a change of bend and direction. The *three-loop serpentine* will be your first goal, but if you are trying to divide a 40 m arena into three equal

10m
C
5m
6m
H
M
E
X
B
K
F
A

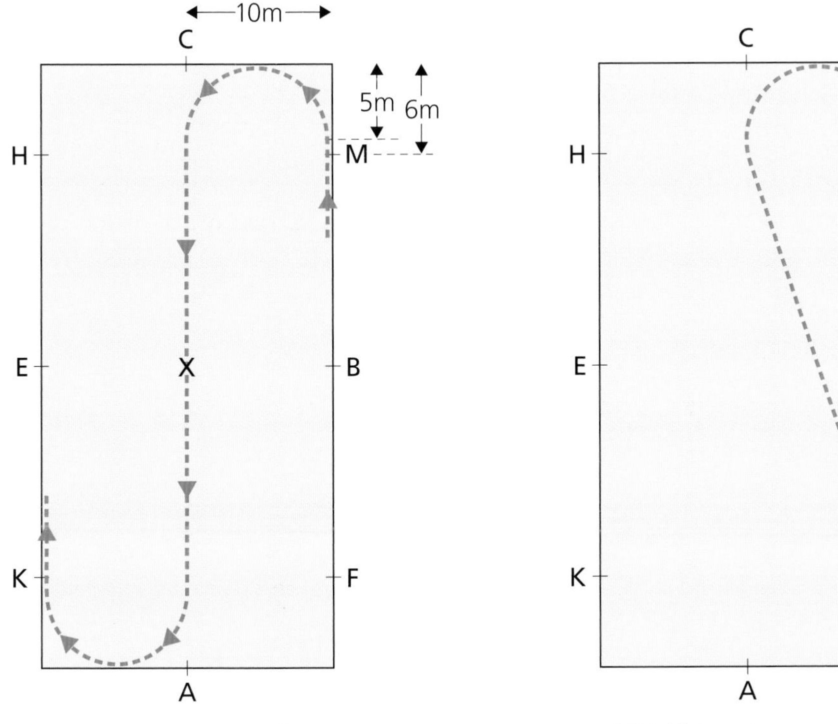

1. Turn onto centre line

C
H
M
E
B
K
F
A

2&3. This pattern can be ridden in either direction

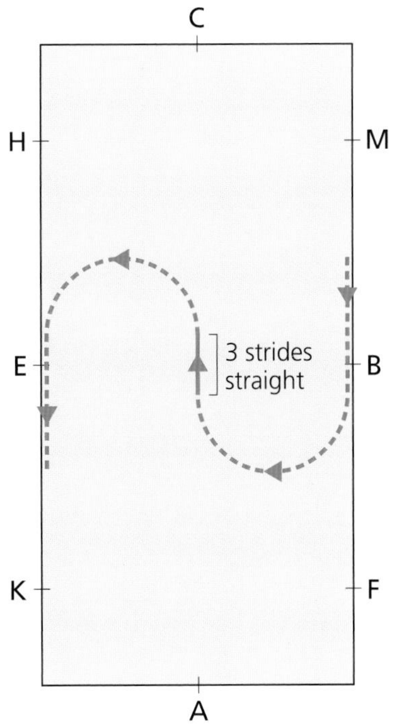

C
H
M
E
3 strides
straight
B
K
F
A

4. Two half-circles to change rein

Various ways of changing direction using 10 m half-circles.

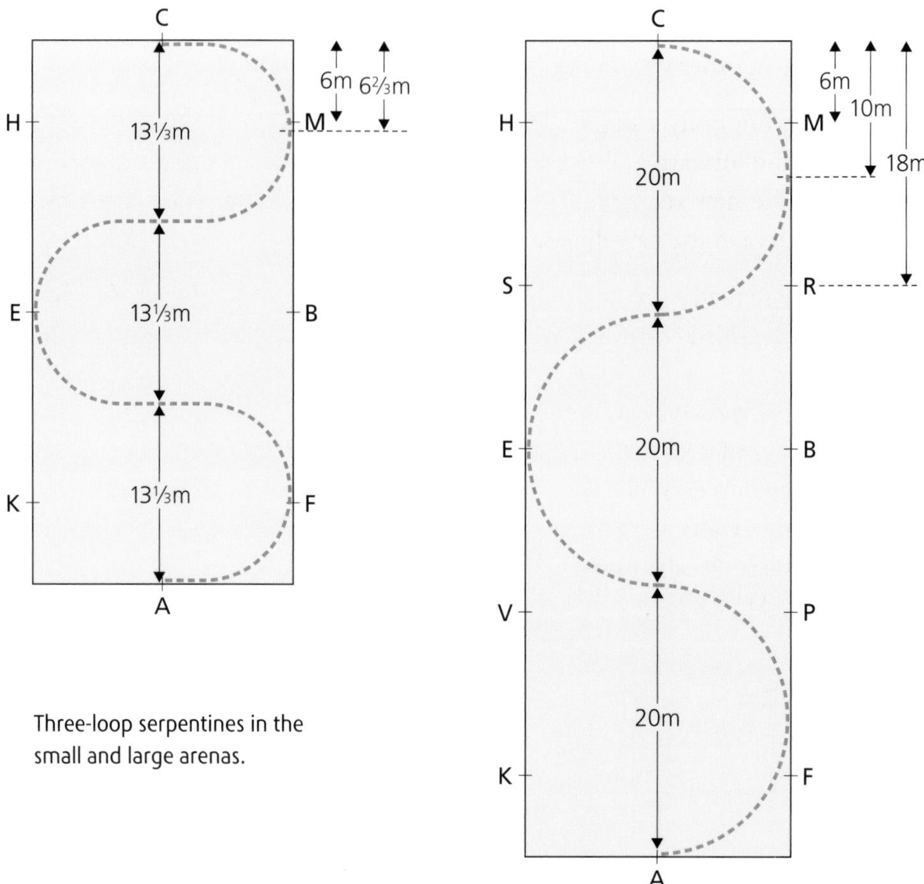

Three-loop serpentines in the small and large arenas.

segments you will find the markers are not very helpful except for checking at the halfway (E–B) point, at which you should have accomplished one and a half loops.

Try visualizing the shape on the floor of your school, then align your horse along the imaginary line you have drawn on the ground (without looking down to find it!). It is also possible to put little markers onto your school fence at home at the points where you should be touching the track – helpful to keep you looking up, but you will be unlikely to find them elsewhere!

Try to make your shape as flowing as possible, with clear bends and a continuous smooth curve on each half-circle.

1. As you approach the centre line, begin to straighten the horse by changing your body position from turned to straight.

2. In rising trot, change your diagonal one step *before* crossing the centre line. This gives him warning that you are about to change direction with enough time for his mind and body to react.

3. Lightly vibrate the new inside rein to begin flexing him (mildly) towards the new direction and at the same time use your new inside leg to press his ribs towards the new outside – *but continue to ride straight for three strides.*

4. As you cross the centre line always ensure that you are heading directly towards the fence – in other words you should be at 90 degrees to the centre line.

5. Now turn your body into the correct position for the next loop. This moves your outside hand forward and in against his outside shoulder to press it towards the inside of the new turn, and completes your weight change, thus beginning a smooth curve in the new direction.

6. Repeat the sequence in the opposite direction for your next change of direction and onto the third (final) loop.

The *four-loop serpentine* can be ridden on a younger horse in the big arena but it should be left until later in the smaller one. The distribution of loops is a little easier as you put two into each half of the school, being halfway through the figure at the half-school line (E–B). In the long arena each of the four half-circles will be of 15 m diameter while in the short arena each will be of 10 m, demanding a greater level of suppleness and balance.

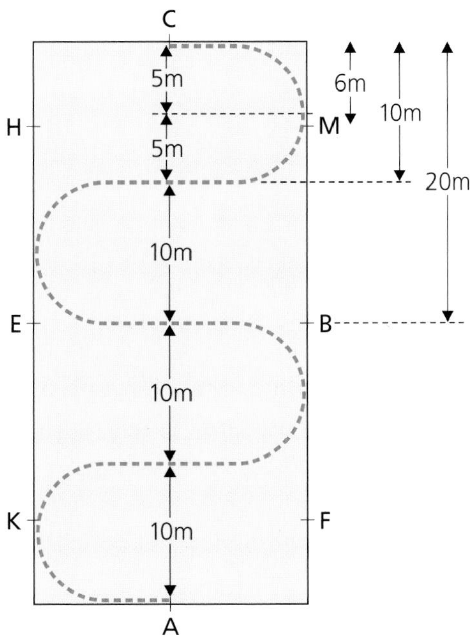

Four-loop serpentines in the small and large arenas.

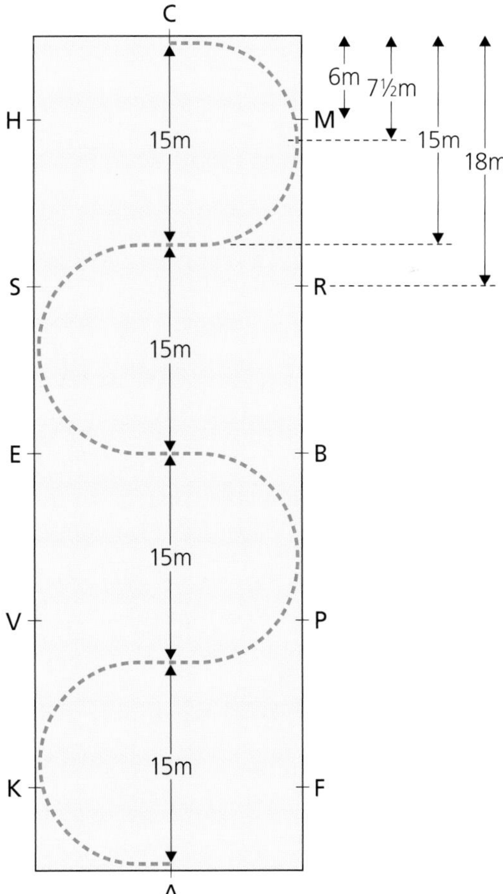

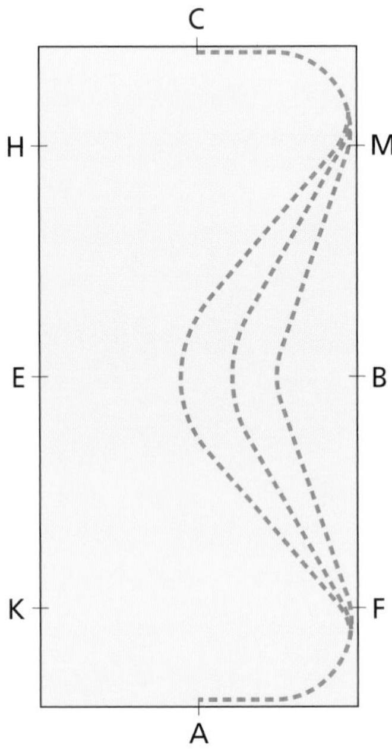

Examples of shallow loops.

Shallow Loops

The changes of direction these require are more subtle than in the other patterns described. They should be ridden as they lead on later to other exercises. The depth and positioning of the loops can be of your own choosing, but some suggestions are offered in the accompanying illustration.

Training Value

1. Since you must work both sides of the horse's body equally, changes of rein are a necessity.
2. The process of realigning the horse's body to the new bend is a challenge to his balance and so helps develop his coordination.

There are further patterns for changing the rein at higher levels of training, but for the earlier stages those mentioned above should be used. Changes of rein should be frequent during a schooling session to avoid the muscles on one side of the horse's body becoming over-tired, and they can be used as both rest and reward when moving from his stiffer side to his softer side. Cultivate the habit of varying your pattern of rein changes.

TROUBLESHOOTING

I can't keep him straight on centre lines

Straightness on centre lines will only be easy after a lot of training. Initially his body will be too crooked and his balance too variable, and the more you try to correct his wobbles, the worse it will get!

See p.164 for how to ride a successful turn onto a centre line, then instead of trying to correct him if he goes off line, simply ride more positively forward towards C – the more forward (without hurrying) you go, the straighter your line will be.

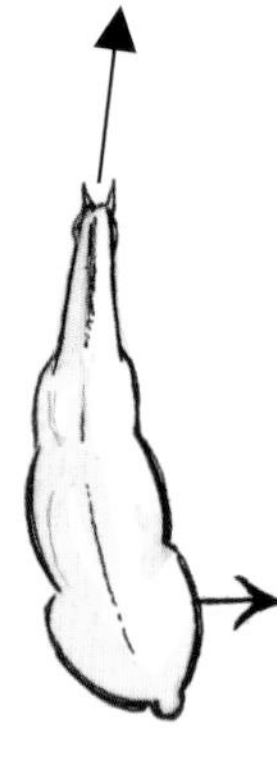

He travels haunches-in in canter

This problem will be easier to correct fully further along in his training – once he has learned shoulder-fore and is balanced enough to perform it in canter.

If he is truly cantering haunches-in, it is because of his natural crookedness. On the other hand, he may be falling out onto his outside shoulder, using the fence as a form of mental support (or trying to stay beneath your weight if your seat has slipped to the outside). The visual effect is almost the same – it is just that, in the second case, he has more weight loaded onto his outside foreleg.

Once you have confirmed your own straightness, the solution to both is to replace his shoulders in front of his haunches by moving them slightly inward away from the fence. *Never* try to push the haunches outward – this disengages his hind legs and may result in him becoming disunited.

To move his shoulders inward:

- Turn your shoulders towards the inside of the school, letting both your hands come slightly to the inside. Your inside hand will lead his shoulders inward while your outside hand presses the rein against his outside shoulder with an inward/forward push.
- Ensure that your weight stays to the inside and doesn't slip out as you turn your upper body.
- Use more inside leg *at the girth* to encourage his inside hind to step directly forward under his body rather than to the side of it. Try to feel him stepping under your inside seat bone.
- You may need to make a fresh effort to turn his shoulders every three or four steps, as he is likely to find this hard work.

I can't keep him aligned on my figures

Always align him by placing his shoulders in front of his haunches.

Thrust originates in the haunches, but direction of travel is determined by the orientation of his shoulders – in other words, if his shoulders are to the left of his haunches, he will travel towards the left, even if he is bent to the right and you are trying to turn towards the right. His head and neck only indicate where he *might* go, and it is perfectly possible for him to turn his head to the right yet travel to the left.

Do not try to reposition his haunches behind his shoulders as this will result in stiffening (resistance) or 'fishtailing' when he swings his quarters from one side to the other to avoid engaging them.

Placing his shoulders where you want them depends on the correct use of your steering aids – see Positions Left and Right, p.38, The Corridor of the Aids, p.40, and Chapter 8 – Steering.

Always remember: you must ride from rear to front, so learn to focus on what you are *feeling* as opposed to what you are seeing.

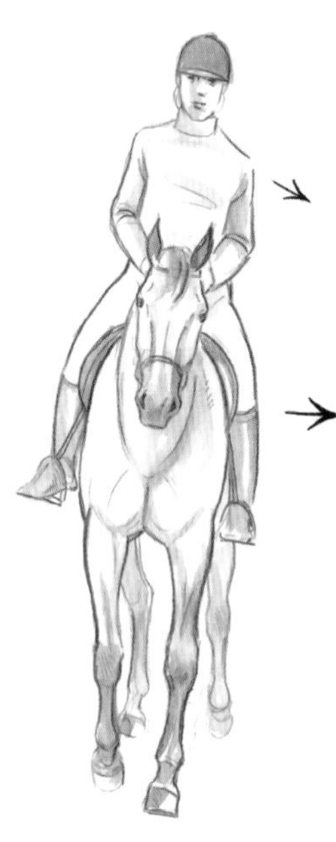

He leans over in corners

Review: *He falls in on circles* (p.155). The mechanism for correcting corners is basically the same, but use the following pattern: ride small circles (10 or 12 m in trot, depending on his suppleness, or 15 m in canter) in *every* corner. Use the feeling of pressing his ribs to the outside throughout all portions of every circle. Keep circling until he travels through the corner as you want him to, then move on to the next corner and repeat.

As discussed earlier, every corner is a portion of a small circle; by frequently placing full circles into corners, he begins to anticipate the necessity to arrange his body into an inside bend and fairly soon he will bend through each corner. Whenever he leans over, change your corner into a full circle.

He swings his haunches out in turns

1. Check your weight distribution in the saddle. If you slip to the outside in turns he will need to swing his haunches out to recover his balance.

2. He may simply be lacking suppleness and this will happen less as his body becomes more able to bend.

3. He may be pushing against your outside leg. If you notice some accompanying stiffening, hollowing or ears back, this may indicate discomfort and you should get his back and saddle checked.

4. If he is pushing back simply out of ignorance then you need to teach him to yield to your leg – use turn around the forehand and leg-yielding (Chapters 14 and 15) to help him understand that he should move *away* from leg pressure. Then try your turns with clear outside leg position and pressure. To begin with, ask for very little bend – this will make it easier for him to remain correctly aligned. Only once you can control his haunches should you re-introduce a little more bend to your turns.

14 Going Sideways

Having now ridden your horse forward on simple straight and curved lines, it is time to start teaching him about sideways aids. This is not because we want to produce shoulder-in or half-pass for competition purposes (yet), but because lateral movements are your main tools for straightening, suppling and strengthening.

You began to educate him in his lateral responses when he was a baby (or as soon as you purchased him) – asking him to move away from the pressure of your hand in the stable, accompanied by the command 'Over'. Now is the time to review exactly *how* he moves over, and to use that lesson as the basis for the next step – *turn on the forehand*, or better yet from a training point of view *turn around the forehand.*

Turn on the Forehand

BUILDING BLOCKS

The building blocks for turn on the forehand are:

- Yielding to leg pressure.
- Rein aids for 'Stop'.

This most basic of lateral exercises involves the horse pivoting around one stationary foreleg and is the means you will use to open and close gates. In terms of gymnasticizing his body, however, it has no value. Because the forefeet are denied forward motion, the hind feet will move away and toward each other without crossing. He may even be tempted to cross one hind leg behind the other – thinking backward (a serious no-no). Because of these constraints, the turn around the forehand, described below, is of far greater value.

Turn around the Forehand

BUILDING BLOCKS

The building blocks for turn around the forehand are:

- Yielding to pressure.
- Response to restraining rein aids (i.e. as in the approach to a halt).

In this movement the horse is permitted to move a little forward, with his forefeet describing a circle about the size of a dinner plate whilst his hind legs cross one in front of the other in *every* step.

Each step should be the same size, and each prompted by your leg aid. You should have sufficient control that you can either stop or walk him forward out of the exercise at any point you choose.

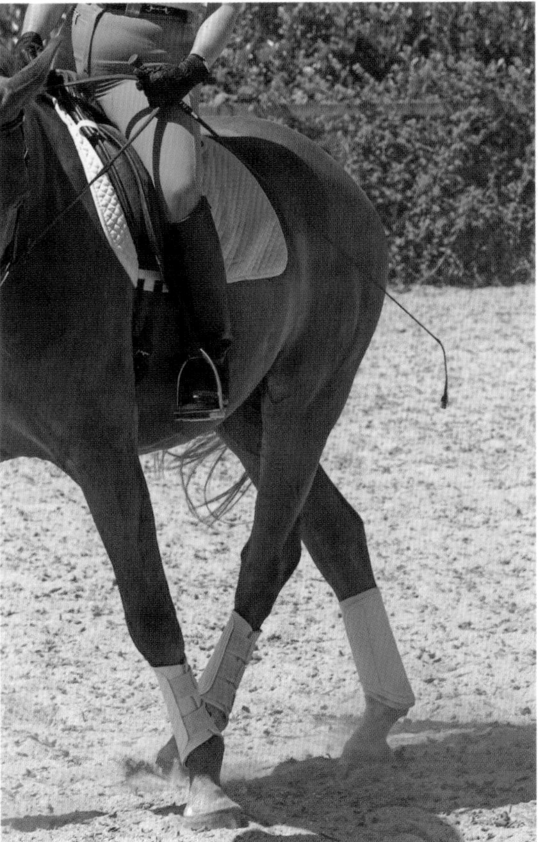

Turn around the forehand to the right (haunches travel to the right), with slight left positioning and his left (inside) hind clearly crossing *in front* of his right hind.

Requirements

1. A slight bend to one side. As an example, let's say to the left.
2. The horse remains calm and in a round outline.
3. He steps slowly forward around a tiny circle with his forefeet.
4. He crosses his left hind leg in front of his right hind in each and every step.

Exactly the same things are done to the other direction.

Aids

1. Approach the exercise in walk, anywhere in the centre of the school.
2. Begin to ask for halt with half-halts (vibrations down the reins) and sitting tall, but before he stops:
    - Turn your shoulders into position left to create the slight bend.
    - Use your left leg slightly behind the girth with rhythmic squeezes. Try to time each aid to coincide with his left hind leg lifting into the air – you can then push it across beneath his body more successfully.
    - Keeping your elbows in and down, use small squeezes (half-halts) of your right fingers to prevent him from stepping forward too much, or falling out through his right shoulder. Try to synchronize these half-halts to the same moments as you apply your leg.

Your outside (right) leg should hang passively until you want to step forward out of the exercise.

Don't worry too much at first about the timing of your aids – this comes with practice (for both of you) and should be a goal for you, not an immediate requirement unless you are already quite experienced.

Outside Assistance

As the horse is still at the earlier stages of understanding your aids, you may require some help from the ground. This will involve someone standing beside your left leg, placing a hand on your horse's side just behind your leg and pressing in the same way as you would to move him over in the stable. Also, use the command 'Over'.

Always make certain that your assistant is aware of the possibility of the horse kicking out. The assistant should stand as far forward as possible whilst still being effective.

An assistant can also help you to develop your feel and timing by calling 'left' or 'now' each time your horse's left hind begins to lift. Concentrate on what you are feeling under your seat and leg in this moment. By using your leg in this appropriate moment, your horse will come to associate your left leg aid with lifting his left hind, (and your right leg with his right hind), which makes many things simpler later on, e.g. squaring up in halt.

Gradually remove the outside assistance by reducing the hand pressure, then removing it altogether. When the horse moves away without this help, have your assistant stand away while you try on your own, still using the voice command. Finally, do it without the voice.

Training Value

1. The horse learns to move away from one leg in a calm, unhurried manner.
2. You start to enlarge his understanding of the requirement for his forehand and his quarters to do different things at the same time.
3. He learns that you require him to cross one hind leg *in front* of the other.
4. His lateral suppleness is increased. As he crosses his hind legs he tilts his pelvis to the left (in this example), so mobilizing his lower back (loin area) and hips.
5. To cross his hind legs he has to bend his hind leg joints, thereby improving their flexibility.
6. He learns to associate unilateral leg pressure with lifting a hind leg (in the example given, left leg pressure with lifting his left hind). This will be invaluable later when teaching such things as square halts and eventually, piaffe.
7. *Only when you can control his haunches can you control the horse.*

TROUBLESHOOTING

He pushes back against my leg

He may not be clear in his understanding of what is required of him (i.e. to yield to your leg pressure), or he may be deliberately resisting your aid. The latter could be a result of youth (testing his limits), discomfort (muscle soreness/lameness/saddle fitting problem, etc.) or over-zealous/over-strong use of your leg aid. You will almost certainly find this resistance only occurs, or is more marked, in one direction – when he is bent to his naturally stiffer side. Not only will he find it more difficult to produce the bend this way, but it also demands that he flexes the joints of his stiffer hind leg to cross it, which he may find uncomfortable, or be reluctant to make the required effort.

Review his understanding of your aid:

1. Begin in the stable – put your hand on his flank and ask him to move over, using the vocal command 'Over'. Does he move away from you or does he push back? As discussed earlier, this is where his education should have begun as a foal, but if it was missed out or insufficiently repeated he may need remedial work.

2. If he pushes back against your hand, sometimes all that is needed is an open-handed smack to remind him, always ensuring you are standing safely out of reach in case he should kick (remember, horses can cow-kick forwards as well as backwards). If this does not work you may need to use a tap with a schooling whip on his quarters, holding the whip horizontal with the ground. Again, be very careful to remain in a safe position (beside his shoulder). Also, keep your other hand on his headcollar so that you are turning his head and neck towards you – this will help to encourage his quarters to move away.

3. Once you have instant obedience to your demand to move over, check how he is moving his legs. He should lift the hind leg nearer to you *first*, and cross it in front of the further hind leg.

4. To help him understand, touch his nearer hind leg with the whip as he lifts it and encourage him to cross the leg over. Horses respond differently according to where on the leg you touch them, and in what manner (a push, a tap or a light smack), so you must experiment to find out what is most effective with your individual. Again, be careful to stand out of reach of his hind leg. To begin with only ask for one step at a time – stop and praise him each time he responds correctly. *Always remember this is about educating, not bullying* – keep everything as calm and relaxed as possible while still insisting that he gives you the response you want.

Asking *Tommy* to lift and cross his left hind by touching it lightly with the whip. Note where I am standing: out of reach of his hind leg.

5. Now try this outside the stable but still on the ground. Allow him a little forward motion as you ask him to take several steps in sequence, keeping things slow and calm. Continue to use the verbal command and dispense with the whip if possible, using just the pressure of your hand against his side in the area where your leg will lie when mounted.

5. Ensure that he responds in the same way to another handler. Don't forget to advise them of the safest position to stand.

7. Now you are ready to try this mounted. Ask for turn around the forehand in the normal way, but have your helper also asking him from the ground in the same manner as above. Apply your leg aid in the same moment as the horse lifts the leg nearer your helper. If the whip aid is still necessary (it may become necessary again now you are on board) then use the leg in the same moment as the whip touches him – your goal is that he associates your leg aid with lifting the hind leg on that side. Always remember that the whip should be used as lightly and precisely as possible to achieve the desired result – it is an aid, not a punishment. Initially, try just one step at a time then build up to several steps in a sequence.

8. Gradually dispense with your helper as described above.

He walks forward too much

1. At first his lack of balance will make this exercise difficult for him. Be patient and ask for one step at a time, allowing him to stop between steps. This will give him time to balance and think about what he is being asked to do.
2. If you are inexperienced, your coordination may not be clear. Have someone help from the ground, holding his inside rein as if they were asking him to turn around from the ground, but you give the leg aids. Gradually take over the rein aids with your helper still in position near his head. When you feel in control, try again without help.
3. Use more half-halts on the outside rein. Try to make them quicker rather than stronger. Keep your outside elbow closed against your side and use quick, tiny closures of your fingers and soft flexions of your wrist.
4. Moderate the strength of your leg squeeze – he may be more sensitive than you think.

He runs backward

1. He may be frightened.
2. You may be using too strong a rein contact.
3. You may be leaning forward (one of the aids for rein-back).

Check your body position, then try with a less strong rein contact and take it slowly, one step at a time. If he continues to go backward, use a stronger leg aid and try one step sideways, one forward, one sideways, one forward.

He goes above the bit

Either you are too strong with your hands or he may be too weak as yet to find this easy and comfortable. Always ensure that there is no physical cause – back, saddle, teeth, etc.

Try with a softer contact and allow him a bit more forward motion to make the exercise easier. Concentrate on getting him to cross his hind legs, and don't worry too much if the turn is large.

15 More Sideways

Once you have taught the horse to move calmly away from one leg, you are ready to begin leg-yielding.

Leg-yielding

BUILDING BLOCKS

The building blocks for leg-yielding are:

- Turn around the forehand.
- Response to half-halts on the outside rein.

This movement asks the horse to move forwards and sideways at the same time and can be performed on many different patterns, and with more or less difficulty. It can be ridden in walk, trot (both rising and sitting) and canter, and does not need collection so it is useful for young horses and older, stiffer horses.

Leg-yielding will help *the horse* develop his balance and will improve *your* suppleness and coordination.

Requirements

1. That the quality of his gait does not change during the exercise.
2. That he remains relatively straight along his spine, with just a small flexion at the poll *away* from his direction of travel.
3. That he crosses his legs.

4. That his speed remains the same before, during and after the movement.
5. That he remains balanced and in a round outline throughout.
6. That his shoulders always travel *slightly* in advance of his haunches.

Aids

1. Start with the young horse in walk, then later in trot. Begin with the simplest pattern described below.
2. Initially position him with his shoulders well ahead of his haunches to make it simpler for him to understand what you are asking.
3. For this example, turn your body slightly into position left, allowing your weight to drop a little into your inside seat bone and stirrup.

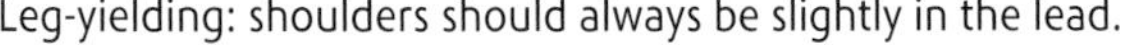

Leg-yielding: shoulders should always be slightly in the lead.

Introducing leg-yielding: shoulders well in the lead, to help the young horse understand what is required.

4. With small vibrations on the left rein, encourage a minute left flexion. You may find it helpful in the earlier days to move your fist and forearm into an 'open rein' position (p.35). Do *not* take this rein across his neck to push him sideways – the point of the exercise is that he yields to your leg; this is why it is called *leg*-yielding, not *rein*-yielding!
5. Close your outside (right) fist against his withers with the rein lying snug against his neck to prevent him from falling onto his right shoulder. You must also keep your elbow close to your body – any gap gives him room to escape outward with his shoulder.
6. Use your left leg *at the girth* in rhythmic squeezes to press him sideways across to the right. The speed of these squeezes should be in the same tempo as his gait before you began the leg-yield. Ultimately, you will want to coordinate your squeeze with the moment he lifts his left hind into the air – you can then displace it sideways more effectively. If he does not respond, do *not* move your leg further back – use it more strongly in the same place and at the same speed and, if necessary, back it up with a tap of the whip.
7. Keep your right leg back in 'outside leg' position, but slightly off his side. When his understanding of lateral aiding is more established, your outside leg will simply hang passively against his side, but in the earlier stages it is helpful to remove this leg completely from his belly to avoid any accidental aids that could block his lateral response and lead to confusion. In this position, if his hindquarters move sideways too fast, his belly will swing into this leg and be prevented from going into the lead. You may need to use an occasional outside leg aid to ask him to go more forward, but other than this your right leg hangs passively.

If he is not going sideways enough, or you want to go more directly sideways (increase the angle) try to coordinate half-halts (squeezes) on the right rein with the moment you press your left leg against his belly.

Do *check*, either with the use of a mirror, or a helper on the ground, that you have your weight to the *inside*. It is quite easy to ride what appears to be a good leg-yield with your weight to the wrong side. The visible result is little different, but the value in training terms is very different: with your weight to the outside, the horse is falling gently sideways to stay underneath you. With your weight to the inside he must step underneath you and carry you sideways, thereby building strength and improving his balance. See Chapter 8, p.88 for a full description of how to distribute your weight *without leaning to one side* in your effort to push him over.

If things go wrong, slow down, or even stop and start again – give him the chance to work things out. Picture yourself trying to write with your non-dominant hand; you might be able to do it slowly, but you won't be able to write at the same speed as you can with your dominant hand. With practice you would get more equal; so will he.

Patterns

These are given in increasing order of difficulty for the average horse:

1. From the inner track/quarter line/centre line to the track. The horse's body is almost parallel to the track with his shoulders just slightly in the lead (see left-hand photograph p.185).
2. On a diagonal line from A to B or C to E as in the right-hand photograph on p.185.
3. Along the fence (see photograph below).
4. On a spiral – see Chapter 12, p.153.
5. From track to centre line, parallel to the track.
6. Across the full diagonal, also parallel to the track.
7 From the centre line with a change of flexion and direction.

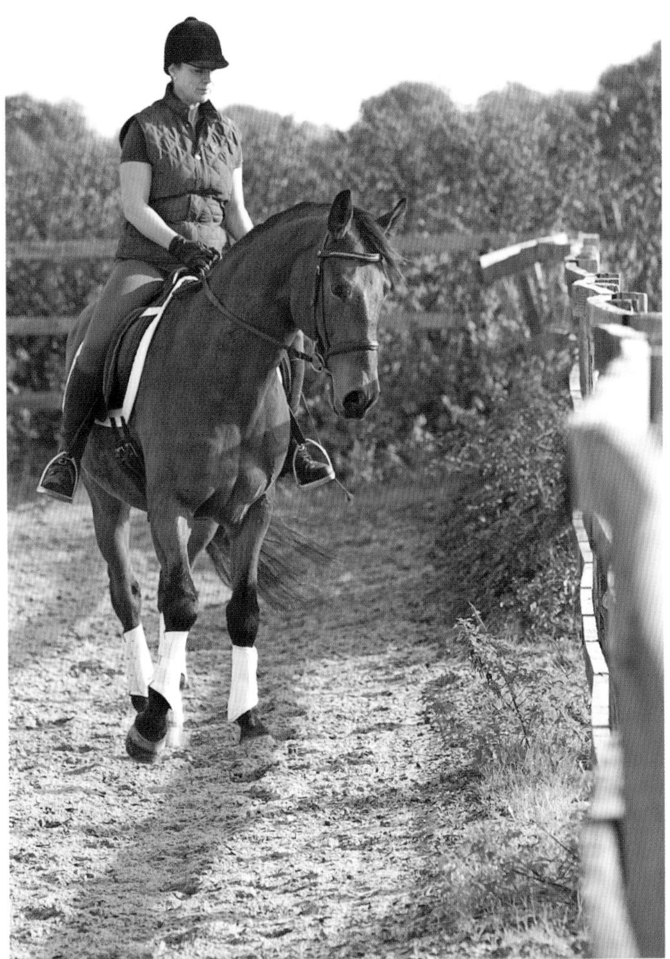

Leg-yielding along the fence: my body is in position left, with my outside (right) rein closed against his shoulder to control the amount of neck bend. My outside (right) leg is slightly away from his side to allow his haunches to move to the inside of the track.

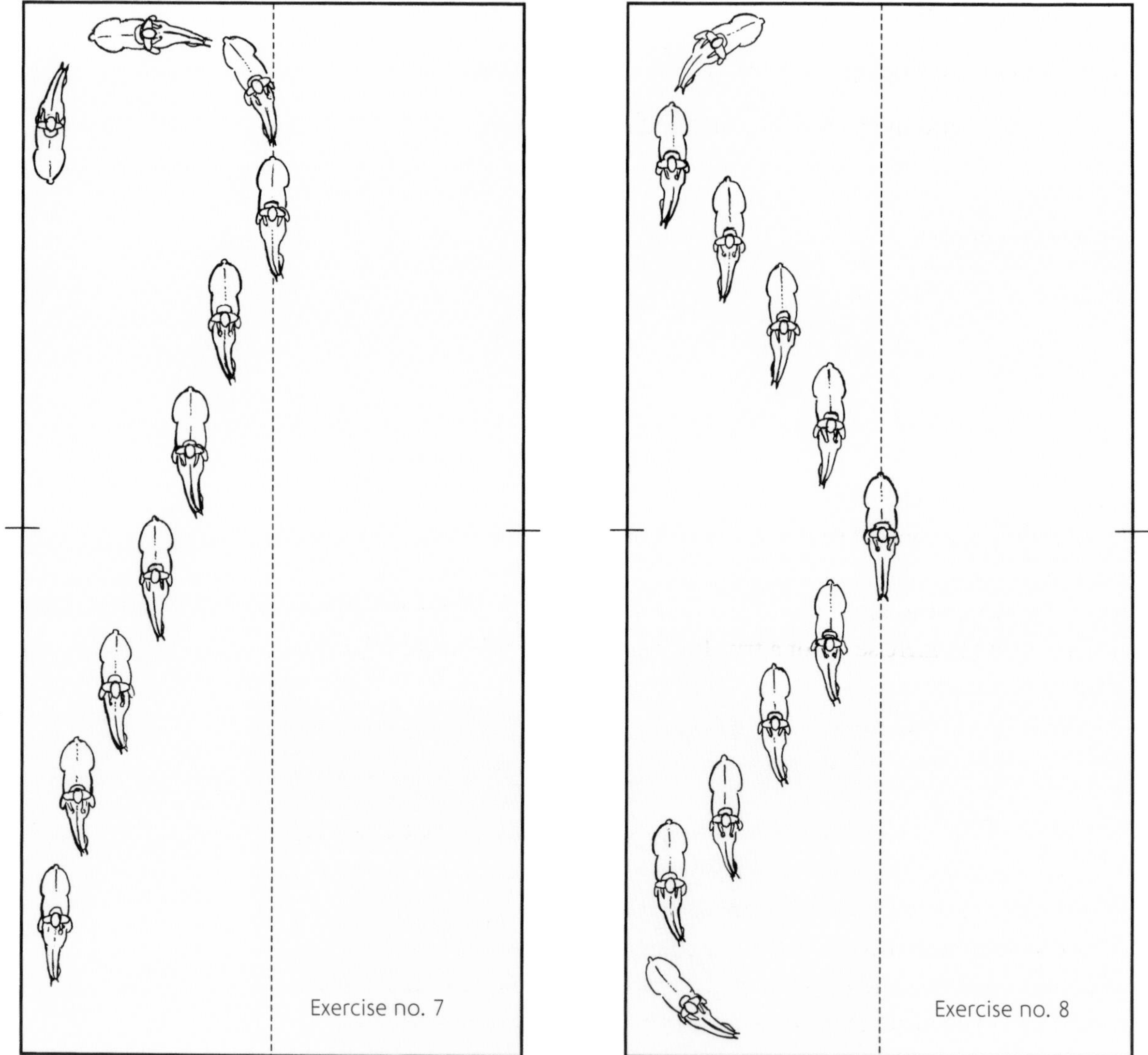

Line Leg-yielding patterns 7 and 8.

8. As a zigzag, changing from one direction to the other, and later making multiple changes of direction.

9. Any of the above can be performed at a steeper angle to increase difficulty as the horse becomes more proficient.

Training Value

1. Leg-yielding teaches the horse the difference between forward- and sideways-driving aids.

2. It improves his balance.
3. It is a tool for controlling straightness.

In addition, the patterns listed above can be adapted to target:

- Bend.
- Suppleness of back.
- Suppleness of hind leg joints.
- Obedience to the sideways-driving leg.

The particular values of the patterns listed above are as follows:

1. **Inner track to track** teaches obedience to the sideways aids and is a suitable way to introduce the concept of moving sideways away from the leg.

2. **On a diagonal line** can be used to increase bend throughout the horse's length. In this form the exercise is not a true leg-yield as you would require for competition, but you can use his desire to move his shoulder towards the wall to help increase lateral bend on his stiffer side. You will probably only need to do this exercise in the one (stiff) direction.

3. **Along the fence** is very suitable for a horse who 'runs through' the bridle or one who struggles with the concept of travelling forward/sideways at the same time, as the fence prevents him from moving forward. The angle to the wall can be varied according to need: a less supple horse, or one who is confused, can be ridden at a minimal angle (just enough to cause the hind legs to cross), while one who tries to 'run through the bridle' can be positioned more acutely, as shown in the diagram overleaf.

4. **On a spiral** is good for a horse who tends to rush as it focuses his attention inward all the time, as opposed to seeing an invitingly open school in front of him. It is also ideal for setting up trot to canter transitions as it both engages his inside hind and helps him find a correct bend throughout his length.

5. **Track to centre line** represents a more advanced stage, asking the horse to move away from his psychological support – the fence – into the open school, thus demanding more obedience to your aids.

6. **Across the diagonal** makes similar psychological demands to 5 above, but asks for more crossing of the legs, thereby increasing all the physical demands.

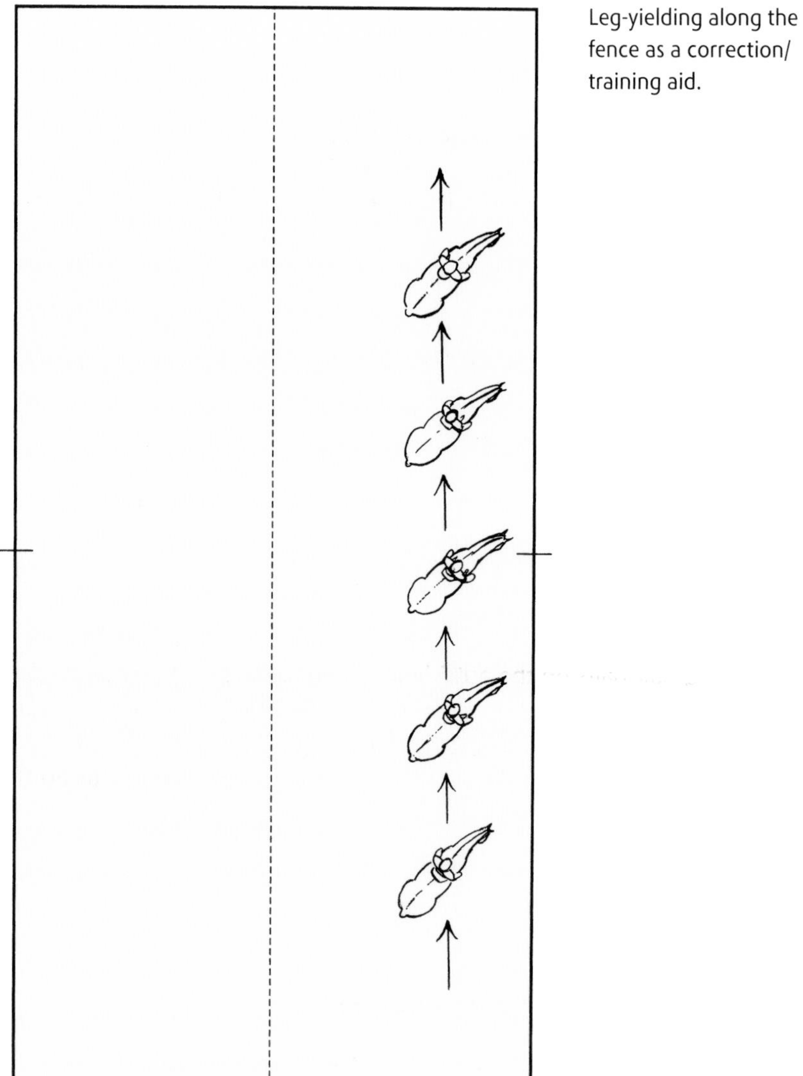

Leg-yielding along the fence as a correction/training aid.

7. **From centre line with change of flexion and direction** is a sophisticated pattern of leg-yielding, asking not only for a change of flexion but also good control of the horse's shoulders to put them into the lead in the new direction, challenging his obedience to your aids for bending and positioning, plus his balance.

8. **Zigzag** increases suppleness as the horse crosses first one hind, then the other. It also teaches equal obedience to each leg and allows you to check that he is travelling equally forward/sideways in both directions.

TROUBLESHOOTING

He runs forward when I ask him to go sideways

This may be a result of misunderstanding, incorrect aiding, panic, loss of balance, or wilfulness.

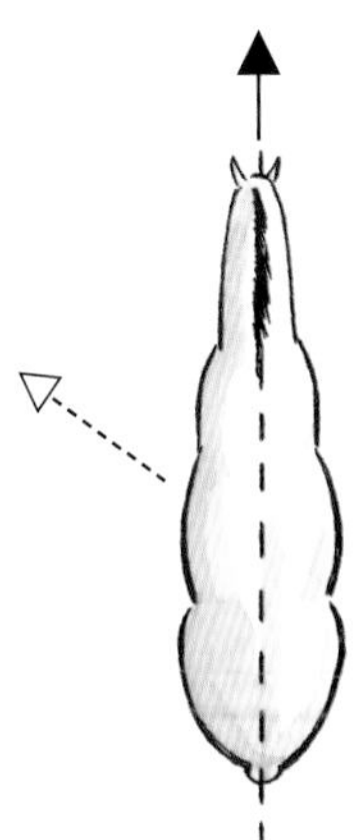

1. Review your aiding:

   - Monitor the speed with which you close your leg on his side – it should be in the rhythm of the gait, not faster. Remember that the speed of your leg aid tells him the speed at which he should be responding.
   - Are you using a strong aid? He may be panicking at the force of your leg closure: the sideways aid should be no stronger than the forward aid – it is the *combination* of leg, seat and hand aids that tells him forward or sideways, not the *strength* of the aids.
   - Are you making half-halts on the outside rein, and are these coordinated to the same moment as your leg aid? The half-halt causes a hesitation in his forward movement and with the leg applied in the same instant his only other option is to step sideways.
   - Are you using both legs instead of just the inside one? You may be confusing him with an aid on the outside that is stopping him from moving sideway. Keep the outside leg back but slightly away from him.

2. Review his understanding of your sideways aiding:

   - Ride turn around the forehand, making sure that he moves sideways only when you apply your leg aid – if he moves faster than you are asking then do just one sideways step then stop; another sideways step then stop. Repeat until he waits for your aid before moving. Keep everything calm and slow – give him time to think and associate your leg aid with his response.
   - Ride leg-yield (starting in walk) with his face turned towards the fence – see diagram this page. In this position the fence prevents him from running forward without you having to resort to strong rein aids. Again, keep the whole situation calm and relaxed – try to keep your contact as soft as you can so that he doesn't become stressed in his mouth. Use more half-halts on the outside rein (refer to Definitions p.24 to clarify *inside* and *outside*) and open your inside hand away from his withers to increase his angle. You may need to back-up your inside leg with a coordinated tap of your whip in time with your leg aids.
   - Progress to the above exercise in trot.

Open inside rein, with my whip touching him just as his inside (right) hind begins to lift. This enables me to influence his hind leg to lift with more speed and energy, and to make a deeper crossing. My inside heel should be lower.

- Ride leg-yield on the spiral (see p.153) but ensure, as you travel outward, that the speed of unwinding the spiral is yours, not his. If he hurries (either forward or sideways) ride only two steps outward, then circle, then two more steps outward and again circle until you finally reach the 20 m circle. Repeat until you are in control of every step.
- Once you have reviewed these exercises, go back to the one where you had the problem and try again with this degree of control in your mind.

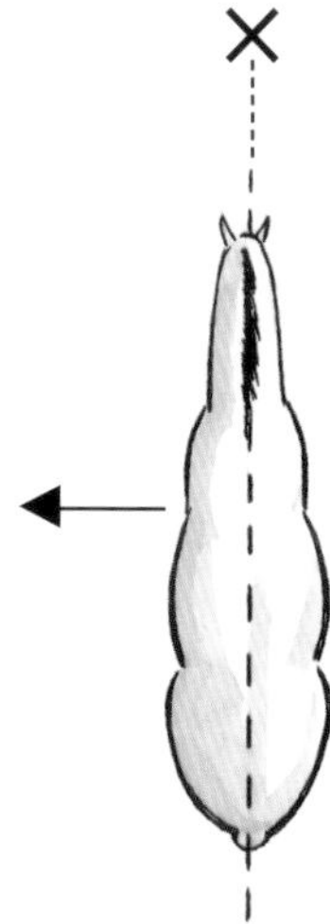

He runs sideways without going forward

This can be caused by panic, too strong a rein contact, or may simply be an evasion: by swinging his hind leg too far across he can avoid bending the lower joints, moving it as a stiff, straight leg, using only his hip joint.

- Check your position in the saddle – if your weight has slipped to the outside he may be rushing sideways to stay underneath you! His body is simply making a natural attempt to regain balance by stepping under your joint centre of gravity that you have displaced to one side.
- Check your aids:

1. If you are too strong in your rein contact you will be stopping his forward motion and he will be doing exactly what you are asking! Try a longer length of rein, and/or find a more forward feel to your contact (see 'The Wheelbarrow Push', p.90).

2. Are you using too strong a leg aid and either frightening him or in fact asking him to go sideways too much? Try using a much gentler aid and see what happens.

- If you are sure you are not the cause, try using the spiral exercise as described immediately above – only allowing two steps sideways then at least two steps forward before you allow him to go sideways again. This will involve some use of your *outside* leg (normally passive in leg-yielding) to arrest his sideways motion and send him forward again.

- Try the same thing using a leg-yield in a straight line from the track towards the centre line – he is less likely to rush sideways if you don't give him a fence to run towards. Again, only allow him two side steps before going forward in a straight line. When he is travelling forward ask for leg-yield again. You will probably need to use this type of corrective exercise for some months before you are in full control of his lateral displacement.

He pushes back into my leg when I ask him to go sideways

Review the same topic in the previous chapter, p.180.

Once you can achieve a complete turn around the forehand (360 degrees) in each direction you are ready to go back to patterns. Use the following associated exercises to help him understand:

- At A, turn onto the centre line.

- At D, ride a complete (360 degrees) turn around the forehand then as soon as you are facing C:

- Leg-yield to the wall, continuing to push him away from the leg you were using in the turn – e.g. if you turned him away from your right leg, you will leg-yield towards letter E.

- As he has learned to yield to your right leg in the turn around the forehand, he will continue to yield to it as you take him towards the wall.

- Ride other leg-yield patterns and if he pushes back into your leg, immediately remind him by making another full turn around the forehand, then return to your interrupted pattern.

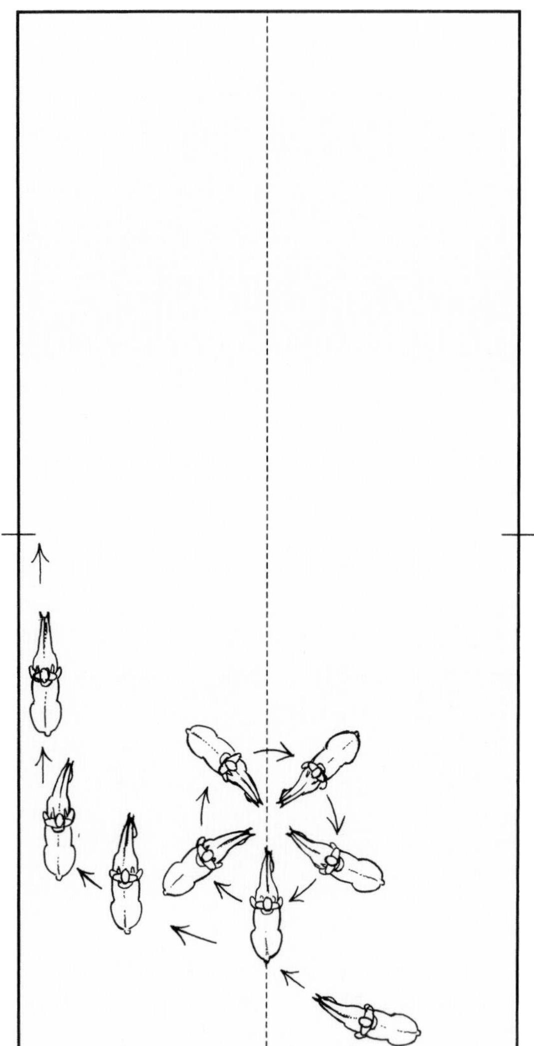

Exercise to teach better acceptance of the sideways-driving aids.

- If he is slow to move off your leg without actually pushing back against it, try a stronger leg aid – do *not* move your leg further back; this won't help and it will almost certainly put your weight in the wrong place. If he is still unresponsive then back-up your leg aid with a touch from the whip, synchronized to the same moment as you close your leg. You may need to experiment with the whip to find the most effective place to touch him – on the flank, the quarter, or lower down on the leg itself. You may even need to put your reins in one hand so that your whip hand can reach down to touch his leg.
- Check that you are not clamping your legs on with too much strength – horses will often push back if they feel you are being unjustly harsh. Use a rhythmic on/off squeezing, not a tightly clamped calf or raised heel. If you are not getting the response you would like it is better to back up your leg aid with a light tap of the whip than to use a very strong tension in your leg muscles – also less exhausting!

Here I am using the whip to touch *Merlin* high up on his quarter. You will need to experiment to find the most effective place to touch your own horse.

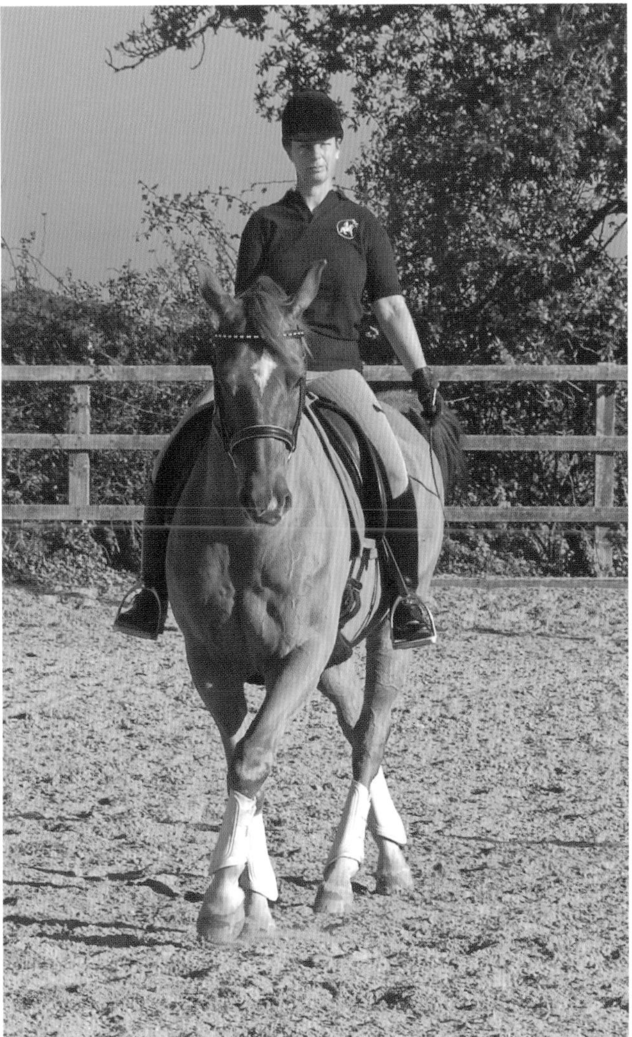

He won't go sideways

There are three possibilities here:

1. Your riding is making it impossible for him to respond. You may be:

- Out of balance. Check your position – you may be over-emphasizing your weight aid to the extreme inside, and he will very earnestly refuse to move sideways in case you fall off!
- Blocking him by using your outside leg as well as your inside leg. If you push with both legs, he won't know which one to move away from.
- Restricting him with one or both hands. Check that your contact is allowing forward enough for him to be able to travel forward/sideways.

2. He is ignoring your leg aid. To tackle this:

   - Press your schooling whip against his belly just behind your leg to emphasize your sideways-driving aid. If he still ignores your leg:

   - Tap him with the whip in the same place and at the same moment as you apply your leg. Try a small tap first then increase the sharpness (but not the frequency) until you get a response.

   - If he still ignores you, put both reins into your outside hand and with the whip in your inside hand reach down and tap him on the hind leg. Again, match the speed and moment of your taps to your leg aids.

3. If he is not ignoring you then your problem is almost certainly that you have moved his haunches into the lead, making it almost impossible for him to be able to go sideways.

This is where mirrors or a pair of eyes on the ground can be of real value. To have his haunches in the lead you will have:

- Not positioned his shoulders correctly at the start;
- Used too strong a leg aid or
- Too strong an outside rein, slowing his shoulders too much relative to his haunches.

To correct this you should:

- Always try to begin your leg-yield by positioning his shoulders slightly into the lead. If you are riding from the quarter/centre line out to the track you will generally be staying on the same rein, so no change of flexion is needed. As you make the turn onto your chosen line do not quite straighten onto the line – think of beginning your leg-yield before you have quite finished your turn. This allows his shoulders to begin the movement slightly in the lead.

- If you find part way through your leg-yield that, for whatever reason, his haunches have moved ahead, correct this by repositioning his shoulders into the lead. You can do this by moving both your hands, as a pair, in the direction you want his shoulders to go. This will take your inside hand inward towards his withers and your outside hand away from his shoulders to invite them to travel outward. Do *not* change your body position, which should be turned slightly away from the direction you are travelling. You should only need your hands in this position for two or three strides, until his shoulders are ahead again, then they must be returned to their normal place relative to your body (see Positions Left and Right, Definitions, p.38).

He bends his neck too much and falls out through his outside shoulder

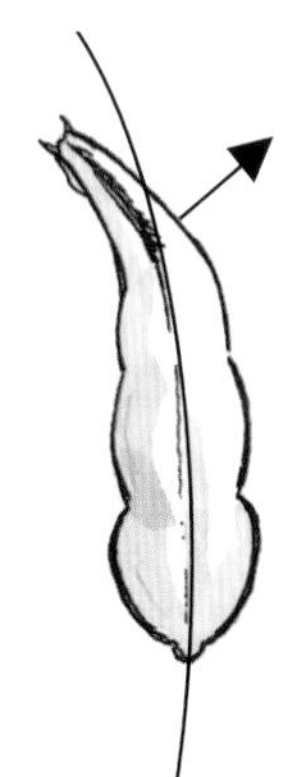

This is his natural crookedness trying to reassert itself and probably happens only when he is travelling in one direction – with his 'soft' side to the inside.

1. Check your aiding:

    - Are you sitting centrally in the saddle, with a little more weight in your inside seat bone and stirrup (correct) or are you *leaning* to the inside, which has the effect of pushing your seat across the saddle towards the outside? Check this with mirrors or a helper on the ground, or have a video taken so that you can see for yourself.
    - If you are collapsing (leaning) slightly to the inside, correct this by lifting your ribcage up away from your waist, or think about making your whole body stretch taller through that side. This will not only straighten your shoulders, it will also bring your seat central in the saddle again. Do not try to correct yourself just by lifting your lower shoulder.
    - Is your body correctly in position left (or right)? (see Definitions, p.38).
    - Are your elbows close to your body? If you have extended your outside elbow forward or outward, you are letting go of the outside rein (no matter how tightly you have it clenched in your fist) thus allowing him to fall onto his outside shoulder.
    - Are your fingers closed on the rein? If you have opened your hand the result is the same as above.
    - Are you trying to bend him by pulling on the inside rein? This will result in just a neck bend, and also has the effect of blocking his inside hind from stepping forward – exactly the opposite of what you want.

2. Once you are certain you are not the cause of the problem, you should tackle his crookedness by:

    - Riding your lateral work on the problem rein with no bend whatsoever. Keep his neck totally straight no matter how much he wants to bend it. You may find a lot of weight in your outside hand – for the short term do not let this worry you, just ensure that your hold on that rein is passive (elbow closed firmly against your ribcage with your hand close to his withers), with no active backward pulling.
    - Review: *He falls to the outside*, Chapter 12, p.156 and work on the exercises outlined until your skills of placing his shoulders have improved. Go back to lateral work with these feelings in mind.

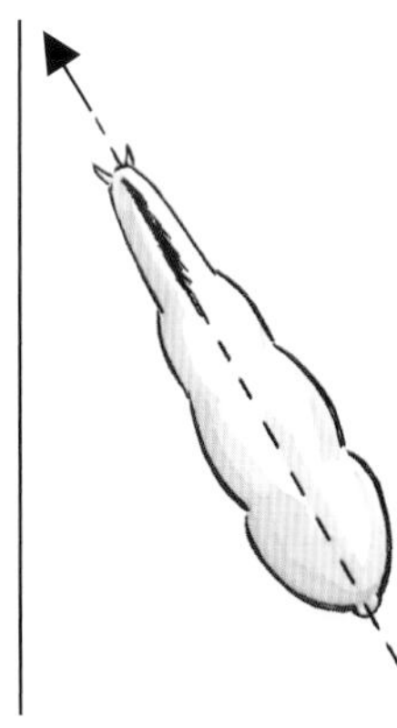

He isn't falling onto his outside shoulder, but his quarters are still trailing

Basically this means that he is simply travelling along a diagonal line, not leg-yielding at all.

1. Review his understanding of moving off your inside leg by repeating the turn around the forehand.
2. Pay more attention to how you position him at the start of your leg-yield – are his shoulders only leading fractionally, or are they too far ahead?
3. Check that your weight is in your inside seat bone and stirrup (see p.88).
4. Once you have begun your leg-yield, try to keep steering his forehand away from the direction you are travelling i.e. in leg-yield to the left, (direction of travel) he will be slightly flexed to the right and moving away from your right leg. In this example, feel constantly as if you are trying to turn his forehand to the right. Do this by increasing your body turn to the right, and thus pressing your outside (left) rein more strongly against his neck. This is necessary to slow the speed at which his forehand moves sideways relative to his haunches.

He goes against my hand, and hollows

This may be because of weakness or discomfort in his back/hind legs, you being too strong with your hands, or him not being genuinely 'through' before starting the exercise. It may also be an evasion.

1. Check his back for soreness/saddle fit, and take a close look at his hind leg action – are you certain he is sound? If in doubt, get your vet to check him over just to be sure.
2. Review your aiding:

- Are you sitting in balance – a crooked rider or a heavy rider (torso lacking muscle tone) will be much harder for him to carry, especially with the increased demands of lateral work.
- Are you pulling back? This is certain to cause hollowing from the discomfort (and frustration) it causes the horse. Review Chapter 8 Steering.
- Are your forward-driving aids sufficient to support the movement? If he is dragging his hind legs instead of stepping them underneath his body, his back will sag and hollowness will result.
- If you are sitting to the trot, is your seat adhesively attached to the saddle? If you are bouncing on his back you cannot blame him for dropping his back

away from the discomfort. You may need to improve your depth of seat by lunge lessons/work without stirrups before you are ready to progress with this work.

3. If you suspect that he may be struggling with weakness, give him the benefit of the doubt and ask for less angle – only so much as he can manage without hollowing. Also continue to perform the sideways movements in rising trot to allow his back to lift and swing – there is no absolute requirement for lateral work to be done in sitting trot.
4. Once you are sure you are not at fault you may need to be firmer with your aiding to overcome his evasion.
   - Keeping your upper body toned and your seat deep, with a softly swinging lower back, ask him to begin the movement. When he starts to hollow keep your hands absolutely still using passive resistance (see Definitions p.35) and send him forward with your inside leg towards your outside rein. You may need to add a feeling of pressing down on the reins without physically lowering your hand position.
   - The moment he complies and lowers his neck, relax your aiding and praise him. Be prepared to do this even if you think he will hollow again – you need to educate him that the reward of cessation of the aid (Definitions p.28) will *always* be there when he submits. In the long run he *must* want to do this work – you cannot and should not need to hold it together with strength.

He becomes stiff/tense and loses rhythm

You have probably asked him for more angle than he is physically capable of at this stage of his training.

Ride at less of an angle to regain his confidence and allow him to relax. This should also recover his rhythm. When he is more balanced and stronger you will be able to increase angle again.

Remember it is *you* who should be in control of the angle – your inside leg determines how much you go sideways; your outside leg how much he goes forward. It is the combination of the two that determine the angle and the consequent crossing of his legs.

He changes speed

Speeding up could be a result of you being too fast with your aids, him losing balance, or him avoiding bearing weight on the engaged hind leg by picking it up too fast. It could also be caused by panic if he does not understand clearly what it is you are asking him to do, or by pain in his back or hind leg. *Always* be sure that he is physically sound before you press the point.

Slowing down is almost certainly because he finds the weight-bearing introduced by the engagement of the inside hind beneath his body very difficult. It could, however, also be a result of extreme physical stiffness or, more rarely, laziness.

If he speeds up

1. Check that your aiding is:
   - Remaining in the rhythm of the gait – squeeze your leg against his side in a rhythmic on-off pattern that is coordinated to the speed with which he lifts his hind legs. Using your aids faster indicates to him that he should speed up.
   - Maintaining tempo (speed of the rhythm) with your seat, especially in sitting trot. See *His trot rhythm/speed varies,* p.139, for a description of how to do this. Keep asking yourself – is this *my* trot? It must be *yours* not his.
2. If he is losing balance, see that:
   - You remain central in the saddle. If your weight is to the outside he may be falling sideways in his efforts to stay beneath you.
   - He isn't falling out through one shoulder. See earlier this chapter (p.197) for work to help with this problem.
   - He understands your sideways aiding clearly. If he is panicked he may be running away, causing him to lose balance and panic even more. Review his reactions to your sideways aiding with a slow, calm turn around the forehand.
3. If he runs faster as an avoidance, you need to insist that he stays slow enough that he dwells for a short time in each stride with the inside hind leg carrying his body-weight. This will build the muscles of that hind leg and quarter and soon he will find the work easier – sadly, unlike the trainer at the gym, you can't explain it to him – you just have to make him do it for his own good.
   - Use the techniques described in *His trot rhythm/speed varies*, p.139, to make him move at the speed *you* choose.
   - You may also need to use a passively resistant contact (see Definitions, p.35) with increased tone in your torso muscles. All in all, a prolonged half-halt.
   - Use the leg-yield pattern with face to the fence (photograph p.187, diagram p.190) – the barrier prevents him from running forward and so helps you keep a lighter contact. Be careful that he does not offer *too much* angle – this allows him to swing his hind leg too far across and avoid engaging it beneath his weight.
   - Use spirals – the bend helps you maintain the position of his inside hind beneath his body and the smaller circles help to control his speed, again without using

a strong rein aid which is counter-productive (blocking) to the engaging effect of the exercise.

If he slows down

Whether this is a result of physical stiffness, or the horse just finding it 'tough going', you need to be patient at first.

- Work on getting the correct angle for your chosen exercise.
- Ensure that he is soft in the contact.
- Check that he is relaxed about the exercise – stiffness may also be a result of anxiety causing him to hold his muscles too tightly.
- When you and he are happy with all of the above then, and only then, ask him to increase his speed back to a normal working gait. Do this by bringing the speed of your leg aids up to working gait.
- Be prepared to reinforce your legs with the whip if necessary: this may range from one sharp tap to using rhythmic taps in time with your leg aids until you attain your desired speed.
- If he becomes tense again you may have asked for more than he is comfortable with on that day. Be patient and increase only by small increments over a number of schooling sessions.
- Sometimes, alternating a few strides of the lateral movement with a few ridden straight forward can take the pressure (mental and/or physical) off him enough for him to regain the working gait. Gradually reduce the number of straight forward steps until the lateral movement is once again continuous. *Be careful* that *he* is not training *you* – if you can *only* get him forward by taking him straight, it may be pure evasion on his part.
- If you are *absolutely certain* that there is no other cause and he is just being plain lazy, then use your legs and the whip as described above and don't take no for an answer!

16 Improving Straightness and Strength – Shoulder-fore, Shoulder-in and Sitting Trot

Now that your horse has some understanding of lateral aiding, it is possible to improve his straightness further.

In the earlier stages, your steering aids were exaggerated – in particular your use of the opening inside rein. You could not ride with your hands too close together because he simply did not have the balance to stay within narrow limits. By now, his ability to balance will be markedly greater and so your demands on his straightness can increase. Remember that he can only move his shoulders out to the limits of your reins, and that is defined by how wide apart your hands are held (see: Corridor of the Aids, p.40), so now you should begin to ride with your hands a little closer together.

This more refined steering aid allows you to start using lateral positioning to place his shoulders more precisely in front of his haunches, both as a correction to crookedness (whether natural or as an evasion) and to increase the weight-carrying demand on each hind leg in turn.

When performed in trot, the relevant exercises outlined below can be executed either rising or sitting, but this is also the stage to start introducing more sitting trot, to help further develop the strength of his back and haunches.

Shoulder-fore

Shoulder-fore involves a little more precise control of the horse's shoulders while not yet pushing him to the physical demands of shoulder-in.

BUILDING BLOCKS

The building blocks for shoulder-fore are:

- The turning aids (control of his outside shoulder).
- Leg-yielding.

Shoulder-fore is ridden at first along the track with the horse's shoulders moved fractionally to the inside. It can be ridden in all three gaits and it can also be performed on circles.

Requirements

1. That the horse remains calm, in a comfortable balance and a round outline.
2. He stays at the same speed.
3. He maintains the quality of the gait.
4. He has a *slight* bend around your inside leg.
5. Viewed from in front, you should see all four legs, with his outside fore aligned between his two hind legs.

Travelling along the track in shoulder-fore left, *Stan* has a *slight* left position and you can clearly see his left hind between his forelegs – in full shoulder-in, his left hind would be directly behind his right fore, and thus not visible.

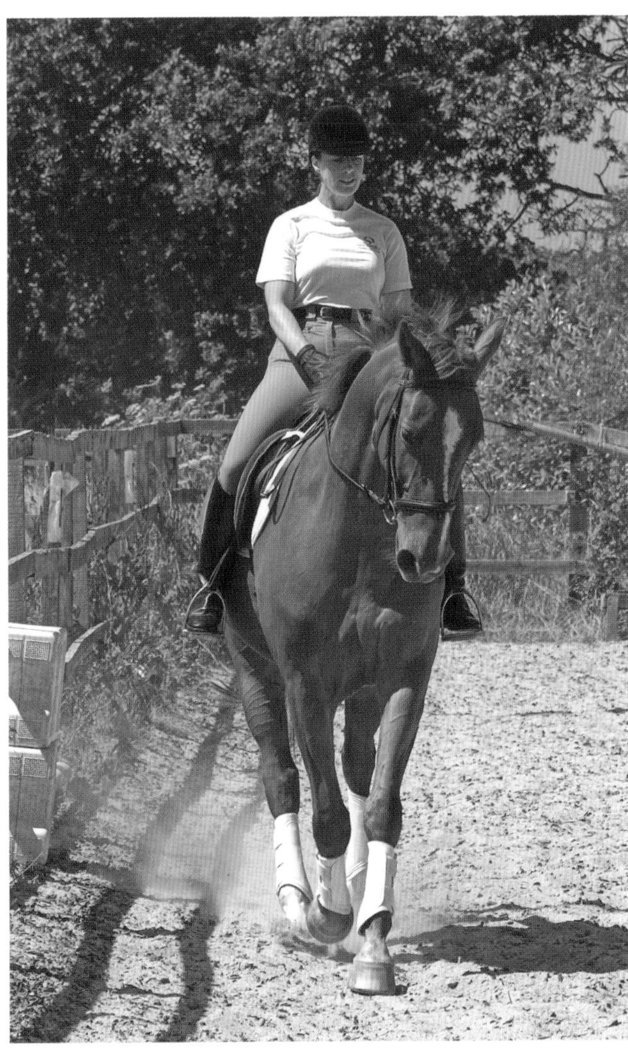

Aids

For shoulder-fore left:

1. Turn your body slightly into position left – this will bring both your hands towards the inside of the school.
2. As your horse turns, expecting to move onto a circle, make a brief half-halt by closing your outside (right) fingers and increasing your body tone. At the same time, increase the strength (but not the speed) of your inside (left) leg aid.
3. As he takes his first step along the wall in the new position, relax your half-halt but be ready to re-apply it if he begins to drift forward from the track.
4. Keep using the stronger but rhythmic (push-relax, push-relax) aid with your inside leg to keep his tempo clear and to push his inside hind forward underneath his body.

For shoulder-fore right, the aids are reversed.

Training Value

1. Increases your ability to control straightness, particularly in canter.
2. Produces increased engagement of the inside hind leg, thereby building strength and suppleness of the joints (try using it also during trot/canter transitions to maximize this effect).
3. Develops the *inside leg to outside rein* connection.

Shoulder-in

The visible difference between shoulder-fore and shoulder-in is as described in the caption of the previous photograph p.203; namely that from a head-on view you will see only three legs – both forelegs and the outside hind – this known as *working on three tracks*. All the other requirements are the same.

BUILDING BLOCKS

The building blocks for shoulder-in are:

- A clear understanding of and good reactions to half-halts.
- Improved suppleness, both to the bend and in the hind legs.

BUILDING BLOCKS continued

- Turn around the forehand.
- Leg-yield.
- Voltes (small circles).
- Shoulder-fore.

With the exception of a greater turn of your body into position left (or right), the aids are the same as for shoulder-fore.

The greatest difference between shoulder-fore and shoulder-in lies in the physical demands on the horse's body. Once into a correctly angled shoulder-in (approximately 30 degrees to the track), he will:

- Have contracted the muscles of his inside ribcage and neck.
- Have stretched the muscles along the outside of his body.
- Be moving his forelegs sideways.
- Be moving his hind legs straight forward.

Training Value

1. Suppling and straightening – shoulder-in is one of the most effective methods of stretching the muscles on the outside of the horse's body.
2. For his hind legs to move straight forward while his shoulders are positioned to one side, his inside hip and leg muscles must work harder than those on the outside, thus improving strength and developing engagement.
3. His weight will be more directly positioned over one hind leg at a time with his hips lowered, improving weight-carrying ability and so helping to develop collection.
4. Improves his balance.
5. Further develops your coordination.
6. Is an ideal preparatory exercise for many movements (e.g. half-pass) and transitions.

Caution

Shoulder-in is a physically demanding exercise and in the earlier stages it should not be overused. Only begin to ask for this much angle when your horse can perform shoulder-fore with ease, and even then do not ask for more than about 10 m at a time. In a short arena, for example, ride shoulder-in from H to E, then circle 10 m, followed by shoulder-in from E to K.

Gradually increase this towards the full length of the long side, but only after several months of build-up work. Eventually, you should be able to ride shoulder-in right around the arena, including through corners, but this comes much later in the career of a dedicated dressage horse.

Sitting Trot

BUILDING BLOCKS

The building blocks for sitting trot are:

- Good rhythm in working trot.
- The horse should have a supple back.
- A degree of strength in the horse's back muscles.
- A relaxed attitude.
- A steady contact.
- A balanced and supple rider position to enable you to absorb the motion without stiffening or gripping.

Somewhere around this stage of your horse's training, you should begin to introduce a little more sitting trot. He should now be strong enough to carry you for short periods sitting (although every horse must be treated as an individual).

Introduce short stretches of sitting trot – perhaps as little as four or five strides at a time. If he stiffens, go back to rising and try again. Keep repeating as he may simply be surprised, and repetition will accustom him to the change. Try also maintaining sitting trot for a little longer following your transitions into trot. Again, rise if he stiffens or labours, but keep repeating until he accepts your seat.

What you are aiming for is that, when you change from rising trot to sitting, and vice versa, there must be no alteration of his outline, speed or rhythm.

Patterns

Gradually increase the length of time for which you ride at sitting trot.

1. First, by a few strides.
2. Then increase to a whole short side, doing rising trot on the long sides.
3. Next sit on the long sides and rise only on the short sides.
4. Gradually build up until he can support you for a circuit or two of the whole school without losing impulsion, or stiffening.
5. As you do more concentrated sitting trot work, remember (particularly on the younger horse) to intersperse it with periods of rising trot to rest his back muscles and recover a loose, swinging back.

TROUBLESHOOTING

He bends his neck too much and falls out through his outside shoulder

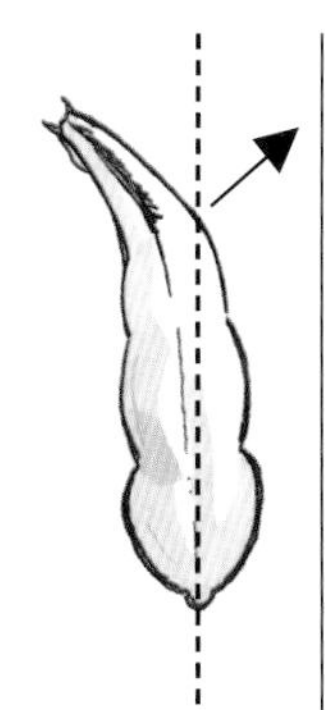

Review the same topic in the previous chapter, p.197.

He gives me too much angle but no bend

1. Start in walk, and think just about having him really bent around your inside leg; feel as if you are pushing his ribcage towards the outside.
2. Ask him to yield softly to his inside bit (see Chapter 10, p.107).
3. Drop your weight a little more into your inside seat bone and, as he begins to move his shoulders away from the track, make a small half-halt (squeeze) just on the outside rein and use your inside leg more strongly in the same moment.

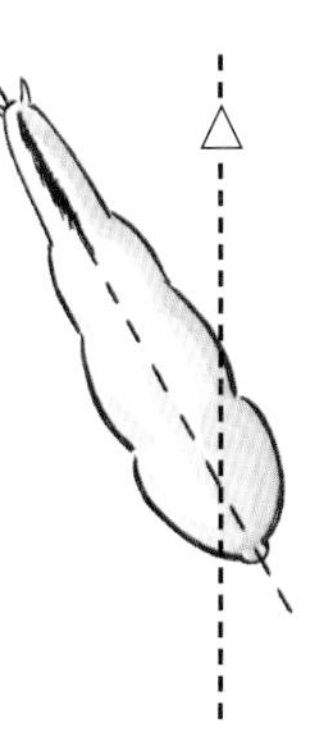

4. He should now travel along the wall in a minimal angle but with a slight inward bend.
5. If he tries to increase the angle, move both fists briefly towards the outside to push his shoulder back towards the track. This will also increase his bend.
6. When you can achieve this in walk, try in a slow trot.

He won't turn his shoulders

This is probably because of a lack of clarity in your aiding, or it could be a deliberate evasion, which is most likely to occur when his soft (easier to bend) side is on the inside, when his weight is more likely to be on his outside shoulder, making it harder to move. There is also potentially a psychological reluctance to move away from the fence.

1. Check your aids. Ensure that you:

- Are turning your body clearly into position left or right.
- Are keeping your elbows close by your ribcage and your fingers closed on the reins so that you do not alter the rein lengths in relation to each other.
- Have your weight slightly more in your inside seat bone and stirrup without collapsing your waist/hip (see p.88).

Also, check whether you are driving sufficiently with your inside leg so that he has enough impulsion and carriage to be able to move his shoulders and yet keep going.

2. If all the above are correct and he still won't turn, try:

- Exaggerating your body turn.
- Increasing your weight in the inside stirrup – but make sure that you don't lean over.
- Turn onto a 10 m circle and after one step begin lateral-driving aids. Do not be worried at this stage about where you end up in the school – it is just important that he is obedient to your lateral aids.
- Review the exercise on p.157 on riding circles in counter-bend to increase your skills in placing his shoulders relative to his haunches.

He goes against my hand and hollows

Review the same topic in the previous chapter, p.198.

He becomes stiff/tense and loses rhythm

You may have asked for more angle than he is yet able to make comfortably; he may be travelling too fast for his balance to be easy, or you have used too strong an inside rein.

Repeat a little more slowly, with less angle, and ensure that you are *pushing* his shoulders round with your *outside* rein, not *pulling* with your *inside* hand. With your fingers and wrist, create a small vibration on the inside rein to ask him to soften and yield to your contact (see p.110), thus lowering his neck and lifting his back, which will bring about relaxation of his whole frame. This, in turn, will improve his rhythm.

He tilts his head in lateral work

1. You may be causing this by using one rein more strongly than the other, making him carry his head on one side to try to relieve the pressure on that side of his mouth.
2. Tilting can also be an indicator of unequal use of his two hind legs resulting from:
   - An underlying physical problem.
   - A lack of alignment of his spine.
   - Comparative weakness on one side.
   - A stronger contact on one side that will block the hind leg on that side from stepping properly forward.

If his muzzle tips to the left it indicates he is not stepping through with his left hind leg, and vice versa.

3. It may also indicate a problem with his physical ability to bend throughout his length, but particularly in his neck and poll. This latter may be a matter for the vet and probably, by referral, the physiotherapist.
4. Check your aiding:
   - Ensure that you are carrying your hands level.
   - Make sure you have equal weight in both your hands, or slightly more in your outside hand (this is an indicator of correct connection from inside leg to outside hand).
   - Ensure that you are sitting balanced and straight in the saddle.

   Having eliminated physical issues and aiding problems, to correct an unequal use of his hind legs you should:

   - Deliberately lighten the contact on the side towards which his muzzle is tipping, even if this is the outside.

- Increase the strength of your driving aids to send his hind legs further forward beneath his body.
- Do not panic if this results in excessive neck bend in the short term – once you have his hind legs stepping equally forward you can reorganize your contact into the normal fashion.

Tilting can be concealed short-term (for the length of a competition) by riding with one hand slightly higher than the other (muzzle goes left, lift your right hand), but you cannot *correct* it like this, only disguise it.

He stiffens/hollows/changes rhythm when I sit to the trot

If you have followed the instructions given in this chapter and his acceptance of your sitting trot is still a problem, you must check:

- His back.
- The fit of his saddle.
- Your adhesion to the saddle. Do not try to sit too lightly – this will only make you bounce. You must sit absolutely tight to your saddle with a loose, swinging back to absorb the motion. Do not worry about sitting down – he won't break! Which would you rather carry on your own back: a rucksack that is fastened snugly or one that is loose and bouncing? If you have a *problem* with sitting, you should take some lunge lessons, or work without stirrups on a more established horse.

17 Direct Transitions and Simple Changes

Once the horse can perform transitions between consecutive gaits with ease, remaining in balance and a steady outline, he is ready to try direct transitions, i.e. transitions that miss out a gait.

As with all transitions, do not rush the preparation – the *quality* of the way he performs each transition is far more important than *when* it occurs. Always remember that each and every transition is an opportunity to build up his strength, suppleness and obedience – but only if you always ask for them when he is perfectly prepared.

BUILDING BLOCKS

The building blocks for direct transitions are:

- Response to the forward-driving aids.
- A degree of balance.
- A degree of straightness.
- The ability to stay in a round outline in simple transitions.

Direct Upward Transitions

These are the easier type: moving into a more onward-bound gait puts the horse's hind legs further under his body, making it easier for him to balance.

Halt to Trot

This should be the first you try.

Requirements

1. That the horse moves directly from immobility into trot, with no intervening steps of walk.
2. That he achieves this by flexing (bending) the joints of his hind legs then pushing (springing) off them, not by dragging himself forward with his shoulders and forelegs.
3. That his outline remains round, with a continuous soft contact.
4. That from the first step his trot is the best quality (length of stride, rhythm, tempo and elasticity) he can produce at his current level of training.

Aids

1. Establish an immobile but attentive and straight halt (see Chapter 7).
2. Close both your lower legs (keep upper legs relaxed) with a little more strength than when asking for halt to walk.
3. Without tensing your buttock muscles, find a feeling of springing your seat forward and upward, as if you were already in sitting trot – you should be using your deep stomach muscles for this.
4. If he walks, keep asking for trot – it may take several attempts before he figures out what you are asking of him. You can gradually reduce the number of walk steps until you lose them altogether.
5. Once in trot, begin to rise within a couple of steps and ride positively forward, focusing on his rhythm, tempo and outline.

Walk to Canter

Teach this once halt to trot is established.

Requirements

1. That the horse moves directly from walk sequence to canter sequence with no intervening trot steps or shuffling.
2. That he 'sits down' and springs off bent hind legs.
3. That he remains round in his outline and soft in your hands.
4. That he immediately finds a balanced, correct canter and sustains it until you tell him otherwise.

The moment of transition from walk to canter – 'crouching down' behind and using his back as a lever to elevate his forehand.

Aids

1. Establish an active but relaxed walk. Pay particular attention to the tempo being crisp (marching speed), and to his attention being fully on you.

2. Ensure a clear bend around your inside leg, with your weight slightly more in your inside seat bone (see p.88).

3. Take note of his footfalls – *there is only one moment in the walk sequence when it is possible for him to change to canter sequence.* This moment is *as his outside forefoot is on the ground.* Use his outside shoulder as a guide, just as you do to check your diagonals in rising trot (see p.131). *You need to make your aid as his outside shoulder moves back.* Until you become adept at feeling this moment, take a quick peek at the outside shoulder and, as it moves back, say to yourself: 'Now… now…now…' Then look up and keep saying it at the same speed.

4. Ask for canter in the 'now' moment by sliding your outside leg back (from your *hip*, not your knee) along his ribs, close your inside leg beside the girth, *and slide your inside seat bone forward along the saddle.* Imagine your seat bone to be a match that you are striking along the saddle – hence a 'strike-off'! With a more educated or a sensitive horse this seat aid may be *all* you need.

5. Maintain rein contact throughout – if you lose it (or throw it forward), your aids may be misinterpreted as 'Go faster/bigger in walk,' or 'Fall on your forehand and jog'.

6. Once in canter, immediately establish an active, forward-thinking gait.

Training Value of Direct Upward Transitions

1. The horse's response to your driving aids will become crisper.
2. If performed correctly, his hind leg joints will become more supple.
3. The muscles of his hindquarters will be strengthened.

Direct Downward Transitions

These are harder for the horse than the direct upward transitions, as they require greater strength and balance, and they should be taught more gradually.

Trot to Halt

This is the direct downward transition that should be taught first.

Requirements

1. That the horse takes more weight onto his hindquarters as he performs the downward transition.
2. That he remains straight.
3. That his outline remains round, with his mouth closed and his jaw relaxed.
4. That he moves directly from trot to halt without intervening walk steps.
5. That he stands still in halt.
6. At a more advanced level he should finish in a square, engaged halt (see Chapter 18).

Aids

1. Take sitting trot.
2. Move both your lower legs back slightly and close them gently to indicate to his hind legs to step forward/under.
3. Close your upper legs to inhibit movement of his shoulders.
4. Using the muscles around your pelvis, hold your seat still in the saddle without clenching your buttocks.
5. Lift your diaphragm (see p.72).
6. Close your fingers to produce a non-allowing contact. If he is genuinely accepting the bit this is all you need to do with your hands. If he becomes anxious or contests the contact, vibrate both reins softly to help him stay relaxed in his jaw.

7. If he initially takes a few walk steps before coming to halt, just keep asking in the same manner – *do not* increase the strength of your rein contact. It may be some time (days or months) before he is strong enough and balanced enough to achieve a direct transition. If you pull on the reins you may achieve it more quickly, but you will teach him to stiffen his frame, which will block his hind legs from stepping forward/under – the main goal of a downward transition.

Canter to Walk

This is a more advanced transition and should be tackled a little later in his training – not before he can comfortably canter a 10 m circle in an easy rhythm and balance.

Requirements

1. That his canter becomes 'smaller' (less ground covered without losing impulsion) and 'sits down' more (i.e. collects) as he approaches the transition.
2. That he accomplishes the transition by lowering his croup and taking more weight back onto his hindquarters, not by bracing a foreleg to stop himself.
3. That he stays straight.
4. That he remains soft in the contact.
5. That his outline is round throughout.
6. That he walks away from the transition in a relaxed, rhythmic fashion.

Aids

1. Use a small circle to prepare – this brings his inside hind further under his body by virtue of his correct bend.
2. Aim to ride your transition as he finishes the circle, when his nose reaches the track; this will be most effective if your school has a fence or wall around it to provide a psychological 'brake' as he approaches it (see right-hand diagram, p.80).
3. A few strides before your transition, use small half-halts on the *inside* rein by moving your inside shoulder back slightly in each stride. This pushes your inside seat bone forward and down, producing a driving force to send his hind leg further under his body *as* your rein inhibits his forward motion.
4. Ask for the transition by bringing your *outside* shoulder back, keeping firm tone in your torso muscles. This drops your outside seat bone down into the saddle, giving it equal weight with the inside one – as your seat in canter should always have more weight in your inside seat bone, this equalization combined with the outside rein half-halt indicates to him to change gait.

5. Once in walk, relax! Ease the rein contact and allow your hips to swing along with the walk – pay attention to this relaxation and to establishing a good walk rhythm, or you will store up problems for later on.

In a more sophisticated form (later in his training) you can achieve the transition with the tiniest of movements: a closure of your fingers and a toning of your upper body. In the earlier days your aids should be more exaggerated and if he drops to trot instead of walk just keep your outside shoulder drawn back and hold your pelvis still (no buttock clenching) until he breaks into walk. Repetitions over a number of sessions will gradually reduce the jog steps until you lose them altogether.

Patterns

Over a period of months, begin to ask for canter to walk transitions in gradually more difficult places in the school. The more gradual the curve, or the longer the straight line, the harder the preparation. You will notice this type of progression if you look at dressage tests of increasing difficulty.

1. Begin as suggested, using an almost complete small circle with the transition ridden facing the fence.
2. As the horse finds this easier, start to ask for the transition halfway around the small circle – as he reaches the centre line.
3. Next, turn across the half-school line (see Definitions, p.17) using the turn to prepare him, and make the transition just before X.
4. Ask on a 20 m circle, first using the fence as before, then anywhere around its perimeter.
5. Turn onto a short diagonal and ask before the centre line.
6. Asking anywhere on a long, straight line will prove how strong his hindquarters are, how balanced he is, and how well he understands your preparation and aids.
7. Asking out of counter-canter (see Chapter 20) is most difficult and should only be attempted when he is well balanced and engaged.

Training Value of Direct Downward Transitions

1. They increase strength and hence carrying capacity of the hindquarters.
2. As a consequence, they help lighten the forehand.
3. They provide the building blocks for more advanced work such as simple changes, flying changes and canter pirouettes.

CAUTION: *never* sacrifice the quality of your training for accuracy. Precision will come with time as your horse becomes more able to perform direct transitions with relaxation and ease – making abrupt (uncomfortable) transitions will only cause anxiety, leading to problems in the long term.

Progression

As your horse becomes more accomplished both in terms of strength and response, you should start to demand that:

1. His upward transitions lift his withers more, so that the transitions become more 'uphill' and less ground-gaining.
2. In his downward transitions he gradually 'sits' more and more during the approach, building greater strength and flexibility into his hind leg joints, with the ultimate aim of developing piaffe and canter pirouettes. Even if you don't plan to take his training that far, you will achieve greater balance and engagement in the new gait if he has genuinely collected on the way into the transition.

Simple Changes

Once your horse can achieve canter to walk transitions, you can ride simple changes.

BUILDING BLOCKS

The building blocks for simple changes are:

- Walk to canter.
- Canter to walk.

Requirements

1. Canter to walk, followed by approximately 2–5 steps of walk, then a walk to canter transition.
2. Initially the downward transition need not be absolutely direct (in Elementary tests), though it must be as balanced as possible.

3. The walk steps *must* be clear, in a good four-beat rhythm, and *straight.*
4. At more advanced levels (Medium tests and above) both transitions must be absolutely direct, with no jog steps.

Aids

1. Ride canter to walk as described above.
2. Relax your aids and allow your horse to settle into clear walk steps.
3. Straighten him (he was previously positioned towards his leading canter leg).
4. Position him towards the new canter lead – move his shoulders slightly to the new side (shoulder-fore) with a slight flexion. *Take time to do this – do not rush it or miss it out altogether.*
5. Ask for walk to canter.

Patterns

Always start with the pattern your horse finds easiest, to build his confidence. This will be either:

- Half a 10 m circle from track to centre line – walk as you arrive at the centre line, making several straight strides on the line – ask for the new canter lead and half 10 m circle to the opposite track, or:
- Turn right at B, use the turn to balance and collect – transition to walk just before X, walk over X – pick up left canter and turn left at E (and vice-versa).

Both of these give you a fairly tight turn, which is the best assistance for providing the balance and collection necessary to achieve the difficult downward transition – see the diagram opposite.

As you progress, gradually ask for the transitions from shallower turns, then further away from turns, then on straight lines and finally the most difficult: from counter-canter to true canter on a straight line – the lead-up work for flying changes. Also increase the frequency: ride simple changes all around the track with only a few steps of canter between each – a building block for tempi changes.

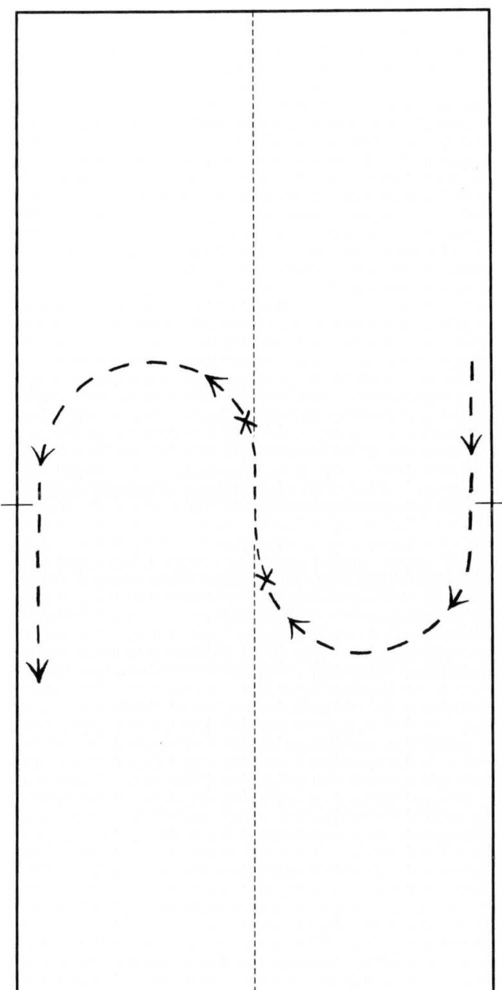

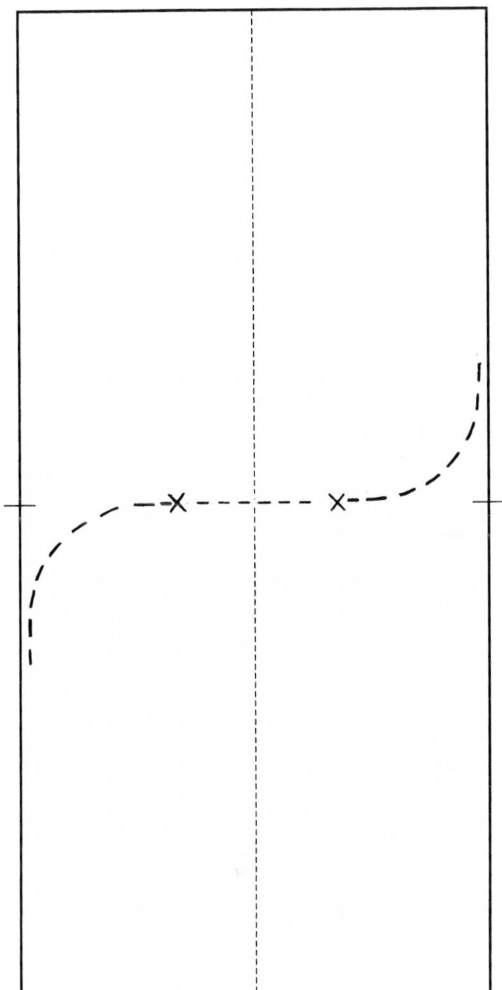

Patterns for introducing simple changes.

TROUBLESHOOTING

He won't go directly from halt to trot – there are always walk steps in between

1. Ensure that he is paying attention at halt – little vibrations on the reins or small squeezes with your lower legs should help recover it.

2. Aid more sharply – kick him or use your whip when he doesn't go. Don't delay – apply the aids strongly immediately he ignores you and don't worry about his outline this once – throw your hands forward and lose contact completely so he has no excuse for not going.

3. Establish another halt. This time, ask nicely. If he goes, great. If he doesn't, *within one stride*, aid strongly again. He must believe you mean it.
4. Repeat this procedure every time he ignores you and soon he will start to cooperate. Once he goes directly into trot most times you can start taking care of his outline and reducing your aids to something more elegant and sophisticated!

He doesn't change cleanly from walk to canter: either he shuffles his feet or he jogs a couple of steps

1. Check your timing (see p.213).
2. Make sure that you have enough activity in the walk – he should feel as if he is about to spring out of the walk before you consider asking.
3. You may need to use a stronger leg aid (or back it up with your whip) a time or two, until he is convinced that you mean it.
4. Make sure that you are giving one clean, crisp aid – not taking your outside leg back too early and pressing it on him for too long.
5. Ensure that you are not dropping your rein contact.
6. He must be relaxed and in a genuinely round outline – if he is hollow or tense over his back this will block the transition.

He hollows in the transitions

Review the same problem in Chapter 7, p.80.

If the hollowing is only in his walk to canter, check:

1. That you have enough activity in the walk for him to be able to make the transition without using his head and neck to lift his shoulders.
2. That you are asking at the correct moment in the stride (see above, p.213). If you ask at the wrong moment he may throw his head up in anxiety because he is unable to do what you ask.
3. If you are happy that the points above do not apply, and he still persists, try putting him deeper, almost overbent, *before* you ask – then when his head comes up, it only moves into a correct position.

He becomes anxious when he knows I am going to ask for walk to canter, and he loses his walk rhythm

You will need lots of time and patience. Never reprimand him, as you will only increase his anxiety. Instead, when he starts to jog:

1. Turn him onto a small circle – anything between 10 and 6 m, depending on his size and suppleness.
2. Ask him to drop his head and work in a deeper outline to relax his back muscles.
3. Keep him walking around this small circle until his rhythm is clear and he relaxes.
4. Once you have this, ask him for canter next time you approach the track and continue on straight in the canter. Alternatively you can go onto a 20 m circle.

Never pull him up to a halt – this will also increase his anxiety. Do not become strong in your contact – use upper leg closure to help slow him down, always being quick to relax your legs once he is in a clear walk rhythm, as this will help him to relax. If you repeat this procedure many times he will gradually learn to be relaxed about the transitions and you will be able to start doing them without the small circle.

He 'runs through the bridle' in direct downward transitions, leaning onto my hands and not going directly from one gait to the next

- Are you certain his balance and engagement are sufficient for him to do these transitions? You may be attempting them too soon.
- Review simple downward transitions – does he clearly understand the requirements to yield to the contact and bring his hind legs under his body? This is even more important when missing out a gait.
- Make more half-halts (vibrations) with your reins to keep the bit moving so he cannot lean on it.
- Are you using enough leg? He must step under to support himself so that he doesn't need to use your hands as a prop. Remember that your legs should both be slightly back (parallel to each other) for trot to halt.
- Try small upward half-halts (tiny flicks upward from the wrist only) to discourage him from lowering his head.
- Use the school fence: make your transition face on to the fence and quite close (see diagram, p.80) – he will be unlikely to run into it, and if he does, he won't do it again!

He hollows and goes against my hand in direct downward transitions

See: *He hollows in (downward) transitions*, Chapter 7, p.83 and review these corrections.

He won't go directly from canter to walk – he always jogs a few steps

First ask yourself whether he is ready to do this. He must have a fair degree of balance and the ability to collect the canter a little before this transition should be attempted. He must also be strong enough in the haunches and supple in his back or he will find it uncomfortable.

If you feel he is physically capable, then:

- Review your aiding – see p.215.
- Try greater body tone to increase the depth of your seat.
- Use a more exaggerated swing back of your outside shoulder – you can refine this when his understanding is clearer.
- Try to make the transition to halt – then simply relax just before he stops, allowing him to walk on. Exaggeration in your mind can make your aids clearer.
- Point him more directly at the fence (see diagram, p.80) – just make sure it is high enough that he won't be tempted to jump it!

He is very tense/unclear in his walk rhythm after the transition down from canter

Causes of this are:

1. You were too strong with your hands and so made the transition uncomfortable.
2. He stiffened his back (probably because your contact was too strong) so the transition was uncomfortable.

3. You are too tense in your legs/back/seat/hands.

4. He knows there is an upward transition coming soon (e.g. to canter in simple change) and is excited.

Once you have ensured that he is comfortable in the transition by being more relaxed yourself, you should take a long-term approach to establish his relaxation: every time you make this transition, as soon as you achieve walk push your hands forward and lengthen the reins to put him into free walk on a long rein. Stay in free walk for as long as he needs to become relaxed.

Once you can achieve this, try riding a 20 m circle in canter at E or B and make your downward transition in the last stride of the circle as you approach the marker, then ride a 10 m circle in medium walk. The bend and engagement of the small circle will help to contain any tendency to rush/jog, and you will find it easier to put your inside leg on to ride him forward in the walk.

Clearly, you cannot do this in competition, but if you take the time to do it at home he will become relaxed and will be confident to walk away from the transition in a good outline and rhythm that will eventually become habitual.

He swings his quarters in simple changes

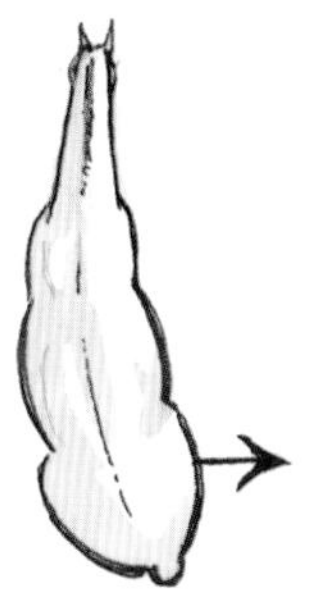

If he is not tense, then you are almost certainly over-riding. Check that:

1. You are not unbalancing him by leaning over to make sure he goes onto the new leading leg.

2. You are not taking the new inside rein too strongly when you ask for flexion – this will cause you to lose control of his outside.

3. You are paying enough attention/giving him enough time to straighten in the walk steps before asking for the new flexion and then canter.

In simple changes, his walk steps are not clear

1. Take more time: anxious riders rush transitions and simply fail to allow time for the walk steps.

2. If his steps are not clear because of tension, go back to canter to walk transitions and stay in walk (on a longish rein) for as long as he needs to relax. See *He is very tense/unclear in his walk rhythm* above and do not pursue simple changes until he is more relaxed.

18 Square Halts and Rein-back

Square Halts

Until now you should have been satisfied with an immobile halt regardless of where the horse's feet were positioned; to achieve a *square* halt with both hind legs engaged under his body requires his understanding of your aids to be a little more sophisticated. Until he can stand immobile at halt, in a steady outline, relaxed yet attentive to you, don't even *think* about trying to square him up.

> **BUILDING BLOCKS**
>
> The building blocks for a square halt are:
>
> - Acceptance of the driving aids.
> - Acceptance of restraining aids.
> - A degree of straightness.
> - Correct response to half-halts (i.e. a rebalancing towards the hindquarters with lowering of the croup – see Techniques, p.37).
> - Response of an individual hind leg to a leg aid on that specific side (started with turn around the forehand).

Requirements

1. That the horse stands relaxed and immobile, with his attention on you.
2. That his weight is balanced over all four feet.
3. That his legs are placed squarely, with his hind legs engaged beneath him (i.e. not trailing behind the point of his buttock) to a degree that accords with his level of training.

4. That his outline is consistent into, during and out of the halt.

5. The transitions in and out of the halt should be smooth, balanced and engaged, with no resistance or stiffening.

Aids

The basic aids for halt were outlined in Chapter 17 under Trot to Halt (p.214). To produce the square halt:

1. Take great care of your horse's straightness as you gradually restrain his forehand (half-halts and closure of your thighs) whilst asking his back end to keep stepping under by positioning both your lower legs back slightly and closing them in a steady but light squeeze. Lift your diaphragm (see photograph p.72) to drop your weight more onto the back of your seat and hold your pelvis still.

2. Make sure that your contact on both sides feels the same – this is essential for the forefeet to stop square.

3. Close your lower legs with equal strength. If you feel him swinging his quarters one way use the leg on that side slightly further back and/or with more strength (you must experiment to find out what works with your individual) until he is straight again.

4. If he tries to swing crooked, keep the transition going until you have him straight, then complete it.

5. Once he has stopped, feel how level your hips are – if one is dropped then he is trailing the hind leg on that side.

To correct forefeet that are not square, lighten the contact on the side of the trailing foreleg and squeeze with just the leg on that side. Lightening your contact on one side invites him to step forward to seek the contact and as soon as the foreleg begins the step, close your fingers to equalize the feeling on both sides of his mouth and prevent any more steps. You will need to experiment to find out exactly when to close your fingers – too soon and he will put the foot back down where it was; too late and he will take a full step forward rather than the half step needed to bring it level with the other foreleg.

To correct hind legs that are not square, keep your contact equal and squeeze with just the leg on the side of the trailing hind. Keep your other leg passively against his ribs. If he has understood his earlier lessons he will lift the trailing hind leg and move it forward – he won't step sideways because you haven't asked for bend and your other leg is against his ribs to discourage sideways movement.

When correcting halts, always ask the horse to step forward – never correct backwards.

Once you have achieved the square halt, relax your legs and arms, easing your hands slightly forward. Relax inside and breathe!

Prior to moving off, ensure that you have your horse's attention by lightly vibrating one or both reins before applying your legs.

Training Value

1. Square halts have both hind legs engaged equally under the body – thus building suppleness and strength equally.
2. By stepping both hind legs forward and under, the horse lowers his croup and so lightens his forehand.
3. They develop more sophisticated responses.

CAUTION: *never punish a horse for making a mistake in halt* – you will make him anxious and ruin future halts. Consider what went wrong in the approach and take care of that next time. Patience and good riding will eventually establish them.

Rein-back

Rein-back should always be used as a gymnastic exercise, never as a punishment. To gain value from rein-back the horse must be relaxed both mentally and physically, and always willing or even keen to go forward following the exercise.

BUILDING BLOCKS

The building blocks for rein-back are:

- Acceptance of your forward-driving aids.
- A calm, yielding acceptance of your contact.
- A degree of suppleness of the horse's hind legs and lower back.
- Shoulder-fore – necessary for you to be able to control the positioning of his shoulders relative to his haunches, should his natural crookedness cause him to step back crookedly.

Requirements

That the horse:

1. Steps backwards with synchronized diagonal pairs of legs.
2. Takes the same length of stride back with each pair.
3. Takes a fair length of stride back.
4. Lifts his feet clear of the ground, not dragging them back.
5. Takes calm and unhurried (but not reluctant) steps back.
6. Moves back straight.
7. Bends his hind leg joints and lowers his croup.
8. Maintains a soft contact and round outline, with his poll the highest point throughout the rein-back and the transitions in and out.
9. Moves eagerly forward again as soon as asked.

Aids

1. Establish an attentive halt.
2. Keeping your upper body toned, incline forward *very slightly* from your hips (not your waist) to lighten your seat slightly.
3. Move both your legs a little back, until both are in 'outside leg' positions.
4. Keeping your elbows low, close your fingers (both hands equally) on the reins to disallow forward motion and at the same time close your lower legs.
5. As the horse takes his first step back, relax your fingers until you have just the weight of the reins in your hands, but without allowing the reins to drop into slack loops. He should continue to step backward until you return your weight to your seat – any excess contact will result in tension and hollowing. If he hesitates or is confused, you may need to make another closure of your fingers before each step, but always relax them as soon as he moves back.
6. Reluctance should be met with more insistent (slightly larger) leg aids, *not* with a stronger rein contact.

To end the backward movement, bring your upper body vertical to replace the weight in your seat and move your legs forward into 'inside leg' position. If you then want to:

halt – close your fingers. If there is any tension in his mouth, vibrate both reins (equally, not alternately).

walk forward – close your lower legs gently. You should already have the soft, allowing contact so you should not need to yield your reins forward more than a fraction.

trot forward – as for walk, but with a slightly stronger leg aid and add the 'springing up' feeling to your seat to lift him into the trot.

Patterns and Outside Assistance

1. If you are trying to teach the horse on your own, start by halting him facing and quite close to a fence. This will help him understand that he cannot walk forward *through* your contact when you close your legs. By using the aids as described with the psychological help from the fence, he should quickly associate those aids with stepping backward. When teaching him initially, also use the vocal command 'Back' that was taught in the handling phases. As soon as he takes a step back, praise him with your voice and a quick touch on his neck. Do not ask for more than one or two steps the first few times.
2. Once he associates your aids with stepping back, next ask him on the track, alongside a fence. Most horses will swing their quarters one way, so at this stage put him with the fence on the side he likes to swing towards, to restrict how far he can deviate from being straight. Begin to ask for three or four steps, not just two.
3. If you have someone on the ground to help, you can dispense with step 1 and start in the track. Once your halt is established, have your helper stand close to the horse's shoulder (but not directly in front – always remember that horses can strike forward with a foreleg, especially stallions). As you apply the aids, have your helper press a hand against the middle of his chest and use the vocal command 'Back'.
4. As he steps back more readily your helper can dispense with the hand, just using their presence and the vocal command. Gradually phase both of these out.
5. Later, when you are in more control of his straightness (as a result of more equality in the suppleness of his two sides, or after corrections – see *Troubleshooting*, this chapter) you will begin to ask for rein-back in the centre of the school, even on the centre line as asked for in more advanced tests.
6. Initially, a really round top-line is important – even if he goes a bit deep – as he will only take correct steps back if he is truly 'through' his top-line.
7. Eventually you will ask him to keep his poll and shoulders higher, using a fractionally more upward direction to your contact, and only the tiniest lightening of your seat, but this must never be done at the expense of a rounded top-line or you will damage the quality of his steps.

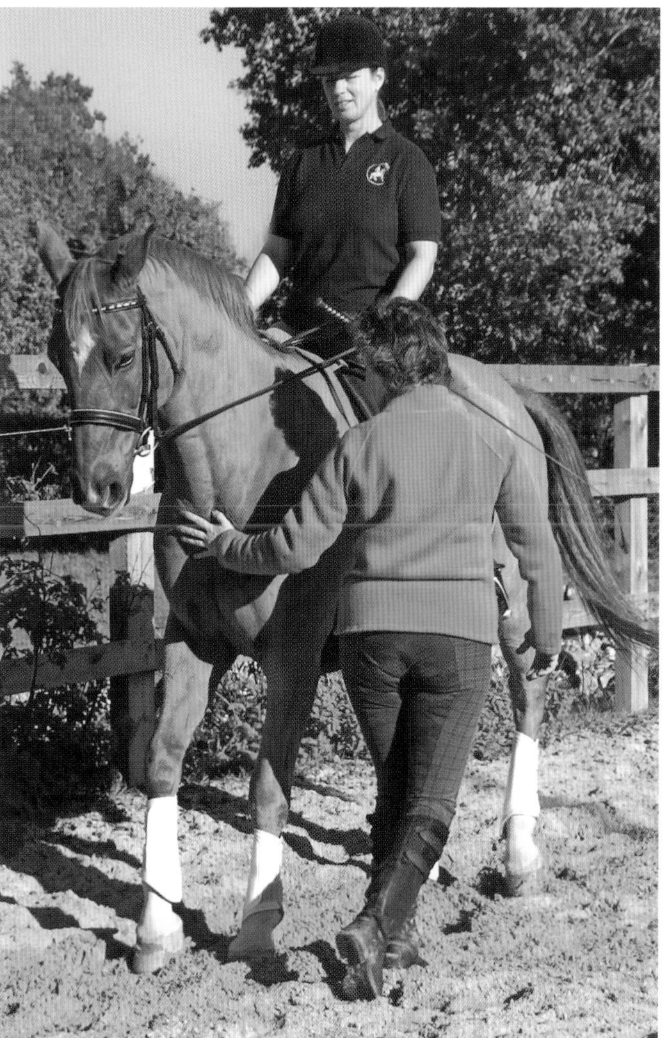

Rein-back with assistance from the ground. Notice that Nikki is positioned out of reach of any hooves.

Training Value

1. Increases understanding and acceptance of your aids.
2. A direct method of flexing the horse's hind legs to lower his croup.
3. Increases suppleness of his back and hind leg joints.
4. Combined with forward transitions, is a great technique for increasing the strength of his hindquarters.
5. A diagnostic tool for assessing straightness!

CAUTION: rein-back must not be used excessively during early training, as it would be easy to damage underdeveloped or weak back or haunch muscles, and it should *never* be used as punishment.

TROUBLESHOOTING

He won't stand still in halt

Horses in the wild rarely stand still unless sleeping, so ridden halts can make them anxious. Being asked to stand still and stay 'on the aids' makes them feel restricted, so try to be as light and sensitive as you can without totally removing your aids. Once in halt, relax as far as possible and only make corrections to straightness by allowing him to step slightly forward, never by pushing his quarters to the side.

If he is young or nervous, talk to him. While you cannot do this in competition, you can help him come to terms with standing still when working at home, and so develop the habit.

Experiment to find at which end of a schooling session he is more likely to stand still: if he has lots of energy it may be near the end; if he is nervous it may be near the start, before his nerves have kicked in. Until he is calmer, only practise halts during the 'good' time, and allow them to be fairly brief, building the habit of standing still gradually.

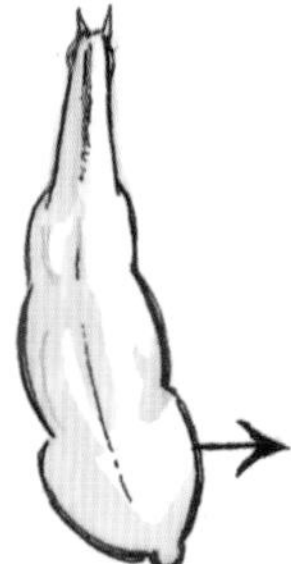

He always swings his quarters to one side when asked to halt

1. First, check your preparation: an unbalanced approach can cause this.
2. Stiffness over his back can make it hard for him to step his hind legs under, causing his quarters to go to one side. Eliminate physical causes first, and then target the suppleness of his back with lateral bending exercises and more frequent transitions.
3. This may suggest a lingering crookedness that must be addressed in all his schooling, not just the halts.
4. During halts (as discussed on p.225) you may need to use your leg on the side to which he swings further back, or with more strength than your other leg, to prevent this.
5. For schooling purposes at home, ride all your halts on the track alongside the fence, with the fence on the side towards which he swings – this will limit how far he can move his quarters and help develop the habit of halting straight.
6. Try approaching and making halts in shoulder-fore. If his quarters always swing to the right, ride shoulder-fore right before and during the halt so that when his quarters move over, he ends up straight. This is a perfectly valid and successful long-term solution as it not only builds the habit of standing straight with his weight equally distributed on both sides; it directly addresses his crookedness by positioning his shoulders in front of his haunches during the downward transition.

He doesn't stop square in front

This suggests an unequal rein contact – the side that is stronger will prevent the foreleg on that side from completing its last step.

During a halt:

- Concentrate on the weight you have in your two hands – do you have more in one than the other?
- Try to determine *who* is taking the stronger contact: you or him. Be honest with yourself. If you are really unsure, ask someone more experienced to sit on him to feel his contact.
- Approach your next halt with the stronger side deliberately pushed forward to lighten it – you will need to keep him straight with your legs and body position.
- If he still halts with the foreleg back (habit), use the technique described on p.225 to move the leg forward. Over time, you should be able to establish a new habit.
- You may notice that his halts are not square in front even without a rider – in this case work with him in hand, halting then lifting the foreleg and placing it square. This will also help form a new habit.

He always trails the same hind leg in halt

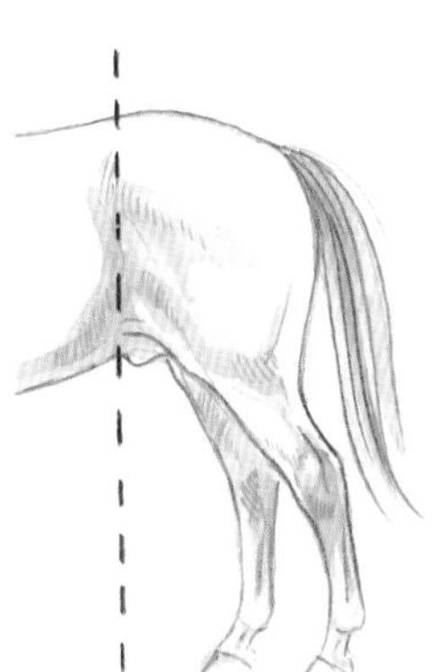

This tells you he is unwilling to step that hind leg under his body and you should try to determine why:

- Is he sore in the back or hind leg?
- Is that hind leg stiff? This could be either a physical problem or a schooling issue.
- Is that hind weak or lazy, therefore unwilling to bear weight?
- Do you use a stronger contact on one side, which inhibits his hind on that side from stepping forward?

Having eliminated physical issues and reviewed your aiding, if he still leaves that leg behind you need to:

- Approach halt with a few stronger leg aids on the appropriate side to activate that hind leg before halting. Be sure to keep your legs parallel so he does not lose straightness.
- Use a stronger leg on that side during your halt aids. Take care of his straightness.
- If he still trails the leg, give him a tap with your schooling whip just before completing your halt. If this causes him to swing his quarters, repeat the process, but with a fence on the appropriate side.

- Someone on the ground can also help teach a new habit by touching him on the trailing leg with a groundwork whip and insisting that he lifts and moves the offending hind leg forward. (A groundwork whip is as long as a lunge whip, but without the long lash – this enables you to tap his legs from beyond kicking range!)

Correcting a trailing leg in halt. Nikki has touched *Merlin* on the outside of his second thigh. You will need to find where your horse is most sensitive – probably somewhere on the back of the hind leg, anywhere from just below his buttock right down to his pastern.

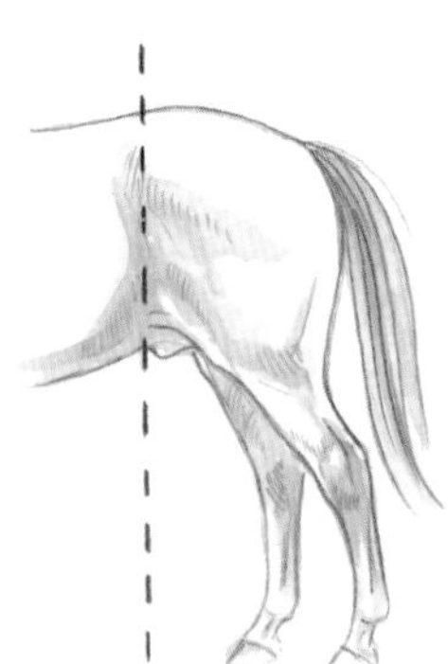

He trails both hind legs in halt (is disengaged)

This could be a result of:

- Conformation – if he is built with his hind legs out behind him you can only reasonably ask him to step a little more forward with his hind legs without causing him discomfort.
- Stiffness in his back. See *He always swings his quarters…* point 2, p.230.
- Lack of engagement in the preparation for coming into the halt – use more leg and less hand during the approaching steps.
- Too strong a contact.
- Hollowing or lack of submission (see Chapter 10).
- Weakness of his back.
- Poor habit.

Once you have determined and corrected the cause, one exercise you can try to help improve habit/strength, is that of rein-back to halt. In other words, rein-back then halt without moving forward – this asks him to get used to standing still with his croup lowered and his back raised. It doesn't matter in the short term if the halt is not square; as his steps backward will be in diagonal pairs he will inevitably have one hind leg further back than the other when you stop. If he offers to square up by taking a *half step* forward, that is even better and you should allow it, but it is not essential: it is the lowering effect on the hindquarters that you are after.

You can also use repeated halting on downhill slopes – he will have no alternative but to step under to balance himself.

He rests a hind leg in halt

Unless there is a physical problem making him sore, he is inattentive or lazy. (Certainly, you want him to be relaxed enough to stand still, but resting a leg is a bit *too* relaxed.)

You should be able to feel him resting – the saddle will drop away from under your seat on that side. Squeeze slightly with your lower leg on the *opposite* side to the resting hind. This asks him to lift the hind he is standing on. If you are quick enough to relax your aid before it lifts clear of the ground, he will have put weight back onto the resting one and will now be standing on both.

He won't go backward

Horses who are very stiff in the back or hind legs find rein-back uncomfortable. Some with certain physical conditions may find it impossible.

First ask him to step back without a rider to confirm that he physically can move back.

Once you know he can, re-cover the steps of teaching him with someone on the ground to help you (p.228). While he may find it difficult, the whole point of the exercise is that it will improve the suppleness of his back and haunches, thus making it easier for him in the long run.

If he is anxious, take plenty of time; ask just a step or two at a time and allow him to move forward if he becomes agitated.

He hollows in rein-back

This is usually caused by too strong a rein contact. If he does not step back without a strong hand you need to review the whole process of teaching rein-back outlined above.

Hollowing can also be caused by lack of strength/suppleness over the back, or by too heavy a weight in the saddle. Check that you are lightening your seat, and that he is physically capable of performing what you are asking (see above – *He won't go backward*).

Occasionally this may be a genuine resistance. If so, then put him over-deep before you ask so that when he lifts his head it comes up into place, instead of above the bit.

He rushes backward

This is most commonly caused by anxiety.

Ask for one step at a time and then walk forward. When he accepts a single step calmly, ask for two then forward. Gradually increase the number of steps until he steps back calmly each time.

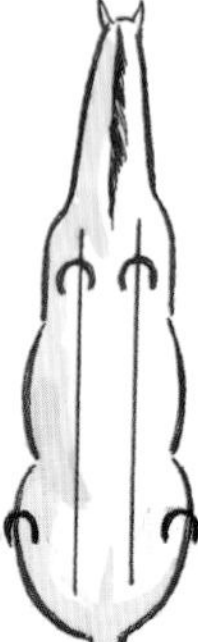

He goes wide behind in rein-back

This is caused by lack of strength or suppleness, or an avoidance of bending his hind legs.

As ever, check his soundness first.

If lack of strength is the issue, leave the movement alone for a while or you risk establishing a habit you will find impossible to change later. Concentrate instead on strengthening him with hill work, pole work and lots of transitions. Only start asking again when he can make a step or two without spreading his hind legs.

Suppleness problems mean that you need to work him in a longer, rounder outline for a while and use exercises to increase the longitudinal suppleness of his back. Ride small circles, turn around the forehand and leg-yielding in this deeper frame to improve his lateral suppleness which, in turn, will improve his longitudinal suppleness provided he remains genuinely 'through' his back during the exercises.

If he is avoiding bending his hind legs, make just a couple of steps at a time before walking forward so he doesn't find the exercise too tough. As his hind legs become suppler you will be able to ask for more correct steps. You can also perform rein-back between two parallel ground poles (about 1 m apart, depending on his body width) and raised slightly off the ground. (You can buy small plastic blocks for this purpose, or make wooden ones with a 'V' cut in the top to hold the pole securely in place.) These will prevent him from stepping to the side. You *can* use poles placed on the ground, but he is more likely to step over these, or potentially trip on them, so make sure that you are not alone when you do this.

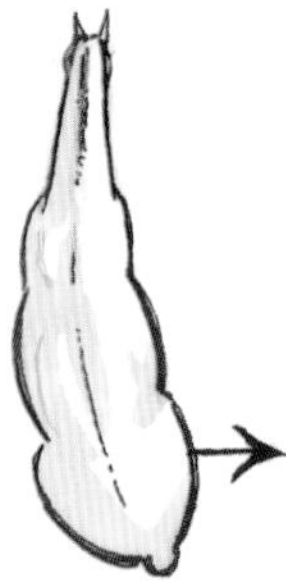

He swings his quarters sideways in rein-back

Stiffness and his natural crookedness contribute to this, as can asking for rein-back from a crooked halt.

Focus on improving both these aspects, and when you do ask for rein-back, position him alongside a fence with the fence on the side towards which he swings. This limits how crookedly he can move and helps establish a good habit of stepping back straight. Alternatively, use the raised poles described above.

You can also start by halting in a slight shoulder-fore position, with his shoulders moved to the side towards which he swings his quarters. As he steps back he will become straight. Over time, as he becomes more genuinely straight in all his work, you will need to position his shoulders gradually less to the side, as his haunches will become less likely to swing.

He drags his feet back

This is usually a result of pulling on the reins, causing him to evade by going too deep, or hollow.

Review your aiding, keeping your rein contact as light as possible. You may need to go back to using help from the ground for a while so that you can achieve more subtlety in your contact.

1. If he is confirmed in going deep, try actively raising his head with upward half-halts before you ask so that any downward movement of his head and neck does not go as far as overbending.
2. If he is confirmed in hollowing, take the time to put him too deep before asking, and ensure that your seat is lightened enough to allow him to lift and round his back as he steps backward.

His steps are too short

To encourage him to take longer steps make sure that he is really round before you ask, and keep the backward steps slow and deliberate; the main contributing factors to short steps are hollowness and rushing. If either of these is also occurring, see the appropriate section above.

He is slow to move forward

If he is reluctant, ride vigorously forward a time or two without worrying about outline or a specified gait. Once he has learned that you mean business you can return to finesse and control.

19 Lengthening and Collecting

Lengthening

Lengthening the gaits describes a progressive increase in the size of the horse's strides (ground cover) but not in the speed (i.e. the frequency) of his footfalls. Lengthening should not be introduced until the working gaits are fully established.

There are two important concepts to grasp before you can achieve correct lengthening:

1. Without correct and adequate preparation (a secure outline, a straight and balanced horse, and increased impulsion) lengthening is impossible.
2. While impulsion is the responsibility of your legs, your seat asks for lengthening.

Some horses show natural ability to lengthen, but others have to be taught. While certain conformations – upright shoulders, croup-high – can limit the ability to truly extend, most horses can be taught to show at least a little difference in stride length.

BUILDING BLOCKS

The building blocks for lengthening are:

- A well-established rhythm.
- Straightness.
- A degree of balance (lightness of forehand).
- Correct response to forward-driving aids and working easily with a fair amount of impulsion.
- Acceptance of half-halts.

Requirements

1. That the horse's strides become longer (cover more ground) without becoming quicker (more frequent).
2. That his strides show the same, or greater, suspension than in the working gait (i.e. they don't become flatter).
3. That his strides are regular, with both hind legs pushing equally and both forelegs taking steps of even height and length.
4. That he stays straight.
5. That his hind legs do not move wider apart than in his working gaits.
6. That his outline becomes a little longer.
7. That his neck should lower slightly but his withers should not drop (i.e. he should not fall onto the forehand).
8. That his balance and rhythm should be maintained, especially as he returns to the working gait after lengthening (i.e. he should not take quicker steps to rebalance himself).

Aids

Rising Trot

1. *Preparation is important:* have your horse moving in a balanced, energetic trot in a good outline before you even think about attempting lengthening; throwing him at it with any of these features missing will only doom you to failure and may damage his confidence. You may also teach him to lengthen in an incorrect fashion that will be hard for him to unlearn.
2. Through a short side, ask for more impulsion with a stronger inside leg aid. If he tries to speed up, restrain him with closed fingers on the reins and a slight closure of your upper legs to allow you to rise at your own speed, not the one he wants.
3. Coming out of the second corner of the short side, straighten him onto your chosen line and ask him to lengthen by:
   - Swinging your hips higher and further forward at each stride, but not faster.
   - Squeezing both lower legs quite strongly but in time with your rising.
   - Pushing your hands a little forward and down to encourage him to lengthen his frame slightly.

When you wish to return to the working gait, in order to reduce the length of his strides, close your upper legs a little more and reduce the height of your rising but keep a rhythmic squeezing with your lower legs to ask his hind legs to step further under (to rebalance). If necessary use a little vibration down both reins: never use rigid or strong hands – this will only make him stiffen and block his hind legs from stepping forward under. If you are coming into a corner then vibrate just the inside rein.

Sitting Trot

Only try this once he is strong enough in his back to support you, and then only if you have a genuinely secure seat.

1. Prepare as for rising trot, above.

2. Ask by increasing the horizontal swing of your pelvis along the saddle combined with stronger leg aids. Your seat must be independent enough for you to move it *at your own speed* as opposed to any other speed he offers you. Remember to offer your hands a little forward and down.

To return to the working gait, reduce his length of stride by using your legs and contact as above and swinging your seat in a smaller motion.

Canter

1. Prepare as for trot, above.

2. If your horse is active enough in the preceding canter, you should only need to offer your hands a *little* forward and he will be keen to lengthen. Regulate the size and speed of his strides by increasing the horizontal movement of your seat along the saddle, making sure that you do not move it any faster. Keep your body upright as you do so – leaning forward will drop him onto his forehand.

3. Monitor his straightness – many horses swing their hindquarters to the inside in lengthened canter. Use a little shoulder-fore positioning (see Chapter 16; also *He travels haunches-in in canter*, p.174) to keep his shoulders in front of his haunches.

4. Continued 'jump' is important – his strides should not flatten. This is the job of your inside leg used rhythmically once in every stride.

To return to the working gait, reduce the size of his strides by holding (without tensing) your seat to a smaller action and use your legs as for reducing the trot – with particular attention to a rhythmic and clear lower leg aid, or he may lose the canter. You may also need to make small vibrations on the inside rein, but as soon as working canter is re-established give a small release of contact to confirm and approve his answer.

Walk

Walk will be the last of the three gaits that you will ask to lengthen. The walk we ride on a daily basis is medium walk; unlike trot and canter we do not ride working walk. Choosing when to introduce extended walk will depend on your horse's balance: he must be able to lengthen his strides without falling onto his forehand. The most obvious indicator of loss of balance in walk is tripping.

Extended walk is ridden very much like free walk on a long rein, with just a slightly shorter rein length. As in the other gaits, encourage your horse to lengthen his strides by increasing the horizontal movement of your seat along the saddle (without increasing the speed of your movement) and by pushing your hands a little forward and down. The most important ingredient in extended walk is relaxation, so his whole frame lengthens and he moves through his whole body – he should look like a panther slinking along. In contrast to the other gaits you can allow him to lower and lengthen his neck quite a lot, just keeping enough rein contact to maintain a round frame.

To return to medium walk, reduce the size of your seat movement (being certain not to tense your buttock muscles) and gradually shorten your reins, using the 'D' shaped action described on p.34. Use your legs alternately to help him maintain the activity in his walk sequence, with more or less strength depending on his sensitivity.

Priorities

When riding medium gaits you must prioritize in the following order:

1. Genuine roundness of the top-line.
2. Straightness on your line/figure.
3. Balance – not on the forehand.
4. Impulsion.

It is no good worrying about impulsion if the horse is hollow. His balance cannot be right if he is crooked. In other words, this is the order in which to sort out any problems that occur.

Patterns

Lengthening can be taught on straight lines or circles once you have determined which your horse finds easier. The following exercises will suit different horses so try them until you find one yours likes.

1. Some will find it easier to begin lengthening on the lunge without a rider's weight to disturb their balance. Having established a good trot rhythm, encourage him to take longer strides by using your voice. Say 'Trot – trot – trot', or click

your tongue in the same rhythm but louder and raise the whip or even flick it towards him. If he is listening to you he should take his rhythm from your voice so the extra energy will produce bigger strides, not hurried ones.

2. Establish him on the lunge circle as above, then allow him to go several strides straight along the long side (you will have to take big steps or run a little), encouraging him as above. The open long side in front of him may help encourage him to stride out for a few steps before you ask him to circle again.

3. When teaching lengthening, initially ask for only two or three strides at a time. The moment he loses balance and begins to run, slow down, rebalance and ask again. This is easy on the circle because you have a continuous curve so you can ask him at any point. If he is correctly bent, the direction of his forefeet will be towards the inside of the circle, and hind feet toward the outside, courtesy of the alignment of his shoulders and hips to the bend, illustrated in the accompanying diagram. (The arrows indicate the *directions* in which his feet will travel, *not* the distance.)

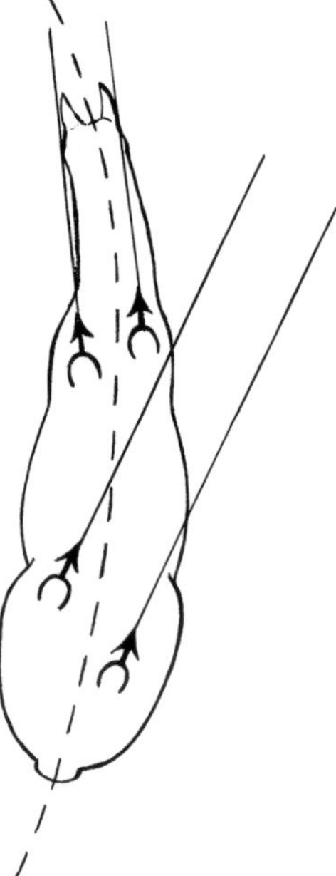

The alignment of the horse's shoulders and hips to the circle, demonstrating the direction in which his feet will be pointing.

This means that his hind feet will be in no danger of striking his forefeet, so he may be more willing to try. (Lengthening in canter provides no such conflict because of the nature of the canter sequence.)

4. Starting from a spiral or from a small leg-yield (quarter line to track) is another option; the engaging effect of the sideways steps can help you build the energy you need.

5. Horses gain psychological support from fences, so ask initially on a straight line along the track. Again, only ask a few steps at a time, taking time to build up as

he understands and gains balance and confidence. This can be two or three sessions with some, two or three *years* with another. Have patience. Much depends on his confidence in his ability to balance. Rushing things at the start can ruin lengthening forever.

6. When he can lengthen comfortably on a long side, try on a diagonal. Use the preceding corner to increase energy then build the lengthened strides gradually and return to the working gait the same way. Do not expect him to lengthen for the whole diagonal just yet – that comes later.

7. Once he is established in shoulder-in you can use this at the start and finish to improve the transitions in and out of lengthening – ride four or five steps of shoulder-in at the start of a long side (this engages his hind legs); straighten him to the track and ask him to lengthen; finish by turning his shoulders inward and driving him forward into shoulder-in. This teaches both of you to collect by driving, not attempting to do so by 'putting on the brakes'.

8. When you ride lengthened strides, *think* of riding the bigger strides slower (like long passage), and the collected strides faster. This counteracts the tendency to hurry in lengthening and slow into collection, both of which are wrong. Using this mindset, your end result will be the same tempo in both.

9. Use a small circle to help you return to the working gait from lengthened canter – this will absorb the extra impulsion into engagement (the circle places his inside hind further under his body) rather than risking losing it by 'putting the brakes on'.

Training Value

The training value in lengthening is found in the transitions at either end, known as *transitions within the gait*. The initial gradual increase and decrease of stride length will, in time, become clear transitions into and out of medium and extended gaits.

Transitions within the gait ask the horse to flex and lower his croup, thereby increasing engagement, which builds strength and flexibility of his hind leg joints and helps him work more 'uphill', i.e. lightens his forehand.

They also demand ever-improving speed of reaction to your driving aids (upward) and restraining aids (downward).

Progression

1. As your horse becomes more established in the medium strides, you will gradually ask for them across whole diagonals or down complete long sides.

2. Next, you will need to show clearer transitions at start and finish (i.e., a less gradual change to and from the medium gait), but this cannot be hurried, especially the transition down at the end, where the potential for stiffening is huge until the horse is really supple, strong and balanced.

3. After this comes a greater increase in the length of the strides, leading toward full extension (the longest strides that the horse can do whilst retaining rhythm and balance.)

4. At about this stage you also need to be asking him to travel more 'uphill', – carrying more weight on his hindquarters as well as pushing – brought about by an increased ability to collect (see next section). You will need to indicate to him the need to stay 'uphill' in his extensions by pressing your hands *slightly* upward as well as forward – it is almost a *feeling* as opposed to an action, just indicating a direction. He will only reach this stage when he is strong enough – about the time he begins Medium level dressage work.

Collection

Collection involves the horse carrying more weight on his hindquarters and less on his shoulders, which he achieves by stepping his hind legs further forward underneath his body and flexing all three hind leg joints. The results are a taller, shorter posture and that his strides (in all gaits) gain height and as a consequence cover less ground.

Collection is *not* an artificial shortening of the frame and strides by using the reins to pull him together and restrict his action.

BUILDING BLOCKS

The building blocks of collection are:

- Suppleness in all the horse's joints.
- An advanced degree of straightness.
- A forward attitude.
- Good impulsion.
- Good acceptance of both restraining and driving aids.
- Strong stomach, back and haunch muscles.

Requirements

1. That the horse's hind legs step further forward beneath his body with well flexed joints (engagement).
2. That he remains straight.
3. That both hind legs continue to lift to the same height as each other.
4. That both hind legs step forward equally.
5. That his strides gain height, and in trot and canter gain greater suspension (expression).
6. That his outline appears shorter, with his neck rising unrestrained out of lifted withers in a harmonious curve from withers to poll, which is the highest point, with his face slightly in front of the vertical.

The degree of collection you should ask for depends on his level of training and, to some extent, his conformation. Not all horses will be physically able to achieve a great amount of collection, but when required in competition it need only be sufficient to perform the stipulated movements with ease.

Preparatory Exercises

A horse's ability to collect will develop gradually out of the schooling process as his stomach, back and haunch muscles become stronger, and is brought about largely by:

- Correctly ridden transitions between the gaits: trot-walk-trot, trot-canter-trot and later, walk-canter-walk, all of these repeated frequently.
- Frequent transitions within the gaits.
- Voltes.
- Shoulder-in.
- Half-halts: at about this stage in his work, you can begin to use half-halts (p.37) not just as a means of re-balancing after a loss of balance, or as preparation for movements, but as a direct means of asking him to carry more weight behind.

Aids

These were described in Chapter 3 under 'half-halt'.

By now you should be able to accomplish your half-halts over no more than two or three strides, and as you start to use them directly to produce collection you will find they will become effective when applied during a single stride, or even (at very high levels of training) two to a stride.

Later, all the more advanced lateral movements will further develop collection.

Training Value

1. To further develop and increase the horse's balance.
2. To increase his ability to lower and engage his haunches and, as a result, lighten and mobilize his forehand.
3. To increase the comfort of his ride: a collected horse is easier for the rider to maintain balance and a deep seat on.
4. He will have more power instantly available.
5. He will respond to lighter aids.
6. Many of the more advanced movements are impossible to perform without collection.

Collection should be started around the beginning of the third full year of training (if you have been consistent, and your horse is strong and supple enough), or when he begins to work on Medium level movements. Although some collected gaits are asked for in Elementary tests, you should not try to get more than you need to perform the movements, and as you should always be working at least one level above the one you compete in, by the time you ride Elementary tests you should have begun some of the Medium work, so you will already be touching on collection.

TROUBLESHOOTING

He doesn't increase his stride length

- Check his back and the saddle fitting – he must be comfortable to enable lengthening to take place.
- Does his conformation permit lengthening? Some horses are simply not built to do this exercise.
- Is he genuinely round in his outline? He cannot lengthen if he is hollow.
- Are you indicating a clear enough difference with the size of your seat movement? Try exaggerating the swing of your pelvis.
- Does he have enough impulsion before you ask? Use stronger lower leg squeezes whilst restraining with a non-allowing (not pulling back) hand to build some contained energy before you ask.
- Are you allowing a little forward with your hands? He must be able to lengthen his frame slightly in order for his strides to lengthen.

- Is the quality of his trot/canter good enough before you ask – i.e. does it have clear suspension? Lengthening can only occur whilst he is in the air, so if his movement is too flat he's not going to be able to do it. You may need to work on improving the impulsion in his working gaits first to bring them up to the necessary quality.

- Is he balanced enough to be able to achieve lengthening? If he is too much on his forehand, his forefeet will come to the ground too quickly to permit increased stride length. Work more on his balance, using transitions between gaits and half-halts, then try again.

- If he is just lazy or ignoring you, use a sharp tap with a schooling whip – sometimes horses just need to be startled into trying it. In rising trot, time your tap with the moment you start to rise – as his inside hind is lifting from the ground – when you can make the most difference to the flight of that leg.

He runs rather than lengthening

1. Running is generally the result of him wanting to put his forefeet down more quickly than his hind feet to enable him to keep his balance. It may also be down to the rider being in a rush to get it over with!

2. Have his saddle checked – correct fit (not pinching) and balance (seat level) can influence his ability to stay in balance.

3. Check his balance before you ask. If he is too much on his forehand, running is inevitable. Use half-halts (see Techniques, p.37) to help bring his weight further towards his quarters and *only* ask for lengthening when his balance is better. This is essential work to be done at home as you do not have this choice in competition.

4. Are you dropping the rein contact? In the earlier days he needs a fair degree of support from your reins. You must ease your hand forward *a little* to allow his frame to lengthen slightly, but never lose contact altogether or he will fall onto his shoulders and run.

5. Are you speeding up your seat movement? Riders often become anxious and ride hell for leather in the hopes of pleasing a judge – which it won't! Change your mental approach and picture your lengthening as being *slower* than your working gait – longer strides have greater time in the air so lengthening should *feel* as though it happens in slow motion.

6. Are you leaning forward? If so, you put excess weight over his shoulders, just where he doesn't need it for his balance.

7. He may become anxious and run. This is usually a lack of confidence in his own ability to balance, so do not ask for more than three strides at a time until he can do those without hurrying. Gradually increase the number of strides but only as

many as he can do without running. This may take months, so be patient and do not throw away all your work by going out and letting him hurry in competition. Medium trot strides are only one or two marks in a test, so sacrifice those marks in the short term with his future in mind.

8. Work on the suppleness and speed of response of his hind legs – more transitions and lateral work. If his hind legs trail when he attempts to lengthen, he will not be in a position to support his carriage; running will result.

He hollows

A horse cannot lengthen if he hollows: as his back drops, his body will stiffen and his strides will shorten as a result. This is most likely to occur if he was not genuinely 'through' (see Definitions, p.20) before you started, or you are pulling on the reins.

- Make sure that he is totally 'through' in his top-line before you ask.
- Make sure that you are not 'left behind' or you may pull on the reins to assist your own balance. If you have trouble with this, try holding onto a 'balance strap' which fits across the front of the saddle between the two 'D' rings either side of the pommel, or a breastplate.
- You may be subconsciously trying to 'pull him up' because of the extra speed involved: become aware of this and try to relax.
- If your contact is over-strong because the horse is anticipating, use repetitive downward transitions in the place where he expects to start lengthening until he approaches it calmly.

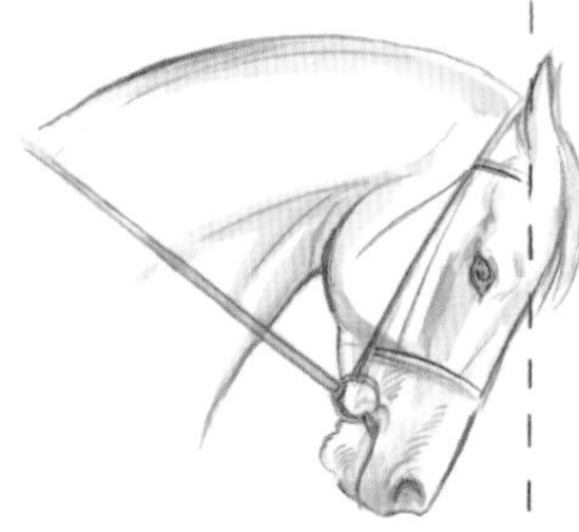

He leans on the bit

His weight is too much on his shoulders, and he may be lazy, using you to carry him instead of doing it for himself.

You need to increase his engagement (through transitions and half-halts) before asking for lengthening then, if he still tries to lean on you, give the reins forward sharply so he loses your support. As horses cherish their balance (see Definitions, p.24) he will quickly change his attitude when he knows that you will not always be there to support him.

He loses rhythm, often falling into canter

Having assured yourself that he is totally sound in limbs and back, and the fit of his saddle is fine, other possibilities are:

1. Lack of straightness on your part – you may be pulling him off balance.
2. Do you lose balance? If you get 'left behind' you will upset his balance. Try using a 'balance strap' or breastplate – see above under *He hollows.*
3. Check the weight in your two hands: stronger contact on one side will inhibit the freedom of one of his shoulders.
4. More straightening and suppling work is needed to make his two sides more equal; he may be pushing harder with one hind leg. Practise leg-yields and shoulder-fore (shoulder-in, if he is capable) and pay great attention to his alignment on all figures.
5. Check his straightness, especially through the preceding corner: he may be carrying his haunches to one side, so he has only one hind leg under his body. Review: *His haunches swing out in turns*, p.94.
6. Did you allow him to totally straighten from the preceding turn before you asked? *Only* ask when he is straight, even if this takes several strides to accomplish.
7. Take greater care with your preparation – use half-halts and focus on his balance both before and during lengthening.
8. If you have eliminated the above and he still does it (he may have one shoulder that is looser than the other), take a slightly stronger contact on the side of the foreleg that gets in advance. While this may limit the degree of lengthening, by disallowing the inequality in front he will not be able to break to canter.

He forges in lengthening

This happens when the front hoof does not quite lift from the ground fast enough for the incoming hind to avoid touching it, and is caused by lack of balance or excess speed.

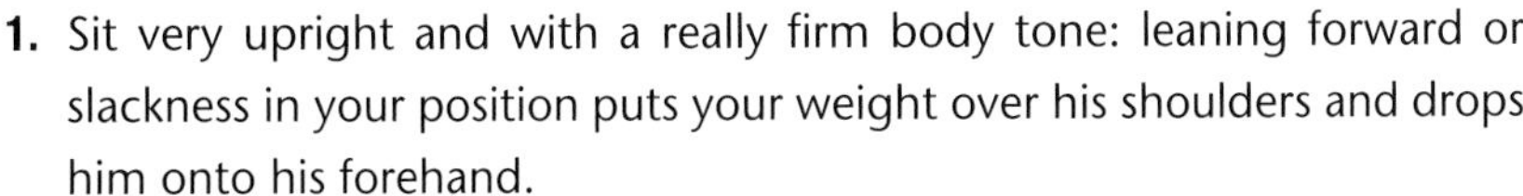

1. Sit very upright and with a really firm body tone: leaning forward or slackness in your position puts your weight over his shoulders and drops him onto his forehand.

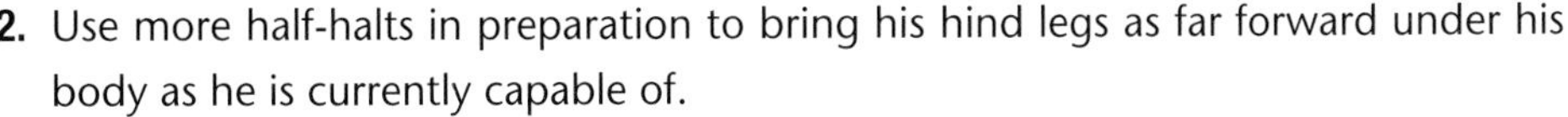

2. Use more half-halts in preparation to bring his hind legs as far forward under his body as he is currently capable of.

3. Check that you are not hurrying him; excess speed will put him onto his forehand.
4. In the short term, moderate the size of medium strides you ask for – as his balance improves you will be able to ask for more.

He goes wide behind

This is caused by asking for lengthening before his hindquarters are strong enough to cope. Once learned, this is a hard habit to eradicate, so reduce your demand immediately and concentrate instead on strengthening exercises: transitions, hill work and small jumps/gridwork.

Try again only when he is stronger, and pay particular attention to keeping his weight off his shoulders – at first, use circles, where it is harder for him to go wide behind.

He takes quicker steps during the transition from medium trot to working trot

This is the result of him stiffening his body, which may be a result of either lack/loss of balance, or an incorrect use of the rein contact (too strong or too rigid).

Start by concentrating on the feel you have in your hands during the transition: if *he* takes a stronger contact, then the issue is one of balance. If *you* are the guilty party, then focus on relaxing your wrists and forearms during the transition.

Check that you are:

1. Moving your lower legs back a little and squeezing them gently during the transition – this asks his hind legs to step forward under.
2. Lifting your diaphragm slightly to drop your weight more firmly into your seat (see photograph, p.72).
3. Vibrating both rein contacts lightly to keep him relaxed in his jaw.
4. Really working with your pelvic muscles to maintain the speed at which your seat swings to your choice (same tempo as the medium), not allowing it to move faster with the quicker steps he wants to produce.
5. At the end of your medium trot try turning him either onto a 10 m circle to help bring his inside hind leg further forward (and work hard at maintaining your seat tempo as you do so) or, if he is capable, into shoulder-in, which will also bring his inside hind forward underneath him and allow you to keep riding positively forward as the movement makes the transition happen for you.

He goes haunches-in in medium canter

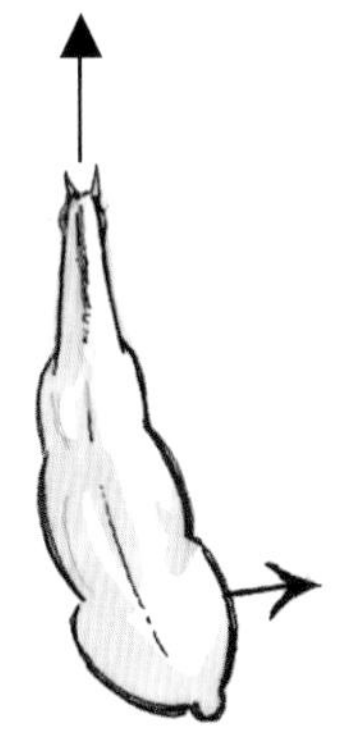

Check that you are not sliding/being pushed to the outside of the saddle – this will allow/encourage him to travel crooked.

Use shoulder-fore as your correction – see Chapter 16. Position his shoulders *slightly in* before you even begin lengthening, then keep them there throughout. Beware of too much neck bend – this must be shoulder positioning only.

He takes off too fast into medium canter

This is generally a result of excitement at the prospect of the bigger canter, and if he knows where you are likely to ask, he can build lots of energy ready to go. In many ways this enthusiasm is desirable, but it must still be under your control.

Work on the medium strides only on a circle for a while, never asking for them at the same spot twice in a row. He will then be unable to anticipate exactly when you will request medium canter, so he will listen more to you. The circle also makes the return to working canter easier as the continuous curve keeps his inside hind leg further forward beneath him than when he is on a straight line. Only ride a few strides at a time, concentrating on the transitions into and out of medium.

When you revert to working on straight lines, use downward transitions each time he tries to rush off until he is not sure what he is going to do, then re-introduce medium strides on an occasional basis.

If he rushes once you are into the medium strides, use a small (10 m) circle to help steady him. Once he is convinced that rushing will only earn him the tough work of a small circle he will be less likely to try it.

He loses impulsion when I try to collect him

You may be asking for collection too early, before he is strong enough to produce lift at the same time as impulsion. Try again using quicker leg aids – alternate legs in walk, together in trot, inside leg in canter – and do not let him slow. If he really struggles, it is probably too soon for this work.

There is also the possibility that you are using too much hand and blocking his hind legs from stepping forward. Try to use smaller, quicker aids given with just your fingers and be sure to keep your elbows and forearms relaxed. Make frequent tiny contact releases to encourage self-carriage and a forward desire on his part.

His balance doesn't seem to change when I collect him

True collection takes a great deal of strength and he may not be ready yet. Do more strengthening work (transitions, voltes, shoulder-in, hill work) and try again in a month or two.

If you believe he has the strength and maybe does not understand what you are asking:

- Use many more half-halts, at least one to each stride.
- Round you lower back more – this is what you are asking him to do so you must initiate with your body what you want him to mirror with his. Keep your upper body tall, but tilt your pelvis more up at the front (deep stomach muscles, *not* buttock muscles).
- Try to find a slower rhythm with your seat but a quicker one with your legs. Collection needs to be very active (from your legs), but moving at a measured tempo (from your seat).

He stiffens when I try to collect him

You are probably using too strong a contact. Collection asks him to physically shorten his body by bringing his hind legs further forward beneath him. Too strong a contact stops him from doing this, causing him to stiffen with anxiety or anger (confusion) as you ask him to do one thing with your legs and another with your hands.

Try with more frequent half-halts, with clear contact releases after each.

He may also not be supple enough yet in his back or hind legs to achieve collection. Do more suppling exercises, including work over trotting poles, to encourage greater flexion of his joints.

He swings his quarters when I try to collect him

This may indicate that he is not yet either supple enough (see above) or strong enough to achieve true collection. Work on improving these two factors and reduce the degree of collection you are asking for until he can achieve a little yet still remain straight.

Swinging may also be an indication of discomfort, probably in the hind leg joints or lower back. Whereas the earlier work has not put sufficient stress on these areas to show up a problem, collection asks far more of him physically in terms of flexion and sustained muscle usage, and a previously sub-clinical problem may suddenly become apparent.

20 Counter-canter

Counter-canter is when you ride in left-lead canter whilst travelling right-handed around the school – see photograph, p.25 – or vice versa. Throughout, the horse must remain slightly bent and positioned towards his leading leg, in this case to the left.

Counter-canter should only be started once his working canter is well balanced, fairly supple and can be collected a little without any tension. It has many benefits but is quite demanding, so never make the exercises so hard that he struggles, or you may damage his muscles.

BUILDING BLOCKS

The building blocks for counter-canter are:

- A canter that is balanced, supple and slightly collected.
- The ability (of both horse and rider) to position the horse's shoulders inward relative to his haunches.

Requirements

1. That the horse's canter strides (speed and length) do not alter.
2. That he does not either change lead or become disunited.
3. That his canter maintains 'jump'.
4. That horse and rider remain upright.
5. That the horse is always slightly positioned (mildly bent) towards his leading leg, not to his direction of travel.
6. That his haunches do not swing towards the side of his leading leg.

Aids

1. Before asking for counter-canter, ensure that the true canter is as balanced and collected (feeling 'uphill') as your horse can achieve, and have him as well connected from your inside leg to your outside rein as possible – so that you can give your inside rein without losing bend.
2. Keep the same aiding throughout both true and counter-canter, although your outside leg may need to be drawn back in a lightly exaggerated position in counter-canter.
3. Your inside leg is responsible for both bend and impulsion, so remember to use it! Counter-canter cannot be ridden exclusively from your outside leg as this pushes the haunches too far over.
4. Keep your weight on your *inside* (p.24) seat bone – allowing your weight to slide to the outside will unbalance him.
5. When you change direction from true canter into counter-canter (see suggested patterns next section) turn him into the counter-canter by moving both your hands towards the new direction (right, in the example above). This will turn his shoulders to the new direction of travel whilst maintaining his bend towards his leading leg. If necessary vibrate the inside rein slightly to help keep him relaxed in this flexion.
6. Once he is in counter-canter, reposition both hands so they are placed correctly relative to his canter lead.

If you find this hard to grasp, go back to riding trot circles in counter-bend (see Chapter 12 *Troubleshooting – He falls to the outside of circles*) until you feel competent at steering him with an outside bend. Then try again in canter.

Patterns

1. Start with a 3 m loop away from the long side. Make all your turns gradual, or you will pull your horse off balance.
2. If you have a very large arena (more than 20 m in width), or you ride on a field, you can start riding large, gentle curves in counter-canter without the constraints of corners to negotiate.
3. Once he can manage 3 m loops, relaxed and in balance, deepen them to 5 m.
4. Deepen them gradually to 10 m, (i.e. to the centre line) and eventually as far as the opposite track. This progression can be quicker in a 60 m arena as the turns are less acute.

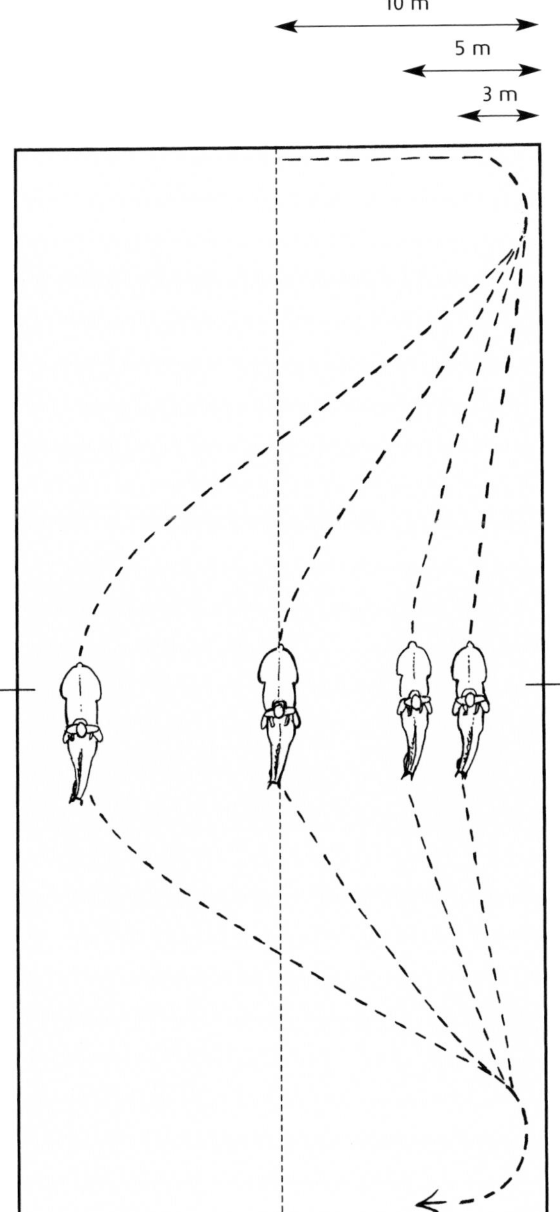

Riding loops of increasing depth in counter-canter.

5. Next, ride a half-circle and return to the track (see diagram p.169). Ride the smallest half-circle you can manage without upsetting his balance and relaxation, positioning it as near to the end of the arena as possible. This will make your angle of return the least acute, which will aid him in maintaining his balance. This movement will be easier in a long arena, where you can return to the track and have many straight strides before nearing a corner.

6. Gradually start asking him to keep the counter-canter through the first corner of the short side. At this stage, ride shallow corners, i.e. one quarter of a 20 m circle, no deeper.

7. Keep counter-canter through the whole short side.

8. Eventually you will ride full 20 m circles in counter-canter, then later, smaller circles.

9. Ride a 20 m figure of eight with one circle in true canter, the other in counter-canter.

10. At Advanced level you will ride serpentines of four and five loops without changing leads, also two 10 m half-circles to change rein, also without changing lead.

Training Value

- Suppleness – he must really stretch the outside of his body to get around the turns in the counter-bend.
- Engagement – his inside hind leg is asked to carry more weight than in other exercises (or he will lose balance), so counter-canter increases strength and enables greater engagement.
- Balance – counter-canter is quite unnatural so the horse needs to develop his balance to a high degree to manage it.
- Straightening – to perform this exercise with ease, his alignment needs to be sophisticated, so any lack of straightness becomes immediately apparent. Counter-canter is also a useful tool for *improving* straightness – if he habitually canters with his haunches to the inside on one lead, riding him in counter-canter on that lead (with minimal or no bend) utilizes the wall as a deterrent to moving his haunches over and teaches him to canter without curling to the side.
- Collection – when the exercise is done correctly, he will use his haunches to lift his shoulders and move them fractionally sideways in each step, developing lightness of his forehand.

TROUBLESHOOTING

He falls out of counter-canter into trot

There are several possible causes:

1. He lost balance, either by falling onto his forehand or by falling/leaning sideways.
2. *You* lost balance/let your weight move, so disturbing his balance or confidence.
3. He didn't have enough impulsion before you started, or he lost impulsion during the exercise.

4. He hollowed and/or stiffened his top-line, possibly because of anxiety about a difficult/unfamiliar exercise, causing his hocks to move out behind his body and so losing impulsion.

5. You asked for this exercise before his suppleness/balance/engagement/degree of collection were ready for it.

6. You tried too hard to keep the bend. By over-bending his neck to the side with a strong rein you either pushed him onto his outside shoulder and caused him to lose balance or you blocked his inside hind leg from travelling forward thus destroying his impulsion.

Start by checking your aiding – weight distribution, leg positions, inside leg to outside rein connection. If these check out, then take the exercise back to a simpler pattern to re-establish his confidence.

Re-assess whether he is ready yet for the more demanding exercises. You may need to do more suppling, straightening and/or collecting exercises before he is ready to try again.

He hollows and/or stiffens

Basically the same causes as above – anxiety, lack of strength or suppleness are the usual culprits here, so follow the same diagnostic approach as above, even if he does not lose the canter.

He changes behind and becomes disunited in counter-canter

Again, as above. Further possibilities are that you did not maintain your outside leg position clearly enough, or he is too stiff in his hind legs to enable him to perform counter-canter just yet.

As always, check your equitation first, but also assess his physical capability for this demanding exercise, and do more work on his balance/suppleness before trying again.

He performs flying changes instead of maintaining counter-canter

Possibilities are:

1. Your aiding is not clear enough – you let your weight slip to the outside, or your leg position changed.
2. He lost balance.
3. He is disobedient – counter-canter is harder work than true canter, so he is avoiding the extra demand.

Exaggerate your weight to the inside of the saddle (without leaning over) and use your inside leg clearly at the girth. Take your outside leg even further back so that there can be no possibility of confusion, and close it firmly on his side – not enough to push his haunches out of alignment, but enough to help turn him.

Never punish him for making a change or you will store up problems for the future (when introducing flying changes). If he changes, simply drop him to walk and ask for the counter-canter again. You may need to put him on a straight line, or make a curved line towards the leading leg to help him pick up the desired lead, but try to keep him relaxed about the whole situation – never let him know he has done wrong.

21 Building Blocks of the Higher Movements

All horses should be trained in the manner and exercises outlined so far, whether the intention is to specialize with the horse in a particular competition discipline or keep him as an all-rounder. These basics apply as thoroughly to the showjumper or eventer as they do to the pure dressage horse, as they enable him to perform with the greatest degree of ease, not only minimizing the risk of him causing himself physical damage but also enabling him to produce the best performance of which he is capable.

For the dedicated dressage horse, once he has reached the stage where he can perform all this early work with relative ease, his training can progress to increasingly higher levels. As ever, it is important to understand which factors represent the **building blocks** of these higher exercises, and to have them in place before the exercises are attempted. In this chapter, we will look briefly at the remaining exercises required of the competition dressage horse in this light.

A good example of the progression from simple **building blocks** to a very advanced level of training is the development of the canter zigzag from its earliest Novice level exercise up to the finished Grand Prix movement:

1. Trot serpentine (moving shoulders from one side to the other with change of direction) ->
2. Serpentine with trot-walk-trot transitions either side of the centre line ->
3. Canter serpentine with simple changes ->
4. Canter serpentine with flying changes ->
5. Canter half-pass followed by flying change ->
6. Canter half-pass one way with flying change to canter half-pass the other way (Prix St Georges test) ->
7. Canter zigzag; half-passes of several metres with flying changes between (Intermediaire I test) ->

8. Canter zigzag; half-passes of specific numbers of strides with flying changes (Intermediaire II and Grand Prix tests).

Travers and Renvers

These two movements are fundamentally the same and are sometimes referred to as 'mirror images'; it is just their position in relationship to the track that defines them.

Travers

This movement is also known as haunches-in, and should be ridden on three tracks or just onto four tracks, with the horse's neck and face pointing straight down the track.

BUILDING BLOCKS

The building blocks for travers are:

- Turn around the forehand (moving away from one leg).
- Leg-yielding.
- Increased balance and suppleness.
- Obedience to the bending aids.

Training Value

Travers improves:

1. Obedience to your outside leg.
2. General suppleness.
3. The carrying capacity of the horse's outside hind leg: his inside hind leg steps away from his body while his outside hind crosses under his body and, whilst on the ground (stance phase) is supporting his weight by itself.
4. Flexion of the stifle joint.
5. Collection.

Travers is an essential precursor to teaching half-pass.

Renvers

Since, as stated, renvers is effectively a 'mirror image' of travers, the building blocks for the two movements are essentially the same. However, renvers, in which the forehand is positioned in from the track, is more difficult to perform than travers, because of the lack of psychological support for the horse when he is performing a movement without his shoulders alongside a fence. Therefore, as additional building blocks, he needs:

- Improved self-carriage.
- More confidence and obedience to the relative placement of his shoulders and haunches.

Training Value

As well as having the training values of travers, when renvers is ridden through corners, or on circles, the depth of crossing of the hind leg is greater, so it is even more suppling and collecting, and can be an ideal preparatory exercise prior to straightening into an extension.

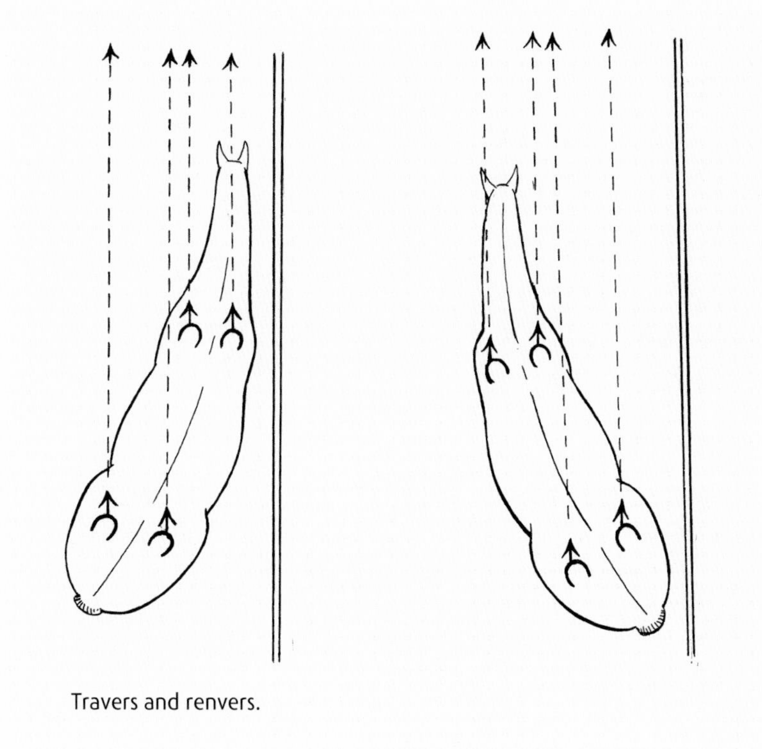

Travers and renvers.

Walk Pirouette

This movement is also known as turn on the haunches. In it, the horse will describe a small circle with his forehand and will be bent towards the direction in which he is turning. His hind feet will keep marching, with his inside hind more or less on the spot in the centre of this circle. He must maintain a clear four-beat walk sequence throughout.

Walk pirouettes are begun as large quarter-pirouettes, then large half-pirouettes, gradually reducing in size, eventually becoming full or double pirouettes. Although only the quarter- or half-pirouette is ever asked for in competition, riding full or double turns allows the development of more engagement and gives more time for corrections within the pirouette.

BUILDING BLOCKS

The building blocks for walk pirouettes are:

- Shoulder-in – to prepare the bend and position the shoulders correctly at the start.
- Travers (haunches-in) – to maintain control and prevent the haunches from swinging out.
- A degree of collection of the walk – pirouette cannot be ridden from medium walk.
- Submission to the bending aids.
- Obedience to half-halts from the hand – to prevent the horse from stepping forward too much.
- Good control of the shoulders and haunches – the shoulders must move considerably faster than the haunches to accomplish the turn.

Although walk pirouette is a fairly advanced movement that requires the walk to be collected, it can be started in its simplest form as a large quarter-pirouette quite early on, and may be required in this form in Elementary level dressage tests. Only a small degree of collection is needed to perform this large quarter turn, and it can be taught before travers is introduced, requiring only basic outside leg control to stop the haunches from swinging out.

Training value

1. Walk pirouettes demand a very sophisticated level of coordination from the rider – you will need to do a different thing with each leg and each hand and keep your weight in the correct place all at the same time! In other words, they are a great way of working on the sophistication of your aiding.
2. Correctly performed with plenty of activity, pirouettes improve the lowering of the quarters, i.e. engagement and collection.
3. They can be used as a more sophisticated way of changing the rein.

Half-pass in Trot and Canter

Half-pass is a forward/sideways movement in which the horse is bent towards the direction he is going, yet his body is almost parallel to the track. His face must look at the marker towards which you are aiming, with his shoulders always travelling *slightly* in the lead compared to his haunches (more so at the lower competitive levels), and his outside legs crossing in front of his inside legs. His balance and the quality of his gait should not change throughout the whole movement.

BUILDING BLOCKS

The building blocks for half-pass are:

- Improved suppleness and engagement.
- A degree of collection.
- Travers.

Half-pass should be started as travers ridden on a diagonal line. This means that the horse will not yet be parallel to the outside track – that comes later as he develops more suppleness and ability to engage.

The essence of half-pass is a *forward*/sideways movement – the forward component must be prioritized over the sideways to develop this movement without compromising the quality of his gaits.

Training Value

1. Increases suppleness.
2. Improves balance.
3. Develops collection.
4. Targets the flexing of the stifle joints.

Flying Changes

Flying changes are a completely natural movement for a horse, achieved by changing canter sequence from one lead to the other during the moment of suspension.

Problems encountered with changes come from asking for them before the horse is sufficiently balanced, strong, engaged, straight and responsive. Once you have improved these factors to the point where he no longer tries to evade your corrections, it is only a matter of teaching him to respond to the aids for changing.

BUILDING BLOCKS

The building blocks for flying changes are:

- A really good quality, forward-thinking canter, with clear and expressive 'jump'.
- Walk to canter with good engagement i.e., really 'sitting down' behind, and with *immediate* response to your aids – no hesitation at all.
- Canter to walk with good collection and staying light in your hand.
- Counter-canter.
- Simple changes, both from true to counter-canter and vice versa, performed on straight lines (long sides) with confidence and ease and a minimum of walk.
- A sophisticated degree of straightness.

A calm temperament makes teaching changes much easier; excitable horses can become quite distressed and will require far more preparation time. Only patience and the prevention of anticipation will succeed with the 'hot' horse.

Tempi Changes

Tempi changes are multiple flying changes, performed at intervals of a prescribed number of strides: every four, every three, every two and eventually every stride.

The chief **building block** of tempi changes is establishing single flying changes that are straight, confident, engaged ('through') and precisely on the aids.

Tempi changes should be introduced gradually, first as a pair, with no particular number of strides between them, then three, also with no counting requirement, taking some weeks before too many in a row are demanded. Once your horse is calm and confident, start to count numbers of strides between the changes, beginning with four-time changes.

Half-pass Zigzags in Trot and Canter

Also known as 'counter-change of hand', zigzags involve alternating half-passes to left and right, initially riding prescribed distances (usually 5 or 10 m) before changing to the other direction. In canter this means making a flying change at the change of direction before going into the new half-pass, and they eventually will be (in canter) a counted numbers of strides in each direction.

BUILDING BLOCKS

The building blocks of half-pass zigzags are:
In trot:

- Half-passes that are equal to both sides in terms of bend and sideways displacement.
- A sophisticated degree of suppleness and balance.
- Quick reactions to the placement of the horse's shoulders.

In canter:

- As for trot, plus established flying changes.

Counter-change of hand can also be performed in passage.

Canter Pirouettes

Canter pirouettes require the horse to perform a small circle with his forefeet around an even smaller circle with his hind feet. His canter must be extremely collected and the pirouette should consist of between six and eight canter strides.

BUILDING BLOCKS

The building blocks for canter pirouettes are:

- Accomplished walk pirouettes.
- A really good quality canter that can be extremely collected – near to the spot – without loss of impulsion or sequence.
- A greatly enhanced degree of suppleness and strength in the hindquarters.
- A really soft acceptance of the bridle, both in respect of restraining (half-halt) aids and bending aids.
- Small circles in canter that have good quality canter strides and are easy to maintain in correct alignment.
- Shoulder-fore in canter.
- Canter half-pass.
- Travers in canter on a circle.
- Greatly enhanced balance.

This movement represents the ultimate in collection of the canter and is only possible after years of balancing and strengthening work. In turn, it can be used as an exercise to further strengthen and collect the horse, and it targets the flexibility of the hip joints.

Piaffe

Piaffe is the ultimate in collected trot, performed 'on the spot', although it must always retain a desire to move forward. In the earlier stages, piaffe should move slightly forward (about 1 m for ten steps in the Intermediare II test) and then, as strength improves, it will gradually come to the spot in the Grand Prix. The horse's haunches will be maximally flexed and engaged and his head and neck as raised as his conformation permits. He should spring from one diagonal pair to the other with elastic, cadenced steps.

BUILDING BLOCKS

The building blocks for piaffe are:

- Trot – walk – trot transitions.
- Clear connection/response of each hind leg to each of your legs – so that you can activate one hind more if it is 'lazier'.
- Very clear understanding and acceptance of soft half-halts on the reins.
- A great deal of strength and flexibility of the hindquarters, developed over years of repeated (correct) transitions.

As well as being an end in itself, piaffe is a wonderful exercise for increasing engagement and collection and can be used as the ultimate preparation for the most difficult movements.

It is possible to perform a pirouette in piaffe, a movement which is permitted in Grand Prix Freestyle tests, and is sometimes used to help keep the horse more active within the piaffe with less prompting from his rider.

With some horses you can develop piaffe best from walk – by asking for a transition to trot whilst half-halting (softly) to limit forward movement – like jogging for a few steps before returning to walk. Others are more easily trained from trot – by bringing the trot steps smaller (whilst maintaining activity) and nearer to being on the spot without letting the horse drop to walk. These earlier steps are called *half-steps.*

Piaffe should be taught before passage. Horses often offer passage first, but once passage is developed it will be extremely hard to persuade him to piaffe, which takes more sheer strength, and passage will usually be offered as an evasion.

Passage

Passage is the ultimate in a cadenced trot, having a slow rhythm and a prolonged moment of suspension. The horse will spring upward from deeply flexed haunches, travelling energetically forward and upward with elastic steps, and seem to hang in the air before coming down again. His forearms should come as close to parallel with the ground as possible, with the cannon bone perpendicular to the ground. His outline and contact are virtually the same as in piaffe.

BUILDING BLOCKS

The building blocks for passage are:

- A great deal of suppleness and strength.
- Piaffe.
- A very clear connection between the swing of the horse's back and the action of your seat – passage is produced 90% by seat, 10% by legs; piaffe is the opposite.
- A sophisticated acceptance of half-halts.

Every horse will develop his own style of passage, some more spectacular than others, but the required ingredients remain the same: a measured rhythm with great engagement and prolonged suspension. The passage should always be a joy to watch.

22 Timescale for the Building Blocks

In an ideal world, with a *very* talented, sound horse and an experienced rider it is possible to train from backing to Grand Prix in four to five years. For the rest of us, both the timescale and the end product are rather different. The most important criterion is that *your horse must be his own calendar.*

This means that he must not be pushed faster than he is mentally or physically able to progress. You should only move on to more complicated/demanding exercises when he is working easily and confidently at his current level.

Equally, this does not mean that he should not be challenged to move on, only that the pace should be dictated by his individual speed of development.

It is during his earlier years – up to about 7 years old – that he is most capable of being suppled physically and developed mentally. After this, his body and mind are less malleable; improvements will be slower and there will be more limit to his potential. So, while care must be taken not to over-push him, there is some urgency for certain work to be done while he is still young enough to benefit fully.

When you buy a horse with limited knowledge, or no knowledge, of his background, one of your first tasks is to determine exactly what his training level is in terms of comprehension and competence, so that you can begin to fill in any missing foundations or early **building blocks** to enable you to take him forward. This entails putting him through all the exercises detailed so far, in order of difficulty, until you find out what he does and doesn't know.

In order, (displayed in their ideal age ranges when starting from scratch), these will be as shown in chart overleaf.

Prior to Backing

- Acceptance of general handling.
- Acceptance of wearing saddle, bridle and lungeing gear.
- Obedience to voice aids.
- Lungeing, to include obedience to forward and restraining aids, and development of good rhythm and a steady outline.

First Six Months under Saddle (3–4 Years Old)

- Calm acceptance of rider's weight.
- Relaxation.
- Obedience to forward-driving aids, and aids for downward transitions.
- Establish good rhythm in all gaits.
- Acceptance of the contact and work towards a feeling of connection from rider's legs into hands, so working in a long but round outline.
- Straight lines, large circles and serpentines.
- Stretching down in walk and trot.
- Transitions between gaits, on straight lines or circles according to which he finds easier.
- Halt and standing still.
- Trot – walk – trot transitions.
- Canter on large circles.
- Forward seat canter.
- Turn around the forehand (towards the end of this period).
- Trotting poles and small jumps.
- Hacking.

Second Six Months under Saddle (3–4 Years Old)

- Smaller circles.
- Serpentines of more than three loops.
- Turns onto the centre line.
- Leg-yielding short distances.
- More engagement in transitions, so less on the forehand in downward transitions and more active upward transitions.
- Halt to trot.
- Begin small periods (few strides) of sitting trot.
- Hill work to improve bending of hocks.
- Pole work and jumps.

Year Two (4–5 Years Old)

- More accuracy in alignment on circles and straight lines.
- Leg-yielding across the diagonals of the school and on spirals.
- Longer periods of sitting trot.
- Serpentines with transitions between walk and trot over the centre line.
- Canter on smaller circles (15 m).
- Beginnings of lengthening in both trot and canter.
- Shallow loops in canter to begin counter-canter.
- Canter across the diagonal with transition to trot at the end, also sometimes a few strides of counter-canter before the downward transition.
- Stretching down in canter.
- Improve engagement of canter to help reduce speed.
- Rein-back.
- Quarter-pirouettes in walk.
- Shoulder-fore leading to shoulder-in.

- Easier direct transitions.
- Continued use of trotting poles but increasing size (height and spread) of jumps.
- More hill work.

Year Three
(5–6 Years Old)

- Most of trot work (after warm-up) in sitting trot.
- More advanced direct transitions e.g. canter to halt.
- Clearer transitions within the gaits and longer periods of medium trot and canter.
- A little collection in walk, and introducing extended walk.
- Simple changes.
- Travers.
- Half-pass.
- Counter-canter around short sides.
- Half-pirouettes in walk.
- Rein-back to trot or canter.
- Begin half-steps (early work towards piaffe).
- Extended gaits.
- With a talented horse, the flying change may be introduced towards the end of this phase.

Year Four
(6–7 Years Old)

- Increase engagement to enhance expression of gaits and enhance the ability to collect and extend in balance.
- Fully establish collected and extended walks.
- Make steeper angles in half-passes.
- Fully establish single flying changes.
- Begin to combine half-passes with flying changes.
- Working (large) canter pirouettes.
- Establish forward piaffe both from walk and trot and into either.
- Start sequence changes in canter, down to two-time.
- Begin passage.

Year Five
(8 Years Old)

- Establish piaffe on the spot.
- Small canter pirouettes.
- One-time flying changes.
- Establish passage.
- Transitions between piaffe and passage, and trot and passage.
- Passage – extended trot – passage transitions.
- Keep developing the horse's strength so that he finds these movements easy – this may mean hill work or even interval training on a gallop, as well as school work.
- Your ultimate goal is that he finds all his work easy and performs it with maximum expression.

Summary of the Goals of Training

For many, what in the talented horse can take 2–3 years may be a lifetime of work. The important things are NOT: the speed at which he develops, or the goals he achieves, BUT:

- That he is taken up through the layers of complexity and demand in a logical, progressive order that does not strain him physically or mentally.
- That this progression builds him into a straight, strong and supple individual who has the greatest potential for a long and healthy life.
- That it produces a partnership in which both horse and rider are relaxed and happy in what they are doing.

Index

Note: Page numbers in *italic* refer to illustrations

abdominal muscles
horse 31–2, 37, 103, 113–14
rider 30
above the bit 115–17, 126–7, 158–9, 183
adductor muscles, rider 30, *31*
against the hand 221, 222
aids
combination 35
corridor 40
horse's sensitivity to 46–7
passive resistance 35, 37
see also named aids and under specific movements
anthropomorphism xv
anxiety, horse 221, 245–6
see also tension
Arabs 145
arena, dimensions and markers 17, *18*
arms, position and function 8, 33–4, 116
assistance
newly-backed horse 70–3
rein-back 228, *229*
square halts 232

back (horse's)
conformation 14–15
dropped 125
hollow, *see* hollowing
tension 137
back (rider's) 35
backing up, in hand 55
balance (horse's) 24, 26
in canter 128, 142–3
on circles 161–2
lengthening strides 245
and outline 105–6, 116–17
in turns 93–4
use of neck 100–1
balance (rider) 8
counter-canter 254
lengthening strides 246, 247
rising trot 138–9
bascules, three 27–8, 114
behind the bridle 118–19, 120–1
bend 22, 41, 90, 148
counter-canter 255
illusion of 148–9
importance of 149–50
outside 157–8
in serpentines 172–3
in shoulder-in 207
biomechanics 95–102
bit
acceptance of 107–13, 117, 159
changing 123
chewing down onto inside 107–9, 117
fiddling 123–4
raising in mouth 124
tongue over 124
yanking at 124
boredom, in schooling 5
breathing, horse's 103
bridle
for lungeing 57, 58
running through 221
bucking, in canter 144–5
building blocks 3, 4
higher movements 257–8
timescale 267–9
bungee, elastic 64–5

cadence 20
canter 19, 133–5
balance of horse 128, 142–3
breaking into trot 144
bucking 144–5
'curling up' 23, *24*
disunited 145, 255
half-halts 143
half-pass 261
hollowing 128
incorrect lead 84–5
lengthening strides 238, 249
rider's position and seat 30, 38, 134, 135, 142, *143*
simple changes 217–19, 223
slow/laboured 144
straightness 23, *24*, 134, 174–5
strike-off 74–5, 85
use of whip 42
see also counter-canter; flying changes
canter pirouettes 264
canter to trot transition 76
canter to walk transition 215–16, 222
centre of gravity, horse 87–8
centre line 164–5
leg-yielding 190
straightness 174
turn onto 171
Chambon 63–4, 69
changing direction
aids 167–8
building blocks 167
figure of eight 170
half-circles 169–70, *171*
long diagonals 168
requirements 167
serpentines 170–3
shallow loops 174
training value 174
circles 150–4
15 metre 153
20 metre 152–3
accuracy 152–3
aids 41, 151–2
building blocks 150
falling in 155–6
falling out 156–8
importance of bend 149–50
impulsion 161
lengthening strides 240
outline of horse 110–11, 158–9
outside (counter) bend 157–8
requirements 151
spirals 153–4
training value 154
troubleshooting 155–62
coaching 12
collection 22, 242–4

aids 243
definition 242
preparatory exercises 243
requirements 243
training value 244
troubleshooting 249–50
communication, effective 3
competing, versus schooling 29
conditioned response 48
conformation 13–16
consistency, in training 49–50
contact 21, 26
alternating 109–10
in canter 144
circles 41, 158–60
collection 250
'floating' 33, 81, 119
following 129
horse's acceptance of 107–13, 117, 159
inside rein 41
lengthening 245, 246
passive resistance 111–13
rigid/strong 103, 121
unsteady 119–20, 159–60
yielding/releasing 22, *22*, 34, 111, 112
contact point 33–4
corners 93, 165–6, 176
corridor of aids 40
counter-canter 24, 25
aids 252
building blocks 251
patters for riding 252–4
requirements 251
training value 254
troubleshooting 254–6
counter-change of hand 263
crest release 22, *22*
crookedness 23–4
and circles 157
halt 230
rein-back 234–5
in transitions 83, 84
in turns 94
see also straightness
croup-high conformation 15

diagonals
changes of rein 168
leg-yielding 189
lengthening 241
diaphragm lift 71, 72
direct transitions
downward 214–17, 221
progression 217
troubleshooting 219–24
upward 211–14
dominance, horse 45
double bridle 119

ears, horse's 47
elastic bungee 64–5
elbows, position 8, 33–4, 197
empathy 11–12
endurance rides 27
engagement 20, 101
increasing 125–6
'swing bridge' effect *126*
evasions 26
excitability 46

falling in 94
circles 155–6
corners 176
falling out 92
circles 156–8
leg-yielding 197
feel, rider 10
feet, horse's 16
picking up foal's 52–3
fence
lengthening along 240–1
use for leg-yielding 191–2
use for stopping 71–2
figure of eight 170
figures
accuracy 4–5
alignment 175
changing rein 168–74
training value 5
Flash noseband 123–4
flexion 22
flying changes 38, 262
instead of counter-canter 256
tempi 262–3
foals, handling 51–3
focus of attention 45
forging 247–8
forwardness 20
free walk 127, 130, 138
front (horse's) 15

gaits
activity 19, 20
impulsion versus speed 20
quality of 17–19
rhythm and tempo 19
see also individual gaits
goals of training 2, 4, 269
ground poles
for improving the walk 136
lunge work 63
rein-back 234

habituation 48
hacking 27
half-circles
changing direction/rein 169–70, *171*
counter-canter 253
half-halt
aids 37
balancing canter 143
before turns 166
lungeing 66
trot-canter transition 74
half-pass 261, 263
halt
aids 225
early training 71, 75
in hand 55
refusal to 79, *80*
square 224–6, 230–3
standing still 230
halt to trot transition 211–12
halt to walk transition 70–1, 73, 81
handling
foal 51–3
weanling 54–5
youngster up to backing 56
hands
actions 33–4
in canter 135
horse leaning on 118, 156, 246
position 8, *10*, 116, 202
rising trot 132
sitting trot 133
widened position 82, 120, 121
Harbridge 64, *65*
harmonizing 118
haunches
control of 91
swinging in collection 250
swinging out in turns 94–5
haunches-in, canter 174–5
head
conformation 14
tossing 124
head (horse's)
tilting 92–3, 122–3, 209–10
unsteady 159–60
head (rider's), tilting 89
heave line 103
herd instincts/hierarchy 44–5

hind bascule 28
hind legs
  action on circles 160–1
  conformation 15–16
  going wide behind 248
  tracking 14–50, 24, 25, 154
  trailing/resting in halt 231–3
hocks, conformation 16
hollowing 115–17, 126–7
  canter 128
  counter-canter 255
  leg-yielding 198
  lengthening 246
  on lunge 68–9
  sitting trot 210
  transitions 80–3, 220, 222
Holme Grove Merlin 22, 103, 104, 195
horse
  basic nature/instincts 4, 44–7
  conformation and physical capability 13–16
  essential training 12–13
  learning 3, 47–50
  memory 47
  physical strength 80, 81, 105, 117, 158–9, 248–50
  postural ring 96–8, 101
  posture 27–8, 95, 98–102, 105
  rider's empathy with 11–12
hyperflexion 99

imprinting 49
impulsion 20
  on circles 159, 161
  loss 249
inside 24, 25
inside leg to outside rein 41
insight, horse's 48–9
'instant results' culture xv
instincts xv, 4, 44–5

jogging 137–8
jowl, thick 14

kicking, on lunge 67

laziness 46, 118, 141
  on lunge 67
  when first 'on the aids' 115
leading
  foal 52
  weanling 54–5
leaning, on hands/bit 118, 156, 246
learning, horse 3, 47–50
leg aids 30–3
  circles 151
  downward transitions 75, 86
  horse's response 31, 48, 117, 141, 219
  newly-backed horse 70–1
  restraining 32
  rising trot 131–2
  sideways pushing 32–3, 185–6, 193–6
  supporting horse's posture 31–2
  turns/circles 90–1
  walk 129
leg position 9, 139
  canter 135
  inside/outside 37–8, *39*
  sitting trot 133
leg-yielding 156
  aids 185–6, 193–6
  building blocks 184
  patterns for riding 187–90
  requirements 184–5
  spirals 189, 192, 193
  training value 188–9
  troubleshooting 191–201
lengthening 236
  building blocks 236
  canter 238, 249
  on the lunge 239–40
  patterns/exercises 239–41
  priorities 239
  progression 241–2
  requirements 237
  training value 241
  transitions 248
  trot 237–8
  troubleshooting 244–9
  walk 239
Leo's Orlando 39
light seat 134, 145
limbs, conformation 15–16
limitations, setting 4
loading 55
loops
  counter-canter 252, *253*
  shallow 174
Lover Boy 39
lunge cavesson 57
lunge whip 59–60, *62*, 67, 68
lungeing
  equipment 58–63
  exercises 61–3
  first ridden sessions 70–2
  lengthening strides 239–40
  side reins 60, 68–9
  techniques 60–1
  troubleshooting 66–9
  on two reins 66–7

manners, young horse 54
markers, arena 17, *18*
medium gaits, *see* lengthening
mirroring 3
mouth problems 112–13, 115–16, 123–4
moving over 53
muscles (horse's)
  abdominal 31–2, 37, 103, 113–14
  isotonic/isometric contraction 101
  postural ring 96–8, 101
  stress 124
muscles (rider's) 10, 30, *31*

nappy horse 42
natural horsemanship xv
neck (horse's)
  and balance 100–1
  carriage 27–8
  conformation 14
  lowering 99–100, 127, 138
nervousness, horse 46
nose
  poking 99
  tilting 92–3
nosebands 123–4
nuchal ligament 96, 99, 102

on the aids
  checklist 27
  definition 26–7
  placing of horse 114–15
on the forehand 105, 125–6
outline 13, 27–8, 98–102
  above the bit 115–17, 126–7, 158–9, 183
  and balance 105–6, 116–17
  on circles 110–11, 158–9
  correct 27, 102–4
  crest high 125
  deep 99, 118
  long and low 13, 98–9, 101
  mechanics of 101–2
  sustaining rounded 117–18
  in transitions 80–3, 83, 105–6, 220, 222
  see also hollowing
outside 24, *25*
over bending 99, 118–19
overtrack 18

pacing 136
passage 266
passive resistance 35, 37, 111–13
pasterns, conformation 16
patience 11
pelvic tuck 103, *104*, 113
pelvis (horse's) 15, 148
piaffe *104*, 265
pirouettes
  canter 264
  walk 260–1
poll
  dropped 125
  flexion 99
position of rider 3, 8, *9*
  circles and turns 87–9, 157
  control 29
  hands 8, *9*, *10*, 116, 202
  left and right 37–8, *39*, 151, 167
  legs 9, 37–8, *39*, 133, 139
  straightness 94, 157, 160, 162, 197, 198
  see also seat of rider
postural ring (horse) 96–8, 101
posture, horse's 27–8, 95, 98–102, 105
pulling
  horse 116
  rider 116, 122

rein aids
  direct 35, 89–90
  indirect 35
  turning 89–90
  wheelbarrow push 90
rein-back
  aids 227–8
  building blocks 226
  outside assistance 228, *229*
  overuse 229
  training value 229
  troubleshooting 233–5
reinforcement 49
reins
  inside 41, 110–11
  outside 41
  rider pulling back 116, 122
  triangular position 82
  wide position 120, 121
  yielding and retaking 34
  see also contact
renvers 259
rewards 28–9, 118
rhythm 19
  circles 161
  leg-yielding 199
  lengthened strides 247
  shoulder-in 209
  trot 139–40, 210
  walk 136
ribcage, displacing 90
rider 7–8
  coaching 12
  consistency 49–50
  empathy 11–12
  feel 10
  honesty 12
  muscle control, coordination,
fitness 10, 34
  patience 11
  suppleness and balance 8
  see also position of rider; seat of
rider
rising trot 30, 131–2, 138–9
routine 47
running
  canter strike-off 85
  lengthening 245–6
  through bridle 221
rushing
  on lunge 66–7
  trot 140

sacral vertebrae (horse) 148
saddle
  correct fitting 138–9
  pushed to outside on circles 162
scales of training 6
school figures, *see* figures
schooling
  variety in 5
  versus competing 29
schoolmaster 10
seat of rider
  aids 30
  canter 134, 135, 142, *143*
  on circles 157, 162
  independence 28
  lengthening 245
  light 134, 145
  relaxation 33, 137
  rising trot 131
  sitting trot 132–3, 198–9
  walk 129
  see also position of rider
security, horse's need for 45
self-carriage 21–2, 96
sensitivity, horse 46–7
serpentines 170–3
shallow loops 174
shoulder-fore 202–4, 230
  aids 204
  requirements 203
  training value 204
shoulder-in
  building blocks 204–5
  caution for use of 206
  to improve lengthening 241
  training value 205
  troubleshooting 207–10
shoulders (horse's)
  anatomy 149
  conformation 14
  falling out/onto 92, 156–8, 197
  placing in front of haunches 175
  width in relation to haunches 23
showing, mare and foal 52
side reins 60, 68–9
simple changes 217–19, 223
sitting trot 132–3, 139, 141–2, 206–7, 206–8, 210
speed
  circles 161–2
  leg-yielding 199–200
  turns and corners 93
  versus impulsion 20
spine (horse's), flexibility 148
spirals 153–4, 189, 192, 193
spooking 106, 154
spurs, correct use of 43
square halts 224–6
Stan 203
standing still 230
Stanley 112
startling 106
'stiff' side 121–2
stiffening
  in collection 250
  counter-canter 255
stirrups
  riding without 8
  standing in 139
stomach muscles, *see* abdominal
muscles
stopping, newly-backed horse 71–2
straight lines 163–5, 174
straightness (horse) 2
  assessing 165
  canter 23, 24, 134, 174–5
  centre line 174
  circles 157
  functional 23, 24
  in halt 230
  leg-yielding 197
  lengthening 247, 249

rein-back 234–5
transitions 83
true 23
straightness (rider) 94, 157, 160, 162, 197, 198
strength (horse's) 105
circles 158–9
collection 249–50
lengthening 248
transitions 80–1
stretching
after work 102
in free walk 127, 138
submission 21
suppleness
horse 154, 234
rider 8
supraspinous ligament 96
'swing bridge' effect 126
systematic approach 3

tail 15, 148
teeth 123
tempi changes 262–3
tempo 19
tension
causes 118, 140
downward transitions 222–3
rider 137
shoulder-in 209
walk to canter transition 221
test movements 5
'throughness' 20, 118
timescale, training 267–9
Tommy 181
tongue, over bit 124
Tormenta 108
tracking 14–50, 24, 25, 154
training problems 4, 6
transitions
building blocks 73
downward 75–6, 83, 86
early training 70–6
hollowing 80–3
lungeing 60–1, 63
straightness 83
to/from lengthened strides 248
training value 76–7, 243
troubleshooting 77–86
upward 70–1, 73–5, 80–2
see also direct transitions
travelling 55
travers 258
trot 130–3
half-pass 261
lengthening 237–8
quality of 19, 130–1, 140–1
rhythm 139–40, 210
rising 30, 131–2, 138–9
sitting 132–3, 139, 141–2, 206–8, 210
standing in stirrups 139
troubleshooting 140
variations 133
trot to canter transition, early training 81–2
trot to canter transition 74–5, 77
trot to halt transition 214–15
trot to walk transition 75–6
trot/walk/trot exercise 77
turn around the forehand 178–83, 191
aids 179
building blocks 178
requirements 179
training value 180
troubleshooting 180–3
turn on the forehand 177
turns 165–6
aids 87–91, 166
onto centre line 164
troubleshooting 91–4, 176
tying up 53

vocal commands
lengthening strides 239–40
lungeing 60–1
newly backed horse 70, 71
voltes 150, 243

walk
extended 239
free 127, 130, 138
quality of 17–18, 136
riding 129–30
stretching of head and neck 127, 138
troubleshooting 136–8
variations 130
walk pirouette 260–1
walk to canter transition 212–14, 220–1
walk to trot transition 74, 81
weakness, signs of 105
weanlings 54–5
weight aids 87–9
circles 151
counter-canter 256
leg-yielding 192, 195
'wheelbarrow push' 90
whip
bucking/kicking against 145
correct use 41–3
leg-yielding *195*, 196
lunge 59–60, *62*, 67, 68
short/jumping 78

zig-zags
half-pass 263
leg-yielding 190